DIANE ARBUS

A CHRONOLOGY

APERTURE

DIANE ARBUS

A CHRONOLOGY

BY ELISABETH SUSSMAN AND DOON ARBUS

1923–1971

DIANE ARBUS

A CHRONOLOGY

The first part of my story is mostly taken from my imagination.

You also must use some imagination.

I am not born yet . . .

—DIANE ARBUS, 1934 AUTOBIOGRAPHY,

SEVENTH-GRADE CLASS ASSIGNMENT, FIELDSTON SCHOOL

1923

Diane Nemerov, the second child of Gertrude (née Russek) and David Nemerov, is born in the family apartment at 115 West 73rd Street in New York City on March 14, 1923. The Nemerovs' oldest child, Howard, is three. David Nemerov is the merchandising director of Russek's, one of the city's leading fur emporia, founded in the late 1880s by his father-in-law, Frank Russek, a Polish émigré, along with two other Russek brothers.[1]

I came into the world at 1:30 a.m. on Tuesday, March 14, 1923. I was a 9 lb. baby, very large, roly poly, blonde and blue eyed.

— 1934 AUTOBIOGRAPHY, SEVENTH-GRADE CLASS ASSIGNMENT, FIELDSTON SCHOOL[2]

When I was very young I was blond and red-cheeked and round. I was cranky, always crying, yelling, screaming. I remember that we lived then mostly in warm climates (although we must have lived in New York in the winter) and I can always remember the feeling I had. I always felt as if I was very warm and tired and there was a hot sun on me and I had been asleep. I didn't want to wake up and people would try to wake me and I'd be angry at them; I'd yell at them and hate them. I think I always had a sort of haze of sleep around me then. I don't mean that in any symbolic sense—I mean really physically.

— 1940 AUTOBIOGRAPHY, SENIOR CLASS ASSIGNMENT, FIELDSTON SCHOOL[3]

I remember the first dream I remember having. It was a picture of the upper right or left-hand corner of my room as I would see it from my bed. It was quite dark but vaguely lighted so that I was able to see the walls and the ceiling meeting and a ball of black wool sitting on air in the corner with one end a little untwisted.

— 1940 AUTOBIOGRAPHY, SENIOR CLASS ASSIGNMENT, FIELDSTON SCHOOL

1924–1926

In September 1924, Russek's moves to its new headquarters, a McKim, Mead, and White building on the southwest corner of Fifth Avenue and 36th Street, which was originally built in 1905 for its previous occupant, the Gorham Silver Company.[4] The new location coincides with the expansion of Russek's as a department store specializing in women's fashions. David Nemerov is a key proponent of this development.

The Nemerovs move to 1133 Park Avenue at 90th Street.[5] *This house I remember quite faintly*, Diane notes in her seventh-grade autobiography. *It was here that I cut myself with a china doll.*[6] Her brother, Howard Nemerov, refers to the same incident in his memoir, *Journal of the Fictive Life*, published in 1965: *The scar on my sister's face. Did she really get that in our struggle for a doll that broke in our hands? I believe so, but this belief is not a memory, or it is a memory of having been told so.*[7]

1927

As a vice president and fashion director of Russek's, David Nemerov, often accompanied by his wife, Gertrude, sails to Europe regularly to attend the couture collections and assess the latest fashion trends. In 1927, the Nemerovs bring the two children with them.[8]

...we started our trip across the ocean to France. We went over on the Aquitania and came back on the same...I don't [remember] our stay at Paris except for registering at the Majestic Hotel. My parents went from Paris to Switzerland and left my six year old brother and my governess and myself in La Touquet, a summer resort in France.

—1934 AUTOBIOGRAPHY, SEVENTH-GRADE CLASS ASSIGNMENT, FIELDSTON SCHOOL

[My governess was] French and she took care of me for the first seven years of my life. She had a hard, sad, quite lovely face and I adored her. I don't think I ever talked much to her but I was very happy with her...she always looked as if she had a very sad secret and she would never tell anyone.

—1940 AUTOBIOGRAPHY, SENIOR CLASS ASSIGNMENT, FIELDSTON SCHOOL

1928

In September, following in her brother's footsteps, she enrolls at the Ethical Culture School on 63rd Street and Central Park West, a progressive private school begun by Felix Adler, founder of the Ethical Culture Society (1878). Originally known as The Workingman's School, it emphasizes *moral education, psychological development, teacher training, and the integration of "manual arts" with academics.*[9] The academic curriculum is designed to parallel the evolution of human civilization, from tree dwellers to contemporary society. Students in each grade study their subjects through the lens of a particular time period and culture.[10]

When I was quite little I heard about mottoes and I wanted terribly to have a motto that I would keep all my life. I searched about for a long time before I found, written on pennies, "in God we trust." I thought it was wonderful and I swore I would never change it...It made me very proud to have a motto when I was so young and I wanted terribly to be faithful and constant to it. I always wanted something I could be faithful to forever. I hated fickle people.

— 1940 AUTOBIOGRAPHY, SENIOR CLASS ASSIGNMENT, FIELDSTON SCHOOL

Younger sister, Renée, is born on October 13, 1928.

1929–1931

In the summer of 1929 the Nemerovs move to 1185 Park Avenue.[11]

By her own account, the stock market crash of 1929 and the Depression that follows have little direct impact on her life. One of her few memories of the period is recounted in a 1968 radio interview with Studs Terkel, portions of which are later included in his book *Hard Times: An Oral History of the Great Depression* (1970). Like many of the interviewees in the book, her recollections appear under a pseudonym. She calls herself "Daisy Singer."[12]

I had a governess I really loved when I was young...I remember once going to the park to the site of the old reservoir which was at that time empty, because presumably they had put the water in the new one and there was a cavity and there was a shanty town there...the image is not really so concrete. But you know, it was for me the most palpable potent memory of the other side of the railroad tracks...you know holding the hand of one's governess and feeling...I don't mean to say I envied those people, but just to see that you couldn't get in there, you know, that you couldn't just wander down. That there was such a gulf.

— 1968 RADIO INTERVIEW WITH STUDS TERKEL ON THE DEPRESSION[13]

The family fortune always seemed to me humiliating. When I had to go into that store...I would come on somebody's arm or holding somebody's hand at what must have been a fairly young age and it was like being a princess in some loathsome movie of some kind of Transylvanian obscure middle European country and the kingdom was so humiliating.

— 1968 RADIO INTERVIEW WITH STUDS TERKEL ON THE DEPRESSION

I remember the special agony of walking down that center aisle, feeling like the princess of Russek's: simultaneously privileged and doomed. The main floor was always very empty like a church and along the way were poised the leeringest manikins ever whose laps and bosoms were never capacious enough for refuge and all the live people bowed slightly and smiled like the obsequies were seasoned with mockeries. It seemed it all belonged to me and I was ashamed.

—POSTCARD TO MARVIN ISRAEL, MARCH 4, 1960[14]

1932–1933

The Nemerovs move to the San Remo, an apartment house at 146 Central Park West.[15] After the children's maternal grandparents, the Russeks, move in with them, Diane and Renée share a room: *I used to try to give my sister dreams when we shared a room. I would lean over her, the hair at the back of her neck was wet, in ringlets, and whisper "elephant, waterfall, dancing" but it never worked at all.*[16]

Once I remember my brother was robbed. This is when we lived on Central Park West...he was perhaps 12...I would have been 9...which was three years after the Crash...My brother and I were skating outside of the apartment house where we lived. We were dressed sort of young for our age. He must have looked a bit sissified although he was a good football player sometime later. Anyway, two sort of poor boys called to him and he didn't hear them. I remember feeling terrifically proud that he should be summoned by, you know, just regular [boys]. They were older. So I called to him. And he came over and I very sort of dutifully kept my distance so I wouldn't interrupt this sort of manly exchange which apparently consisted of their demanding his money. I don't remember how much they got... It was probably just a few dollars. But they made a dash for it over the low stone wall and my brother made as if to follow them but he was on roller skates. And I, like some sort of Lillian Gish in some ancient film, restrained him, saying, "Don't."

— 1968 RADIO INTERVIEW WITH STUDS TERKEL ON THE DEPRESSION

1934–1935

Enters Fieldston, the Riverdale campus of the Ethical Culture School. A classmate, Stewart Stern, recalls her this way: *I idealized her so much from the time of my earliest recollection that I don't know if I remember her. She came full-blown with her mature privacy intact, and she seemed to know from the beginning of my recollection who she was and who she was going to be and what her private space consisted of.*[17]

...She could shock you with the directness of what she had to say and with...the way she looked at things...She was like a wonderful film director because when you watch them they're doing such body English to the actors they're directing when they're behind the camera... Her face did that. You could almost look at her and get the story of what she was watching

unfold. It was so naked and so tender and so empathic...I think the thing I remember most is the depth of her earnestness and at the same time the flicker of amusement almost constantly. And one of the most raucous laughs. I can still hear it across the din of the dining room.[18]

Her 1940 autobiography seems preoccupied with questions of loyalty, authenticity, and courage:

We used to go into the park in the afternoons to play games and climb rocks. Whenever there was something a little dangerous or daring to do, like jumping over a wide crevice between rocks or playing a trick on the teacher or teasing one of the strong girls I would be the leader and the first one to do it. I was always considered the most daring but I am sure I was more afraid than the others.

— 1940 AUTOBIOGRAPHY, SENIOR CLASS ASSIGNMENT, FIELDSTON SCHOOL

The Nemerovs' professional involvement in the fashion world coupled with their frequent travel to Europe broadens their knowledge of culture and the visual arts. David Nemerov has a particular interest in Impressionist painting. They encourage the artistic impulses of each of their children.

About this time everyone suddenly decided I was meant to be an artist and I was given art lessons and a big box of oils and encouragement and everything. I painted and drew every once in a while for about 4 yrs. with a teacher without admitting to anyone that I didn't like to paint or draw at all and I didn't know what I was doing. I used to pray and wish often to be a "great artist" and all the while I hated it and I didn't realize that I didn't want to be an artist at all. The horrible thing was that all the encouragement I got made me think that really I wanted to be an artist and made me keep pretending that I liked it and made me like it less and less until I hated it because it wasn't me that was being an artist; everybody was lifting me high up and crowning me and congratulating me and I was smiling—and really I hated it and I hadn't done one single good piece of work. It was the craziest pretense in the world but even though I was pretending I believed in it, for about four years I had visions of being a great sad artist and I turned all my energies toward it when I wasn't an artist at all.

— 1940 AUTOBIOGRAPHY, SENIOR CLASS ASSIGNMENT, FIELDSTON SCHOOL

According to Stewart Stern: *When she picked up her brush for the first time she was simply not doing what anybody else did. We were all trying to be representational and she had no interest in that, except as a kind of satire.*[19]

After two summers at Camp Accomac in Maine (1933 and 1934), she vacations in the country with her family and her young cousins, where she spends most of her time alone, reading: *Although I admit I was proud of it for its own sake, I think I was really happy...I began to believe in myself.*[20]

1936–1938

Meets Allan Arbus (born 1918, New York City), who is working in the advertising department at Russek's. David Nemerov's partner, Max Weinstein, is Allan Arbus's uncle by marriage. Arbus had attended City College (1933–35) but left before graduating.[21] They begin to see each other on Saturday afternoons for walks in the park or tea. Together they attend exhibitions at The Museum of Modern Art, including *Photography 1839–1937* (1937) and *Walker Evans: American Photographs* (1938). After a while, they begin meeting in secret, as well. *In confronting the world, we were really always tremendous allies*, Allan recalls.[22]

In 1938 Diane attends Cummington, a summer school for the arts in western Massachusetts. Victor D'Amico, her art teacher at Fieldston, recommends her to the program: *She has exceptional ability and shows a definite sense of composition, color, and form in painting. Her style is highly individual and her manner of expression unique. We have tried to develop her powers without damaging her personal gifts in any way.*[23]

While at Cummington, she studies with the painter Herman Maril. She meets Alexander Eliot, who had spent a year at Black Mountain as a student of Josef Albers and is also in the Cummington painting program.[24] Eliot later comments: *Her painting was very like the photographs were going to be: extremely reverent, extremely reverent in the face of the object.*[25] But her frustration with the medium persists. The following November, she writes Eliot: *Sometimes...I feel as if I could just take anything and know it my way and paint it but it doesn't paint as well as I know it.*[26]

1939–1940

Chooses art as her major at Fieldston. D'Amico (who was named director of education at The Museum of Modern Art in 1937) is her advisor. The Museum of Modern Art, founded in 1929, opens its building on 53rd Street in May 1939. Fieldston art students visit the museum as a class excursion.[27]

She is selected for Elbert Lenrow's Senior English Seminar, along with nine or ten other students, including Stewart Stern. The students sit around a table with Lenrow at the head of it, whom Stern describes this way: *He was a big, broad-*

shouldered man...{who} always wore glasses...{and} a handkerchief in his breast pocket with a kind of lilac cologne on it. He taught with his eyes shut because he had problems with his eyes. The first class he said, "It's nothing personal. I've seen who you all are, I know you all, you're very attractive people, but I'm going to shut my eyes because I need to save them for my reading."[28]

Students in the class are required to write brief essays on each book they read. Her responses, in style as well as content, prefigure her mature sensibility.

The Bible is wonderful and beautiful. It is man's creation; like the desperate attempt of a race of men, faced with things they couldn't understand, to account for it all and be able to believe in what they had created. They were made and placed on the earth and faced with substance and space, with wet and dry, with soft and hard, with big and small, with dark and light, with pain, with unhappiness, with hunger, with desire—and they couldn't understand it. Everything was so wonderful and so horrible that they had to have something to make them know that everything would be all right. A man cannot believe in what he doesn't understand at all, a man cannot believe in nothing. A man must have a sense that there is an order behind everything, good and bad, an order which is bigger than himself but which he can at least in part understand.

—JANUARY 16, 1940, PAPER ON THE OLD TESTAMENT, SENIOR ENGLISH SEMINAR[29]

Chaucer seems to be very sure and whole and his attitude toward everything is so calm and tender because he was satisfied and glad that he was himself. The way he describes meeting the 29 pilgrims gives you a feeling of easiness; it isn't a frenzied need for companionship—it is a delight he gets in speaking and being with people...you get the feeling that he is a little bit beyond them, but that he doesn't want to seem so. The pleasure he gets from meeting them is part physical, part spiritual. He seems to love physical things, even obscene ones, and from looking at them, he gets a contact with the other person. His way of looking at everything is like that of a newborn baby; he sees things and each one seems wonderful, not for its significance in relation to other things, but simply because it is unique and because it is there. When he describes the nun's daintiness, it doesn't seem as if he thinks that that is a standard of good conduct...rather he turns separately to each one and looks on them as whole miracles not as compounds of abstract qualities, and he seems to know that each one will always be himself and he wants that.

—MARCH 5, 1940, PAPER ON CHAUCER'S *THE CANTERBURY TALES*, SENIOR ENGLISH SEMINAR

[Don Quixote] wanted to be right, I guess, but all the time you feel that he was so un-sophisticated that he could never be quite like other people. And being out of tempo with the world, he felt that he was wrong. His "madness" is a way of being himself to the limit. You feel that suddenly and deliberately he threw off his already limited awareness of the conventions of the world, and threw himself in the world's face defiantly, because he was what he was, and he felt that that was good enough.

—APRIL 16, 1940, PAPER ON CERVANTES'S *DON QUIXOTE*, SENIOR ENGLISH SEMINAR

Graduates from Fieldston in June.

For the next several months she continues taking private painting classes—arranged by her father—with Dorothy Thompson, a fashion illustrator who worked for Russek's,[30] and whom she later refers to as *probably an interesting woman*.[31]

I hated painting and I quit right after high school because I was continually told how terrific I was...it made me feel shaky. I remember I hated the smell of the paint and the noise it would make when I put my brush to the paper. Sometimes I wouldn't really look but just listen to this horrible squish squish squish. I didn't want to be told I was terrific. I had the sense that if I was so terrific at it, it wasn't worth doing.

— 1968 RADIO INTERVIEW WITH STUDS TERKEL ON THE DEPRESSION[32]

While at Harvard, Howard Nemerov writes a series of letters to his parents describing his plans to launch, along with five friends, a literary magazine. He expresses the hope that *Diane will contribute, since we all believe thoroughly in her drawing*.[33]

The Nemerovs move to 888 Park Avenue.[34]

1941

Marries Allan Arbus on April 10, 1941, in a small ceremony. The Reverend Dr. Israel Goldstein performs the wedding in his study at 270 West 89th Street.[35] The couple spends their three-week honeymoon on a farm in Columbia County, New York.[36]

They move into an apartment at 325 East 37th Street, where their bathroom doubles as a darkroom. Soon after, Alexander Eliot moves in across the hall with his wife, Anne.[37] Eliot describes the dynamics of their friendship this way: *I used to talk all the time, but I was inarticulate, really. I mean I couldn't think my way out of a paper bag. And Diane of course said very little. Diane was like a lodestone or a touchstone...In that sense she would be the center of things...And Allan was always very strong on the discriminating side. He could say what the experience wasn't. Always. Wonderfully well. This was a great champion to have around, to clear the air, to say, Not that, not that.*[38] When the Eliots' daughter, May, is born, Alex and Anne choose Diane to be May's godmother.

She receives a Graflex 2¼ x 3¼ camera, as a gift from Allan. Takes class with Berenice Abbott, which primarily covers technical aspects of photography, and teaches what she learns from Abbott to Allan. He proves to be an adept technician. On a vacation in Montauk, Allan takes a series of fashion photographs, using Diane as a model, which inspire David Nemerov to hire them as photographers for Russek's newspaper advertisements.[39]

They visit An American Place, Alfred Stieglitz's gallery for modernist art and photography. They meet Stieglitz and from time to time show him their work. According to Allan, the photographers who interest her most in this period, in addition to Stieglitz, are Mathew Brady, Timothy O'Sullivan, Paul Strand, Bill Brandt, and Eugène Atget.[40]

Howard Nemerov graduates from Harvard and the following autumn enlists in the Canadian Air Force, flying combat missions against German shipping in the North Sea.[41]

1942–1944

Following the entry of the United States into World War II, Allan enlists in the army and is sent to Camp Crowder in Missouri for basic training. When he is transferred to Fort Monmouth, New Jersey, Diane joins him. His subsequent reassignment to the Photography Division of the Signal Corps enables the couple to move back to Manhattan, where they rent a small midtown apartment on the east side.

Diane develops a friendship with Pati Hill, whom she meets at a party. In Hill's own words, she has come to New York from Virginia *to live a bohemian life in Greenwich Village, but by then there were no more bohemians.*[42] Hill is working as a fashion model and as a writer. Diane later describes her this way: *She is enormously complex...her thinking, doing, saying are all three always working simultaneously and fast...(but not much together except as in a dance, to meet, to merge, to bow, to entwine) in ever varying relations to each other...*[43]

When Allan is posted to India in 1944, Diane—who is now pregnant—moves into her parents' apartment at 888 Park Avenue. There is a darkroom in the basement of the building for the use of the tenants. During this period she takes photographs of family and friends, using a 5x7 Deardorff view camera David Nemerov had given them.

She also makes a series of self-portraits that chart the progress of her pregnancy, which she prints and sends to Allan. Her letters to him include detailed descriptions of photographs she has seen, and often the photographs themselves, torn from the pages of magazines. Among these are some of Richard Avedon's first fashion pictures for *Harper's Bazaar*.[44]

In London in 1944, Howard Nemerov marries Peggy (Margaret) Russell.

1945

On April 3, daughter Doon is born. The night before, Diane slips away to New York Hospital alone, leaving behind a note for her parents (which David Nemerov saves and later shows to Allan) asking them not to visit her there: *I've gone to have my baby...since I can't have Allan I don't want anyone.*[45]

In a handwritten note dated April 8 she writes Alfred Stieglitz:

Our baby is a girl...curious and even a little funny. I simply stare at her. I expected to feel deep recognition but I don't. She isn't like either of us but lovely: very alive and with very beautiful shoulders. I love our lack of connection: that she doesn't feel anything towards me and I feel in such an odd, separate way about her.

I expected great changes (first, I expected it from pregnancy, then when it didn't come, I expected it from birth.) but I'm glad I didn't change or at least feel changed. I trust myself better as I am. It was very simple—I have forgotten most of the bad part because of the anaesthetic—but I still know it was simple. I guess events are always simpler than people—which is good.

Born April 3, 8lbs. Her name is Doon.[46]

And to Pati Hill, whose birthday also happens to be April 3: *A girl...I know you hate them but she is quite fantastic. She reminds me of a monkey and makes me laugh...*[47]

When Walker Evans leaves *Time* to become staff photographer at *Fortune*, Alex Eliot, who has been working for the March of Time newsreel company, becomes a sportswriter for *Time* and later its arts editor.[48]

1946

On January 25 Allan is discharged from the army.[49] He returns to New York. For a few months the Arbus family continues to live with the Nemerovs at 888 Park Avenue.

Eventually, they move to an apartment on West 70th Street and, with David Nemerov's financial help, rent studio space at 108 West 54th Street and purchase equipment for their fashion photography business. They resume work on the Russek's account using the credit line "Diane & Allan Arbus."

In addition to the commercial photography of their partnership both Diane and Allan continue to make pictures individually, which they show to Nancy Newhall, Acting Curator of Photography (1943–46), at The Museum of Modern Art.[50]

They are both avid readers. The books in their library at the time, inscribed by Diane on the flyleaf "Diane and Allan Arbus," include works by Plato, Marcus Aurelius, Thomas Aquinas, Spinoza, Schopenhauer, Kierkegaard; Dostoevsky, Melville, Conrad, Gogol; Donne, Blake, Rilke, and Yeats.[51]

1947–1950

After several months, Diane and Allan gather together some of their fashion pictures and take them to Alexander Liberman at Condé Nast. Allan describes Liberman's response as *enthusiastic and very gallante.*[52] One of their first regular clients is *Glamour.* Their main contact at that magazine is Tina Fredericks, the art editor. They also work for *Vogue, Seventeen,* and advertising agencies.

Often dependent upon an imaginative use of props and locations, their style is the result of Diane's art direction and Allan's camera work. *They were always idea pictures,* Allan recalls. *For some reason, we couldn't work without an idea and ninety per cent of them were Diane's.*[53] They are admirers and somewhat baffled students of the work of many photographers in the fashion field: Louise Dahl-Wolfe and Martin Munkasci, as well as Paul Hoyningen-Huene, John Rawlings, Irving Penn, and Richard Avedon.[54]

Allan describes their experience in the business as a kind of balancing act between triumph and despair: *Each month there'd be the magazines we were just thirsting for. And if the pictures in them were good—which usually meant there was something of Dick's [Avedon]—the work would all seem possible again.*[55] Or as Diane puts it: *Every few days, after it had rained like we needed it to, or Liberman had complimented us like we wanted, and the picture was going to be used, and nobody thought it was as bad as it was, then the next day was like a miracle, gratis...*[56] Allan concludes: *And whenever we did a picture we liked, we couldn't go to sleep. We'd stay up all night looking at it. We were just two terrified, totally uninformed, wildly enthusiastic photographers.*[57]

They meet Nancy Christopherson (Bellamy), who, with some help from their friend Pati Hill, is exploring a modeling career. Nancy recalls her first encounter with Diane: *It was mysterious the way we met...Pati Hill had given me a list of fashion photographers to see and I'd been walking up and down with it and the next name on my list was Arbus. That's when I noticed this woman on the street. She looked solemn, profound, and I knew, instantly, I just knew we were destined to be great friends. I entered the studio which was very black and white, very sterile, and met a young man with enormous eyes, very nervous and thin. He interviewed me and he was very nice but my mind was still on the woman I had seen on the street. And then she walked in! I wanted to start the friendship right there...*[58]

Howard Nemerov, who has been living in New York with his wife, Peggy, since the end of the war, working as an editor of the literary periodical *Furioso*, publishes his first book of poetry, *The Image and the Law*, in 1947.[59] The same year, Renée Nemerov, recently graduated from the Dalton School, marries Roy Sparkia.[60]

The Arbus family spends summers on Martha's Vineyard (1948 and 1949) with Alex and Anne Eliot and their daughter, May, and on Lake Champlain (1950) with Nancy and Dick Bellamy and Nancy's five-year-old daughter, Poni.[61]

In 1950, Alex Eliot meets Jane Winslow and separates from his wife, Anne.[62]

1951

In the spring, Diane and Allan sublet their studio for a year and sail for Paris on the *Île de France* with their six-year-old daughter, Doon, and their blue Ford sedan. Alex Eliot refers to this trip as their *sabbatical venture*,[63] but according to Allan: *We were really running away.*[64] In a letter from the ship, Diane describes the transatlantic voyage:

Everyone is sleepy—a little screwed up with boredom (the weather has been cold windy rainy—gorgeous but not easy.) There are thousands of children and old people and almost everyone smiles but no one speaks more than two sentences. It's very queer—everyone is always jumping up as if they had a pressing appointment in some other part of the boat...I speak lots of french to the waiters and stewards and occasionally to the crew. They are charming—very eager to share your bad french with you. We say nothing interesting except that the effort involved on both sides is so sweet that it approaches communication.

—LETTER TO ALEX ELIOT AND JANE WINSLOW FROM *ILE DE FRANCE*, MAY 1951

They arrive in France on May 7. They spend the better part of the spring and summer in Paris with brief trips by car to Burgundy (to visit Pati Hill, who is living on a farm there, writing her first novel), to Versailles, to Brittany, and, for a few weeks in June, to Spain. Diane writes Alex Eliot and Jane Winslow: *God what a place this is—Spain—I would rather be here than anywhere.*[65] And about Toledo:

...The atmosphere was so potent, oriental, flowering with corruption, crawling with nursing mothers, sick animals, swaggering soldiers, blind people screaming out about lottery tickets, priests hurrying about on what looked like pretend urgent business, american phonograph records (like Anchors Aweigh) whining a thousand times over behind the beaded curtains, and those birds I told you about, circling low, even into the ruined buildings (in some of which the balconies remained though the house was gone)...

—LETTER TO ALEX ELIOT AND JANE WINSLOW FROM BARCELONA, JUNE 13, 1951

Eliot reports having wangled two assignments for them from *Time*: color photographs of El Greco's Toledo and of Matisse's Chapel at Vence.[66] They investigate both possibilities, but neither comes to fruition. Diane writes:

I was, still am, obsessed by the desire to do something for...[*Time*]...but the only things that came to me were impossibly ambitious complex things which you haven't the space for...and, very likely they wouldn't work anyway...like the Greco-ish images in Toledo...one boy with a greenish face and incredible long hands, working on jewelry...one priest with small shorn head, lean nose, sharp eyes, who got bigger and bigger down to the bottom of him, under his billowing gown, huge folded hands and great massive feet...But much more...there are Goya images mostly from the drawings (so it wouldn't be color)...one we have seen several times: a blindfolded ass with ears fully a foot long walking in a hopeless circle, pulling a water wheel which is attached to him by a stick with another stick outstretched in front of him...as if tempting him but there is nothing on it...

—LETTER TO ALEX ELIOT AND JANE WINSLOW FROM BARCELONA, JUNE 13, 1951

In September, they leave Paris for Italy, eventually settling in an apartment in Florence for the month of October.

We've just moved in, just now, and I'm tired and not all unpacked, but don't feel like it so perversely decided to write you. The apartment is perfectly beautiful... large, tall, skylighted living room with a fireplace and an easel and an impressive

round table with upholstered chairs whose backs come as high as my head...
Our landlord, Dottor (of law) Gordigiani looked fairly unpleasant in this first
encounter, raising all sorts of vague objections to our using the garden, and
upturning his palm with distressing frequency, but I have hopes that his wife
will be nicer.

—LETTER TO GERTRUDE AND DAVID NEMEROV FROM FLORENCE, SEPTEMBER 30, 1951

We feel very small here. At breakfast the table was so big that we had to keep
pushing the butter, salt, and sugar at each other like at a bowling alley...Last night
Allan and I stayed "in the living room" after Doon went to bed and talked in wee
small voices like we were breaking the silence. So amazing to have a living room,
but especially such an immense one, that we often say to each other, "where shall
we sit?" and when anyone leaves one room, Doon asks, "where are you going?"

—LETTER TO GERTRUDE AND DAVID NEMEROV FROM FLORENCE, SEPTEMBER 30, 1951

...it has been such a wonderful month here. It's even lovely ending, because
it makes so clear the picture of it. We lived so well, accomplished something
photographing and reached a kind of peak of feeling between the three of us.

—LETTER TO GERTRUDE AND DAVID NEMEROV FROM FLORENCE, NOVEMBER 2, 1951

In December they rent a house on a farm in Frascati, outside of Rome, and make
arrangements for Doon to attend the nearby Montessori School. Although the
trip to Europe is intended to provide them a respite from fashion photography,
it is also seen as an opportunity for each of them to pursue their own individual
photography.

...Sunday we almost caused a riot going with our cameras and our great big blue
Ford and the dog, into one of the nearby hill towns and walking around. What
seemed liked thousands of children came scrambling out of every nook and cranny
and crowded around us, jumping and laughing, so that we had to maneuver in a
real complex way when we wanted to go home in order not to have thirty children
riding home on the roof of the car with us...

—LETTER TO GERTRUDE AND DAVID NEMEROV FROM FRASCATI, DECEMBER 17, 1951

1952–1954

As the prospect of their return home approaches, they begin to seek magazine
assignments that may enable them to prolong their stay.

We have two assignments [for *Vogue*], one non fashion...someone's collection of
paintings with the collector...the other, some evening gowns from the collections

here (in color—worse luck...we have to scour Rome today for extra equipment.) This means some extra money, but more important I have several more ideas which they might use that we could do here or in Spain. This besides being a grand opportunity means we could come home as Vogue photographers instead of Glamour photographers who disappeared for a while, and also enables us to stay until we can get the studio back (May 1st) which skirts the problem of having to beg and rent studio space the first two months we are back...Also I'd love to stretch things out a bit and [would] love to go to Spain. All this IF they are interested...

—LETTER TO GERTRUDE NEMEROV AND ROSE RUSSEK FROM FRASCATI, JANUARY 27, 1952

Her method of developing a magazine project in this period, from the original idea to the proposal, research, and pursuit is consistent with the way she later approaches her own personal work.

... I think we will be going to Milan next week for Vogue, then a few days work in Rome for Vogue, then a weeny job in Florence for Glamour. Meanwhile, I have almost completed a lovely mammoth letter to a Vogue editor full of further suggestions which may or may not catch their fancy. Anyway, if we do get the Vogue pages done (it is still not absolutely definite) with some assurance that they will [be] published and paid for, we may do on our own one lovely idea which we had, because if Vogue won't use it, some other magazine probably will. It all depends on whether we can cut some of the red tape involved, which is fantastic. (It involves a certain amount of cooperation of the part of Vatican officials, and the organization of the Catholic church is too big to care, too Italian to be efficient.)

—LETTER TO GERTRUDE NEMEROV FROM FRASCATI, FEBRUARY 14, 1952

While living in Frascati, they receive from Pati Hill the completed manuscript of her first novel, *The Nine Mile Circle* (published in 1957 by the Riverside Press, Houghton Mifflin). Diane had known only what Hill had told her, that it was about a child who killed its fantasy self for the sake of a friend.[67] Diane responds to the manuscript:

Dear P.

The book is beautiful. It enchants so that when I stop reading it I am drunk with it. It's not circular like so many books (where the end is a prelude to the beginning)...it grows as surely as a flower does and its petals get plucked and blown away and in the end I was so sad I thought it must have died. Read it twice with interruptions, and then sometimes just picked up any part. It's very sad, not by anything in the subject of it, but like it's constructed by loss, I mean the losing of its parts, fading, forgetting...whereas most books, even the saddest, are resolved and tied up, each thread to another, so that somebody (author or reader) ends up with a package and takes it home. Really marvelous (the peoples, times, places, meshings, crossings)...and the marvelous absence of an obstreperous, omnipotent author...and the brilliant floating center of it. (I remember wondering ages ago where everything goes when you throw it away, garbage, things you lose, forget, etc and vaguely expecting they'd all turn up in some immense spiritual city dump...but it's like you followed a thousand things and found they all go different places and never stop.)

—LETTER TO PATI HILL FROM FRASCATI, FEBRUARY 16, 1952

I am in bed with a cold and Allan is getting one and every fifth person in Rome has flu. We have been "working" without doing much work. I mean we suddenly were assigned several assignments and invented several more and made all sorts of preparations and hunted for necessary equipment because it all meant we could stay longer. But suddenly, the best paying and also ghastliest assignment has been canceled. And we are relieved and horrified at the waste...(Haven't photographed in ages because of "work")...Dread going home, dread working, dread my family unreasonably. But I don't dread NY or Central Park or lots of places (which I secretly think belong to me).

—LETTER TO PATI HILL FROM FRASCATI, FEBRUARY 16, 1952

After a number of changes in plans, they leave Italy on March 23 and sail home from France to resume their fashion photography business. They arrive in New York on April 7 in time to attend Alex Eliot and Jane Winslow's wedding.[68]

By mid-May they have rented a triplex at 319 East 72nd Street, in a building owned by the sculptor Paul Manship. The studio and darkroom are on the second floor, with a balcony overlooking a spare, white, two-story living room. Along one wall of the living room is a built-in bench with cushions and marble inset coffee tables designed by their friend Arthur Weinstein. Diane writes the Eliots, who are honeymooning in Europe: *Our house is perfectly beautiful in spite of the chaos and full of the loveliest views and the loveliest shadows at night.*[69]

...There are many simple pleasures, like our radiant bedroom, waking up in the morning with sun shining through our curtains and the tangled ivy, and cooking in our glorious big kitchen...and our lovely colored couch cushions, and the bookcase Allan built rising out of the chaos, and the general delight of finding that the choices I had felt so damned by making could materialize into such pleasant surprises...Allan is full of energy and courage and optimism, and builds and paints and wires things and fixes others with a whole assortment of unsuspected skills...

—LETTER TO ALEX AND JANE ELIOT ON THEIR HONEYMOON IN EUROPE, MAY 1952

I am full of human feeling because we don't see hardly anybody, only Nancy by appointment and I don't feel much like talking but when I see a face I think it looks wonderful, so I find myself complimenting everyone with quite a note of wonder in my voice…

—LETTER TO ALEX AND JANE ELIOT ON THEIR HONEYMOON IN EUROPE, MAY 1952

Robert Brown, an actor with whom they become friends, moves into the neighboring apartment with his wife and daughter. He recalls the Arbus home as a refuge in which he spends almost as much time as he does in his own.[70] On occasion, their studio and living room provide the setting for workshop productions in which he has a role. Through him, Diane renews her friendship with Fieldston classmate Stewart Stern, now a screenwriter living in Los Angeles and a friend of Brown's.[71]

In the autumn of 1952, the Arbuses enroll Doon in the Rudolf Steiner School, probably on the advice of the Eliots—May Eliot is a student there. A few years later Diane makes note of the following remarks by Steiner's principal, Henry Barnes, on the subject of progressive education: *In being encouraged to express themselves, the students were made to think that self-expression was the coin of life and that any bill could be paid with it. They didn't realize that experience won from life itself was necessary to cope with reality.*[72] These words appear to have struck a chord with her view of her own experience at Ethical Culture Fieldston School.

She and Nancy Christopherson, inveterate moviegoers, often take Doon and Poni with them. They see many Italian neorealist films: Vittorio De Sica's *Shoeshine* (1946), *The Bicycle Thief* (1948), *Miracle in Milan* (1951); Roberto Rossellini's *Open City* (1945); and Federico Fellini's *La Strada* (1954).

April 16, 1954, daughter Amy is born.

1955

On March 28, Rose Russek, widowed in 1948, dies in her bedroom in the Nemerov apartment at 888 Park Avenue. Three years earlier, in a letter to the Eliots, she had written: *My grandmother is sick…not alarmingly, but sadly ailing, sick and seventy and moving in with my parents, which is like the defeat of a proud spirit who forgot what the fight was all about.*[73]

A Diane and Allan Arbus photograph of a father and son on a sofa taken for *Vogue* is included by Edward Steichen in *The Family of Man* exhibition at The Museum of Modern Art.[74]

According to Allan, Diane's belief in herself as a photographer never wavers, in spite of the fact that she is continually plagued by uncertainty about what to photograph and constantly dissatisfied with the pictures she actually makes. She studies photography with Alexey Brodovitch, art director of *Harper's Bazaar*, at the New School for Social Research. Although she remains in contact with Brodovitch, in the ensuing years she finds the course of little help to her work.

The family moves to a triplex garden apartment with studio at 18 East 68th Street.

1956

Although she has been photographing since the early 1940s, Diane now, and apparently for the first time, starts numbering her negatives and corresponding contact sheets beginning with #1. She will maintain this system for the rest of her career. Among the first of these are a few rolls of 2¼ square negatives made with a Rolleiflex. She soon abandons this format in favor of the 35mm Nikon and only returns to it in 1962 when the square begins to become a hallmark of her mature style. During this period, she experiments with cropping both her images and her prints. Some of the prints are mounted on mat board, trimmed flush to the edges and treated as objects.

She and Allan end their photographic partnership. Her growing frustration with the business and with her role in the partnership (which she regards as essentially that of a glorified stylist) culminates one evening in the company of their friend Robert Brown when her account of a *Vogue* sitting leaves her in tears. In the end, Allan suggests she quit the business and she agrees. *I'm sure she felt like she was deserting the ship*, he says later. *But she was very glad to be out of it.*[75] She continues to do all her own printing in the studio darkroom, while her negatives are still processed and contacted by Allan's assistant under Allan's supervision.

She responds to an advertisement for a photography course taught by Lisette Model, whose work had been published by Brodovitch in *Harper's Bazaar* and exhibited at The Museum of Modern Art. *In the beginning, she brought photographs which were nothing but grain...*[76] Model recalls, a description that mirrors an account Diane later gives to her 1971 master class:

In the beginning of photographing I used to make very grainy things. I'd be fascinated by what the grain did because it would make a kind of tapestry of all these little dots and everything would be translated into this medium of dots.

Skin would be the same as water would be the same as sky and you were dealing mostly in dark and light not so much in flesh and blood...It was my teacher, Lisette Model, who finally made it clear to me that the more specific you are, the more general it'll be...

—DIANE ARBUS, APERTURE, 1972[77]

A number of attempts have since been made by Diane and others to account for the ensuing transformation in her work and, more significantly, in her feeling about photographing. One of several versions offered by Model goes as follows: *One day I said to her, and I think this was very crucial, I said, "Originality means coming from the source, not like Brodovitch—at any price to do it different..." And from there on, Diane was sitting there and—I've never in my life seen anybody—not listening to me but suddenly listening to herself through what was said.*[78]

In any event, as Allan recalls: *It was an absolutely magical breakthrough. After three weeks she felt totally freed and able to photograph.*[79]

1957–1958

Takes a second course with Lisette Model. According to Model, Diane frequently asks to look at her work and Model always refuses. At any rate, Diane would surely have seen the exhibition 70 *Photographers Look at New York*, at The Museum of Modern Art, which includes Model's work.[80]

In a letter to her friends Lyn and Bob Meservey, who are living in New Haven while he is working on his doctorate degree in physics from Yale, Diane writes:

I am terribly behind in photographing—it's almost as if everything has to be done all the time. But at the same time I think I see how to do it. Photographing all day long, I used to get so high and dry, into a sort of a weird and rarefied air that I was not only in danger of never coming home but even of ceasing to photograph... like being in the ocean when the waves make you feel so strong you might swim to Europe...I am full of a sense of promise, like I often have, the feeling of always being at the beginning. (And I had a dream...which made perfect sense at the time and when I woke up it scattered and shattered...into something like 'Balance destroy supply under.' Bob will grin like always. Of course, he'll say, that's obvious.)

—LETTER TO BOB AND LYN MESERVEY, CIRCA 1957

For the sake of an application submitted to the Guggenheim Foundation in 1962, Diane categorizes her work of this period as follows: *children's games; sideshows; secret photos of steam bathers; photographs at the beach; movie theater interiors;*

and *female impersonators*.[81] Locations include Central Park, Times Square and its environs, Hubert's Dime Museum and Flea Circus, the Horn and Hardhart automat, Grand Central Station, the roller derby, rodeo, and circus at Madison Square Garden, Sammy's Bar on the Bowery, Coney Island's sideshows and wax museums, Woolworth's department store, Harlem dance halls, and the Carmine Street pool. She photographs traditional events such as the Macy's Thanksgiving Day Parade, the Feast of San Gennaro street festival, and Easter, Halloween, and New Year's Eve celebrations.

During this period she is also attempting—apparently without success—to find editorial work for herself as a photographer:

...once I made [for Tina Fredericks at the *Ladies' Home Journal*] and didnt never get paid for some pictures of how you shouldn't litter up the place, any place, so I spent a week sifting through cans and finding puddles with floating cigarette butts in them and squashed cellophane and orange peels and broken bottle ends and I followed flying newspapers especially comics because it was some of it color film...running like mad to keep up with dick tracy, and I ended up in the rambles part of the park, because she wanted a pastoral scene defaced with litter and it was autumn and two ducks swim there called charlie and lucy and they swam by the sort of strewn up grass very obediently and amy was with me and all of a sudden she said something in a small voice and came up out of the pond dripping with grasses and litter and tears and water like an angry inept mermaid and I had to scoop her into my arms with the camera and hobble out of the park and take her clothes off in the cab because she was shivering something fierce and carry her naked and giggling into that fancy house on 68th street, meeting one of our unspeakable neighbors on the way and dripping everything all over the lobby.

—LETTER TO MARVIN ISRAEL, SPRING 1960

The Nemerovs move to 60 Sutton Place South in 1957. The following year, David Nemerov, now retired from Russek's, moves to Palm Beach with Gertrude and devotes himself full-time to his painting.

Henry Wolf succeeds Alexey Brodovitch as art director of *Harper's Bazaar* in 1958.

1959

She begins keeping a yearly appointment book as well as a series of small working notebooks, a practice that will continue for the rest of her career.[82]

The appointment books are primarily devoted to day-to-day events: scheduled meetings with friends, acquaintances, or professional colleagues; newspaper clippings or notations about upcoming events or phenomena she means to investigate; reminders of responsibilities related to home or family; ideas for photographic projects, and information about people or methods that may help her pursue them.

The notebooks are more eclectic. They include passages copied from books she is reading and observations made by her friends or happened upon by chance: *In this culture we tend each to think of ourselves as the protagonist of our own drama. There is little precedent for playing a subordinate role in someone else's* — N. (Nancy Christopherson), or *The best revenge is forgiveness. —Salada Tea.*[83] There are proposals for photographic projects and related lists; words, synonyms, conundrums, and thoughts; stories told by people she is photographing; an occasional impromptu release accompanied by a brief description of the picture. There are also the titles of books she intends to get for research purposes and names of people to track down as possible subjects or sources of ideas. From time to time, the contents mingle: a scheduled appointment may appear in a notebook or a project proposal on the page of an appointment book.

It is probably her friend Nancy Christopherson who introduces her to Zen literature and to the *I Ching*. One of the notebooks of 1959 consists in large part of excerpts from Zen literature, including Suzuki, *Zen Buddhism*; Alan Watts, *The Way of Zen*; Eugen Herrigel, *Zen in the Art of Archery*; Wei Wu Wei, *Fingers Pointing Towards the Moon*; and *Zen Flesh, Zen Bones.*[84] Much of what she jots down seems concerned with the nature, or the illusion, of time and appears in the notebooks between passages copied from Dostoevsky's *Notes from the Underground* and Bram Stoker's *Dracula.*[85]

In May, at the suggestion of *Esquire* articles editor Harold Hayes, she meets with the magazine's art director Robert Benton. The magazine is planning an issue devoted entirely to New York. She shows pictures to Benton, who is interested in her 35mm photographs taken inside darkened theaters. On May 7 she writes in her appointment book: *Benton wants movie pics, likes waxworks.*

Sends Benton subject ideas, as well as prints and contact sheets. She annotates some of the images with brief typewritten notes glued on verso of mounts. A picture of an eyeball from the horror movie *The Man Without a Body* is captioned: *An experiment by an eminent British doctor in keeping separate organs alive with a whole system of flashing lights and buzzing wires, dials and gauges, prior to grafting them on to people who happen to need such spare parts.*[86]

By this time she has almost entirely ceased cropping her images. With rare exceptions, she is printing the full 35mm negative as a vertical or horizontal rectangle in the center of an 11x14 sheet of photographic paper, leaving a border some two to four inches wide surrounding the image.

Moves in August with Doon and Amy from 18 East 68th Street to 131H Charles Street, a converted carriage house adjacent to the 6th Precinct police station in Greenwich Village. Allan moves to 71 Washington Place where he establishes a studio and darkroom, and continues his work for fashion magazines, keeping the name of their former partnership, Diane and Allan Arbus. She still shares his darkroom, and the family meets regularly for long Sunday breakfasts at Charles Street. Although this is in fact a separation, they do not tell their parents until three years later. (As Diane notes in a letter to Model on September 25, 1962: *I finally told my family that Allan and I were living apart and they suffered a whole series of delayed hysterical reactions, ranging from poignant to revolting.*)[87]

In October, begins work on the New York issue for *Esquire*. The original plan to assign her all photography in the issue is soon abandoned in favor of the concept of an independent photographic essay.[88] Collaborating with Benton and Hayes, she develops a project about the city from the *posh* to the *sordid*.[89] In a letter to Benton, she elaborates:

...I have been looking in the Redbook [the Yellow Pages] under clubs. There is one called the Tough Club and the Scientific Introduction Service and something called Ourselves, Inc. I was looking for some club that would look good for the upper in the sense of respectable reaches like Harold Hayes was talking about. Something like the D.A.R. or the W.C.T.U. or a society for the suppression of something or other like vice or sin. Maybe his secretary could find one such. Brady once photographed the D.A.R. and it was, in the French sense, formidable...I will go anywhere. The Edwardian Room and the Salvation Army.

—LETTER TO ROBERT BENTON, CIRCA OCTOBER 1959[90]

The spectrum of photographic permissions Hayes helps her obtain during the course of the project ranges from the Grand Opera Ball at the Sheraton East Hotel to a trackman in the tunnel of the city subway system, from a children's dancing class at the Colony Club to the Greenwich Street Women's House of Detention.[91] One such request from Hayes is addressed to Walter Arm, Deputy Police Commissioner:

Dear Sir:

In connection with a special issue of Esquire on the subject of New York, we have assigned Miss Diane Arbus, 131H Charles Street, New York 14. N.Y., to photograph various aspects of city life. For some of her work she will need a Police pass. Detective Wanderer, with whom we spoke on the telephone this morning. suggested that we write to you for this permission.

Is there any way in which she could have special permission to accompany on police calls officers working out of the Charles Street Precinct? Thank you very much for whatever you can do for us.[92]

The *Esquire* assignment crystallizes for her some of the moral issues that have traditionally haunted photography and that will continue to preoccupy her in one form or another. From the pragmatic point of view, as she writes Benton: *The releases are sometimes a problem: if people are grand enough they have learned never to sign anything and if they are degraded enough they can't.*[93] And more poignantly: *Couldn't the comment be foreborne or foregone? Tuesday I saw a man lying on the steps of a church on Lex Ave under a sign saying Open for Meditation and Prayer, with his fly open and his penis out. I couldn't ask him to sign a release, could you?*[94]

Toward the end of November, she meets Marvin Israel, a painter, graphic designer, and former art director of *Seventeen* magazine (1956–58). In the early stages of an enduring friendship as lovers and colleagues, they write to each other nearly every day.[95] Both are struck by ironic parallels within their separate histories: parents in the women's clothing business, an Ethical Culture education. As she puts it a few months later in a postcard to him:

...Our bourgeois heritage seems to me glorious as any stigma, especially to see it reflected back and forth in the mirror of each other...It is magic, and magic chooses any guise and ours is just perhaps more hilarious than to have been Negro or midget. It always makes me laugh in the middle of some unbelievable instant to think how our parents would approve of each other. That is the joke we are on them and us and it. To be so Jewish and rich and middle class and from good families and to run so variously away from it that we come full circle and bump into each other. Like they say in the comics*?!!#$?Boinggg......

—POSTCARD TO MARVIN ISRAEL, JANUARY 19, 1960

1960

As a continuation of the *Esquire* project, she investigates and photographs bodybuilders, beauty contests, debutantes, derelicts at the Christian Herald Bowery Mission, Boy Scout meetings, youth gang meetings, a condemned hotel on Broadway and its residents, many of the performers from Hubert's Museum (including Andrew Ratoucheff, a Russian midget who does impersonations of

Maurice Chevalier, and Hezekiah Trambles, known professionally as Congo the Jungle Creep, both of whom appear in the final published article), a pet crematorium, and members of the Jewel Box Revue's touring female impersonator show "Twenty-Five Men and a Girl." In the margin of a letter to Marvin Israel, she writes: *I would like to photograph everybody.*[96]

Her letters include detailed accounts of her photographic expeditions, punctuated on occasion by thoughts about the nature of being a photographer, about the power and responsibility of the enterprise:

The debutantes had to repeat over and over to each person who shook their hand on the receiving line, their name and the name of the place where they came from. There were about sixty of them. And maybe a thousand to shake their sixty hands. And those thousand mostly told the debutantes who they were too. Me and the press photographers were blessedly quiet.

—LETTER TO MARVIN ISRAEL, CIRCA JANUARY 1, 1960[97]

I am photographing sluggishly but yesterday I found a nearby waterfront hotel whos inmates were so gracious and dippy that I photographed 5 of them and they signed releases and invited me back to see the rest...

—POSTCARD TO ALLAN ARBUS, ST. THOMAS, VIRGIN ISLANDS, CIRCA JANUARY 2, 1960

I went to the Grand Central ladies room to find your nomads but the matron said there was only that one Negro lady with the rag shoes and she hadn't seen her for a long time.

—POSTCARD TO MARVIN ISRAEL, JANUARY 4, 1960

I am not ghoulish am I? I absolutely hate to have a bad conscience, I think it is lewd...There was a lady stretched out on the ground...fallen, I think, yesterday weeping and saying to the cops please help me with one shoe off and covered with a blanket waiting for an ambulance which came, on lexington ave and 57th Street. Is everyone ghoulish? It wouldn't anyway have been better to turn away, would it?

—POSTCARD TO MARVIN ISRAEL, JANUARY 5, 1960

I think it does, a little, hurt to be photographed. Please may I someday photograph your house, your ark, your things?

—POSTCARD TO MARVIN ISRAEL, JANUARY 5, 1960

She makes several visits to Mother Cabrini, a disinterred saint, and reports that, according to an illuminated scroll on the wall: *{She}...had been buried in Chicago and...when she was canonized they dug her up and there was just a skeleton of her with shreds of flesh, they said luridly, clinging to it...They make it sound like a frightful faux* *pas on the part of god...*[98] In her current incarnation, *Mother Cabrini's bones are covered with wax so no wonder she looks like the waxworks and her coffin is crystal so no wonder she looks like snow white...*[99]

I got a terrible impulse to photograph her and I tremulously did which wasn't legal so I pretended to be praying and pregnant and once I used the long lens and that camera makes such a fearful groan and clamor that I almost was praying.

—POSTCARD TO MARVIN ISRAEL, JANUARY 15, 1960

...A talk with the man from the Christian Herald (Harry Baronian) which runs the Bowery Mission so he could see what I was like and what my intentions were...he said the Bowery is going to be torn down and the men will move somewhere and make a new Bowery and then the Christian Herald will build a new mission for them. How indefatigable everyone is.

—POSTCARD TO MARVIN ISRAEL, JANUARY 15, 1960

I went to the Mr. Universe Health Parlor and while I was waiting for the manager who proved to be a very sharp, bearded, flirtatious, snobbish, sculptor, pianist, ex-Mr. Universe, one man was weightlifting a bar with 325 lbs of weights on it, making heartrending grimaces and worse little series of gasps when suddenly he cried for help and stood there like Atlas in despair till two other guys rushed over to relieve him. It was uncanny because he couldn't put it down or drop it.

—POSTCARD TO MARVIN ISRAEL, JANUARY 18, 1960

I am sitting in the meat market waiting for the heads...

—POSTCARD TO MARVIN ISRAEL, JANUARY 19, 1960

There was a somewhat fantastic struggle between me and the pastor [Rev. Olford] of the Calvary Baptist Church over my soul...He is a real Baptist preacher who speaks like Maurice Evans, looks like a sort of David Niven and was born in Africa...There were several henchmen and they all wanted [to convert] me so badly that one of them even pushed me bodily thinking thereby to nudge my soul...I think they thought I would encourage ...[the derelicts] to follow, like the judas calf...[100]

—LETTER TO MARVIN ISRAEL, CIRCA JANUARY 22, 1960

Two weeks later, Harry Baronian, acting as a kind of self-appointed impresario, arranges her first encounter with Walter Gregory, a legendary Bowery character known to neighborhood residents as the Madman from Massachusetts, whom she has been hoping to photograph:...*He has only one eye and the other is a small and pretty crescent folded absolutely shut like an eternal wink, and he is indeed quite drunk but pretending to be drunker...and his nose is folded once over sideways, like someone had tried to press him flat like people do to flowers...*[101]

...When I came in the madman looked furious and thrust his finger in my face saying who was I and lifting a bentwood chair over his head in a fine demonstration of madness he told me to say boo which I did and every time he got too mad harry would hum the stars and stripes forever and madman would drop everything and salute...and look like he was about to cry, murmuring about how he was undefeated middleweight champion of the us navy and belonged to the fbi.

—LETTER TO MARVIN ISRAEL, JANUARY 29, 1960

I don't press the shutter. The image does. And it's like being gently clobbered.

—POSTCARD TO MARVIN ISRAEL, FEBRUARY 4, 1960

Someone told me it is spring. but everyone today looked remarkable just like out of August Sander pictures, so absolute and immutable down to the last button feather tassel or stripe. all odd and splendid as freaks and nobody able to see himself, all of us victims of the especial shape we come in...[102]

—NOTE TO MARVIN ISRAEL, CIRCA SPRING 1960

The female impersonators are the real examples of playing a single role because each one forms only one kind of woman which has precious little to do with the kind of man they look like and you cant see one behind the other. It looks like a leap into a new doom....

—POSTCARD TO MARVIN ISRAEL, MARCH 17, 1960

This photographing is really the business of stealing...I feel indebted to everything for having taken it or being about to.

—POSTCARD TO MARVIN ISRAEL, CIRCA APRIL 1960

In a postcard to Israel, she suggests the following distinction between being a painter and being a photographer: *You invent what I discover.*[103] And on another occasion, makes a wry allusion to her own journalistic curiosity:

In the times yesterday there was something about a movie by Fellini [*La Dolce Vita*] about a reporter for a flossy picture magazine who in doing a story about Roman high, low and wild life falls utterly into it and is corrupted, lost, damned. Hmmm.

—LETTER TO MARVIN ISRAEL, CIRCA APRIL 20, 1960

On the April 19 page of her 1960 appointment book, apparently searching for a title for the *Esquire* article, she writes in pencil (and crosses out) the following musings on *Alice in Wonderland*: *I fell into it like Alice*; *Hayes and Benton were the White Rabbit*; and finally, *The journey was vertical and dizzying like Alice's.* The *Esquire* project is published in July as "The Vertical Journey: Six Movements of a Moment Within the Heart of the City." Although she supplies detailed descriptions for the pictures in the six-page photo essay, only brief captions based on her texts are used.[104]

Even before completing "The Vertical Journey"—and months before its publication—she is exploring ideas for her next project. In late April she writes Israel: *It appears as if I can have another assignment so to speak for Esq if I can think of one, (I am to lunch with them on Monday and they sound benevolent though they may outgrow it by then.)*[105] The new project begins to evolve out of the one before like another branch of the same tree and is shaped, in part, by language:

Last week I looked up the word anomaly because I always thought it meant a fish out of water but I knew I was wrong and I was right. It means something not subject to analogy or rule, or something odd or strange or exceptional...and I saw the connection between freaks and eccentrics, the exception to every rule.

—LETTER TO MARVIN ISRAEL, APRIL 20, 1960

At the suggestion of Charlie Lucas, manager of Hubert's Museum (*the great Mr. R.C. Lucas also known as Woofoo, Impresario Extraordinary, Inside Talker who's like I think that I will never see again...*),[106] she visits a number of small-town circuses, fairs, and carnivals, including Wirth's Circus in West Hempstead, Long Island; World of Mirth Carnival in Plainfield, New Jersey; Hunt's Circus in Palisades Park; and a carnival in Hagerstown, Maryland.[107]

...And backstage in the sun and mud squinting spangled mothers spank their squealing children or stuff plastic milk bottles into their mouths and I back up to get more in the frame and bump into an elephant...If in the big circus the art is to make something which has become easy look difficult again, here it is not quite to be able to do it at all.

—LETTER TO MARVIN ISRAEL, APRIL 20, 1960[108]

Throughout the year she seeks and maintains contact with everyone who may help lead her to where she wants to go. There is Joe Loebenthal, *the man from the Dept of Corrections who knows about gypsies and white slave trade.*[109] There are the magicians James Randi (The Amazing Randi), who is also an expert on parapsychology,[110] and Milbourne Christopher, whose act, she says, *includes a trick of explaining a trick by a further trick, which is the supremest kind of eloquence...like a witty rejoinder in the dialogue with God...*[111] There is William Gresham, author of *Nightmare Alley*, a 1946 noir novel of carnival life;[112] Long John Nebel, host of a radio talk show whom she listens to regularly because of his unpredictable panoply of guests; and Joseph Mitchell, whose pieces in *The New Yorker* seem the work of a kindred sensibility.

Each subculture she begins to explore turns out to be, not only a territory unto itself, but a key to deciphering the rules of another, apparently unconnected, subculture so that the world, as she puts it, *seems…not so much small as done with mirrors.*[113] By the same token, what looks like a dead end often turns out to be a hidden door to an unlikely subject she hadn't thought to pursue.[114]

…I am delighted to be on the track. I am really dick tracy. only when I get on the trail it lengthens…Everything is corroboration so that although the trail lengthens it is a lot like the farther afield you go the more you are going home. as if the gods put us down with a certain arbitrary glee in the wrong place and what we seek is who we really ought to be…

—LETTER TO MARVIN ISRAEL, NOVEMBER 13, 1960

Running parallel to—and sometimes intersecting—the research and amateur detective work during the course of the year are the more aimless, yet in many ways equally significant, ventures:

Friday night…I went into a Child's—I mean the restaurant…and at a near table there was a couple and the woman was an incredible spastic, very plain and pale and middleaged like lillian gish, like an out of order mechanical doll. She was eating her custard when I came in and dancing while she was eating it, seven motions for every once the spoon got to her mouth. The man was very tall and thin, graceful fatherly agile cheerful, affable, talkative, when they got up he held her coat for her to dance into and her face didn't ever change, she looked terribly plain and dazzled, like someone seeing visions, and after she got into her coat he bent over like a tree and kissed her.

—LETTER TO MARVIN ISRAEL, CIRCA JANUARY 19, 1960

I am on the train in New Jersey, very sleepy and only roused by the barrenness of what is out the window, winter grass and, once, yellow mud and sometimes pink earth…The wedding was not very good. The bride looked like a fashion editor and this is a blind spot for me and the church was like an airplane hangar but I feel better just walking among strangers…

—POSTCARD TO MARVIN ISRAEL, APRIL 13, 1960

…I am in Coney Is. In a glorious hotel I will show you when you get back. It is like a merry-go-round in a garden, never saw such a glorious place. My room is the color of blue ice cream. Last night there was a wild storm first the surf was pale and white and wild and foggy and the wind was fierce so everyone was flapping, blowing, whirling, running and the few swimmers leaped and giggled with hair dripping like snakes across their faces, then it poured so that the streets were flooded. I walked home sloshing through a sort of lake mid calf deep, littered with garbage and swirling like mad, feeling for the place where you step down off the curb because it was too deep under to see. Today is glorious. Happy Independence Day. How is it? Independence, I mean.

—POSTCARD TO DOON ARBUS, AT CAMP INDIAN HILL, STOCKBRIDGE, MASS., JULY 4, 1960

Yesterday I went all wet and bedraggled to the preliminaries of the miss america contest where they were choosing miss new york city...The categories of judging were 1. personality in a bathing suit. 2. personalityinaneveninggown and 3. talent which counted double what the other two categories counted...It took about ten hours of interviews, sashaying and performing what they called their talent and the poor girls looked so exhausted by the effort to be themselves that they continually made the fatal mistakes which were in fact themselves...Our only hope for judgement day is that god judges us for personalityinaneveninggown while we are in a bathing suit...

—LETTER TO MARVIN ISRAEL, JULY 15, 1960

I went to the assembling of the columbus day parade. women in long capes lined with orange silk and girls with flagpoles coming up from between their legs and ancient veterans and boys in marine battle dress and girls with SACRED HEART written on their left breast, acres of them...I have phorgotten how to photograph. Every once in a while that happens. Still its not bad.

—LETTER TO MARVIN ISRAEL, OCTOBER 13, 1960

Last night I went to a church dance on henry street for neighborhood kids some of whom are gang kids. It was terribly dark, marvelous dancing, very natty guys, everybody negro except about 4 people including me and the priests who wore their full regalia and looked very splendid sweeping through and among the dancers like cats watching mosquitoes...

—LETTER TO MARVIN ISRAEL, CIRCA NOVEMBER 1960

...I spent one fine day on 42nd st, a dark day which started to rain a little...and oh that street was wonderful, everyone winking and nudging and raising their eyebrows and running their hands through their marcelled hair and I saw one of your seeing blind men and a man like you have told me about with the pale ruined face-that-isnt-there and a thousand lone conspirators...

—LETTER TO MARVIN ISRAEL, CIRCA NOVEMBER 1960

Around mid-November she appears to be on the verge of purchasing a new camera, probably another Nikon. Allan recalls her asking him to test some lenses: *I must have tested five lenses*, he says. *Nothing was sharp enough for her.*[115] The dissatisfaction with her relationship to the camera will recur at various intervals throughout her career, often signaling an impending change in her work. On this occasion, having borrowed Israel's camera in the interim,[116] she writes:

...I need my new camera badly. Meanwhile, I only use yours for which I thank you, it seems to me very fine, even intellectual and aristocratic but it is like I am pretending to photograph. I cannot believe it really is doing it. I have to keep hoping and IMAGINING which I hate, and nothing looks so wonderful that I just want to stay with my eye to the keyhole forever like with that other camera which is just a damn seductive liar where you see what you're going to get but you don't get what you saw. So I am turning over a new leaf but the page is stuck.

—LETTER TO MARVIN ISRAEL, CIRCA NOVEMBER 1960[117]

Toward the end of the year, in preparing to write a proposal to *Esquire* on the subject of eccentrics, she reports: *I have been holed up in the public library with Kirbys Wonderful Museum of Remarkable Characters and Wilsons Magazine of Curious and Odd Memoirs and Anecdotes and I am agog with stories...*[118] She also sends a letter to her brother, who has been teaching at Bennington College in Vermont, in which she gives the following description of what she hopes to do:

I am working on something now, the eccentrics I have so long thought of, or rather people who visibly believe in something everyone doubts, and remembering a commodity of dreams [the title of Howard Nemerov's collected short stories, published by Secker & Warburg, London, 1960] I wondered if there were any such anywhere round your vicinity which would provide me the excuse and oppty for a visit...Any imposters, or people with incredibly long beards, or ones who believe in the imminent end of the world, or are reincarnations or keep lions in their living room or embalmed bodies or even skeletons or have developed some especial skill like a lady in Florida who is meant to eat and sleep under water, or affect some remarkable costume or other, or collect things to the point of miserliness? Don't trouble about it, or bother to answer, unless when you look up from the page the Messiah comes wandering out of the woods. Anyway how are you? and what working on? I am fine except obsessed. mch lve d.

—LETTER TO HOWARD NEMEROV, CIRCA FALL 1960[119]

In response to the proposal she submits to Benton and Hayes in November, *Esquire* assigns her the story. Presumably at her request, Hayes provides her a brief To Whom It May Concern letter of accreditation.

1961

The Eccentrics preoccupy her throughout most of the first half of the year and account for the contents of three of her notebooks (No. 4, No. 5, and No. 6).

In some cases, her search is merely a matter of finding potential candidates she already knows, like Joe Allen, a contortionist from Hubert's, also known as the Backwards Man.[120] (*Joe Allen is a metaphor for human destiny — walking blind into the future with an eye on the past*,[121] she writes on a page of her appointment book, and in one of her notebooks: *The Backwards Man: the man who can see where he was... nostalgia...*[122]) In other cases, locating the people she describes as *a few of the most lyrical, magical, metaphorical*,[123] requires more ingenuity.

...I found William Mack the sort of furry rasputin who is courtly and tedious and sinister, remarkably like someone who will appear in the daily news newly dead...a retired german merchant seaman and moslem convert and that sort of union square etymologist who can derive any word from any other...He is given to saying things like that moses wasn't a jew and shakespeare didn't write any plays which make me quite tired to hear and I never know what to say in reply. But he is very splendid looking, like a seer who has forgotten his own secret or an anachronism who wishes it was obsolete. proud, formidable and airless like an unprincipled martyr...the world is full of fictional characters looking for their stories.

—LETTER TO MARVIN ISRAEL, JANUARY 12, 1961

On January 19, she travels to Washington with Max Maxwell Landar, *an 80-year-old man about 4 feet high who pretends to be Uncle Sam because he thinks people would like to think he is.*[124]

He took me to Washington for the Inauguration [of John F. Kennedy], walking the entire way from one end of the train to the other, proclaiming his mission. The plan was for me to photograph him being the First Man To Shake The Hand of Dwight D. Eisenhower When He Was No Longer President but we couldn't get close enough. Instead we slept on benches in Union Station...and he climbed the Washington Monument in a blizzard, all 898 steps of it...solemnly delivering his oration to George Washington at the bottom, for an audience of the five guards and me.

—"THE FULL CIRCLE," *HARPER'S BAZAAR*, NOVEMBER 1961

An entire subcategory intrigues her for a while: the Spiritualists, or Psychics, or, as she puts it on one occasion, "Sensitives." She considers including in the story both Andy Sinatra (*The Mystic Barber, who teleports himself to Mars and says he is dead and wears a copper band round his forehead with antennae on it to receive his instructions from the Martians*[125]) and Bishop Ethel Predonzan of the Cathedral of the Creator, Omnipresence, Inc. of Astoria, Queens. This prompts Harold Hayes to send her the following cautionary note:

Dear Diane,

Two things:

We've had a legal ruling that under no circumstances are we entitled to publish photographs of people under any conditions other than those represented to the subject. That is, you can't take a picture of someone for the purpose of showing him as an "eccentric" unless that person knows he is being shown in this light.

Two, all this comes up because we received a couple of calls in the office from some distressed people (most recently, Bishop Ethel Credonzan [sic] of Jamaica, Long Island) wanting to know why we are printing pictures on spiritual subjects...I do believe that you'd better stay exactly within the letter of the law when describing your assignment to anyone you desire to photograph.[126]

Immediately preceding or following this letter from Hayes, Diane receives a phone call from the Bishop herself:

the bishop called again to say that some man has been casting doubt on me, saying that Esquire is not a spiritual magazine and that I am just trying to make a fool of her but she hates this man and he is not spiritual, in fact he is a press agent and this morning the Lord told her to beware of jack bell which is his name and He talked very nice about me and He said of me, she is innocent, and the bishop prayed over the telephone for the ball of fire to be made manifest in my photographs and she wept and she blessed me and said no one could hurt us and I agreed.

—LETTER TO MARVIN ISRAEL, CIRCA 1961[127]

By the beginning of June, Diane has narrowed down the subjects for the Eccentrics story, made and printed the photographs, and is starting to write the text to deliver the project to *Esquire*.[128] In July, she sends a letter to Doon, who is working at a summer theater in Maine:

...I spent the weekend of the fourth holed up writing about twelve hours a day on the rest of the Odd People and taking walks and eating pickles and I finished it and they are most terrifically pleased and so am I. I am hoping to start on another assignment or two, similarly long range kinds, right away, for which I have several delicious ideas...I have been in a queer empty excited state ever since I finished the assignment, waking at 4 or 5AM restless as a jumping bean and going for a walk and to the movies where I then don't want to stay and feeling alternately haunted and blessed.

—LETTER TO DOON ARBUS, CIRCA JULY 1961

The completed story, entitled "The Full Circle," includes portraits of six people with accompanying texts on each. In addition to William Mack, Sage of the Wilderness, and Uncle Sam, there is Jack Dracula, The Marked Man; Miss Cora

Pratt, The Counterfeit Lady; His Serene Highness Prince Robert de Rohan Courtenay (*the rightful Hereditary claimant to the Throne of the Byzantine Eastern Roman Empire*) and Miss Stormé de Larverie, The Lady Who Appears to Be a Gentleman. (Stormé, whom Diane first encountered in 1960 in connection with her work on "The Vertical Journey," is in fact the girl in the Jewel Box Revue's female impersonator show "Twenty-Five Men and a Girl.")

When Henry Wolf becomes the first art director of Huntington Hartford's new cultural magazine, *Show*, Marvin Israel replaces Wolf as art director of *Harper's Bazaar*. Israel—who had studied with Brodovitch at Yale—is both temperamentally and philosophically allied with the Brodovitch tradition. He envisions the magazine as a forum for challenging, nurturing, and celebrating the photographers and artists it publishes. He and Richard Avedon, *Bazaar's* staff photographer since 1945, form an immediate bond as co-conspirators, committed to pushing the magazine into uncharted territory.

Esquire was wildly appreciative but...they admitted they probably plan to leave out Stormé and Cora for lack of space and I said I didn't know if I would agree to let them have it in that case.[129] Meanwhile Marvin called them to say he'd like to publish it [in *Harper's Bazaar*] if they don't which must have made them jump and which would be wonderful but unlikely so as it stands no one has bought it and everyone likes it and its fine but I'm glad to stop thinking about it because praise is very unsettling.

—LETTER TO DOON ARBUS, CIRCA JULY 1961

In late August, after notifying her that *Esquire* has decided not to publish the Eccentrics, Hayes writes asking her to *destroy or return...whichever you prefer* the letter of accreditation he had given her in connection with the project.[130] She replies: *Enclosed is the letter of accreditation which I am both destroying and returning since I couldn't decide which I preferred. Thank you for it.* And adds: *If I am to deduce that you are feeling injured or outraged or infuriated, I now challenge and dare you to lunch with me. Benton too. RSVP. Yours, Sincerely, Cordially, Truly, Frankly, Fondly, Diane.*[131]

At this juncture, ideas for new projects are beginning to fill her notebooks and appointment book. For *Show*—scheduled to debut in October—she jots down something about a quickie horror movie company, archetypical heroes and villians, as well as *theatrical children and their agents and mothers and makeup and dance lessons and auditions...and the whole world of making believe for real.*[132]

I am fine but still too excited and waking at 5AM again and again. I have a new assignment and several more pending ones for a new magazine called *Show*. The one I am working on first is about HORROR in films, theater, TV, waxworks, spookhouses, any kind of entertainment and although at first I was somewhat cool to the idea maybe that was because I didn't think of it myself because it has begun to...GRAB ME...

—LETTER TO DOON ARBUS, CIRCA AUGUST 1961

The new assignment is nicely different because I don't have to talk to anyone and be nice or take notes and its fun...seeing what is scary and how afraid we are to be afraid. I spent hours in the waxworks watching little kids and pregnant women staring bugeyed at the ghouls and murderers. and next week I will be able to visit the lit up interior of one of those spook rides which I have wanted to see all my life.

—LETTER TO DOON ARBUS, CIRCA AUGUST 1961

The word *horror* itself spawns a series of thoughts on the connection between fear and horror, as if she were in search of a definition: *anxiety is the fear of being afraid*, she writes in her appointment book on July 16, 1961; and in a notebook, *anxiety is fear looking for a cause*, and later, *if anxiety is the fear of being afraid horror is the experience of what there is no need to be afraid of.*[133] The completed assignment— which she submits to *Show* in September, and which is never published—is subtitled "These Are Nightmares to Beguile Us While We Wait." As in the case of her other magazine projects of the period, each photograph is accompanied by its own text. There is a headless man, a headless woman, a monster makeup artist modeling his own handiwork, two human pincushions, and the World in Wax Musée at Coney Island:

Still and always, in the murky half light behind chicken wire, murderers and their victims grapple silently and ambiguously for their last lasting time in the scuffed shoes and crumpled stockings and faded wallpaper of their hell where nothing ever happens or stops happening. A man cuts up his mistress, the Duke and Duchess of Windsor smile faintly, a five year old girl gives birth to a baby, a child is raped in a stone quarry and James Dean looks sheepish. The fee is 30 cents but babies are admitted free and everyone tiptoes about, nervous and rapt and polite as if they are in church.

—HORROR SHOW, UNPUBLISHED TEXT, CIRCA 1961

"The Full Circle"—with the exception of the portrait and text on Miss Stormé de Larverie—is published in the November 1961 issue of *Harper's Bazaar*. This omission aside, the article remains faithful to her original conception. Her introductory paragraph encapsulates her view of those portrayed in the story: *These are five singular people who appear like metaphors somewhere further out than we do, beckoned, not driven, invented by belief, author and hero of a real dream by which our own courage and cunning are tested and tried; so that we may wonder all over again what is veritable and inevitable and possible and what it is to become whoever we may be.* The portraits constitute a major stylistic departure from "The Vertical Journey" photographs. A month or so later, in response to a letter from her brother about the article, she writes:

Dear h

...I been gloomy. Publication, although very splendid, felt a little like an obituary. I have figured out what the next thing to do is but i haven't done it. I want to find something like the eccentric event; (like i have heard of a twins convention[134]...unrealized legends or archaeologists delights or american rites. We'll see. I seem to have forgotten how to proceed. If my illusion is everyone elses disillusion, as it sometime seems, why do i feel so sad? I think i think i have forgotten what wasn't necessary to remember in the first place. Don't feel obliged to answer. I don't hope to stay this way.

—LETTER TO HOWARD NEMEROV, BENNINGTON, VT., CIRCA DECEMBER 1961

1962

The record remains unclear as to exactly when she begins considering the 2¼ format as an alternative to the 35mm, or precisely what begins to drive her in that direction. A yearning for greater clarity seems to be one factor: *I wanted to see the real differences between things...between flesh and material, the densities of different kinds of things: air and water and shiny...I began to get terribly hyped on clarity.*[135] The possibility of a more direct relationship with the person she is photographing may be another factor. At any rate, the transition occupies a good portion of the year and seems at times as fraught and poignant as a romantic triangle.

I am very gloomy and scared. Maybe I have discovered that I have to use the 2¼ x 2¼ instead of the 35mm, but the only tangible result so far is that I can't photograph at all. I am inept and hopeless with the bigger [camera] and I no longer believe the language of the littler one, which I so loved...I can't see beyond my nose to tell you how everything else is.

—LETTER TO LYN AND BOB MESERVEY, CIRCA JANUARY 1962[136]

Lisette Model, with whom Diane maintains a close relationship as friend and colleague, recalls a conversation they had on the subject of this dilemma: *She came once and she said she couldn't work anymore with the Nikon and she bought herself a Rolleiflex and now she cannot work with either one of them. Which has happened to me and which is absolutely clear. And I said to her, Take both of them and take the same picture with the Rollei and with the* [Nikon]. *And that, I think, helped a great deal.*[137] Diane employs this suggestion in a number of instances during the year, particularly when dealing with inanimate subjects.[138] In a September 25 letter to Model, she writes: *I have learned to be happy with the rolleiflex so now I have two cameras and I am proud of that.*[139]

Meanwhile *Infinity*, the publication of the American Society of Magazine Photographers, reprints "The Full Circle" in its February 1962 issue, with William Mack on the cover and all six original portraits and texts. In a note to Marvin Israel, Diane alludes to several of the projects she is hoping to pursue next, whether it be for *Harper's Bazaar*, another magazine, or simply herself:

dear m I wanna do the children the overpriveleged ones (of tycoons and aristocrats and notables and luminaries) who are almost as toomuchblessed as freaks. (even I who was not such an heiress and jewish to boot can remember being afraid of being kidnapped as the most precious possession of someone with a lot to lose). It'll be gorgeous. I'll write what they say. (THE SILVER SPOON)...and I was so tired I cant remember what you said about doing amy [Arbus] in clothes for... [*Harper's Bazaar* children's fashions][140] but if I do could I do her with a series of splendid sour pets like her best friends enormous turtle or a white mouse[141]...and I am looking for the faces of places which I would rather find than anything...and if I could go to photograph the living pictures at the Laguna Beach Art Festival (do you still have the clipping in your pocket?) I would hitchhike...

—NOTE TO MARVIN ISRAEL, CIRCA APRIL 1962[142]

The notion of winners of all kinds intrigues her as well. A list that appears in her 1961 appointment book (*the utmost, the winners, the most, the first, rituals, contests, fame, immortality, Secret Rites*) is a harbinger of the more complete project statement in a 1962 Notebook (No. 8).[143] This is followed by pages of events she has researched and plans to investigate: *singer-sewing contest, soap box derby, eating or drinking (pie watermelon), diaper derby palisades, walkathon st.louis, chess champ, miss appetite, miss fluidless contact lens, yeast raised donut queen, miss peel appeal natl idaho potato wk, tooth health week queen, miss press photog, miss anti-freeze, miss salt water taffy wk.*[144]

In mid-July Diane leaves on a cross-country bus trip heading for Los Angeles, where she intends to remain for about a month to work. She means to pursue, among other projects, a story on fortune-tellers to the stars for *Harper's Bazaar*.[145] The plan is for her to stay with her friends, the actor Robert Brown (who moved there in 1960, to seek his fortune in the movies[146]) and Bunny Sellers, who were recently married.[147] In a postcard to Allan from Tennessee, Diane reports on the cross-country trip.

I have no desire to get anywhere. It is nice to come to a town at 4AM and walk around the block. My brown suitcase is not on the same bus as me thru somebody else's error but perhaps it will find me in the end...May switch to a more devious route to see some Indians later. I sleep and wake a lot of tiny times and forget where I am so dawn this morning came as a sweet shock. Think of you a lot. D.

—POSTCARD TO ALLAN ARBUS FROM TENNESSEE, JULY 16, 1962

Bunny Sellers and Robert Brown are living in Malibu as houseguests in the home of a friend and, apparently, on the periphery of some sort of romantic melodrama. Diane describes the situation this way:

I arrived yesterday and my suitcase was not lost and I wasn't tired but it is all quite hard to believe. I seem to be living in the lap of what is surely the most unutterable luxury in a gorgeous house on the ocean built around and terracing an outdoor room furnished with bougainvillea trees. There are a thousand rooms and nooks and niceties and winding staircases and a largesse I have never seen. Bunny and Robt seem to be the mainstays of this household and there is an explosive drama transpiring of which James Mason, the real James Mason that is, plays one of the characters. They do this with more grace but less conviction than most people but it is all so handsome that one cannot care until one cares too much. Bunny and Robt seem to be paying a kind of emotional rental and we do quite considerable of tiptoeing although the freedom is enormous and the generosity so great that one cannot find a donor to thank. Parties are planned, lives are crumbling, everyone is charming...Fitzgerald should write this letter...I am a little jittery but one nice thing is that other people's problems are more crucial and I look to myself relatively little and simple like I can fit in a brown suitcase and get lost. I am frighteningly dependent in the matter of a car but I may be a help in getting Bunny and Robt out from the under they are in. I mean they are being a bit bled I think...I am at any rate well taken care of and there are a million plans for where to take me. I am just not absolutely sure my heart will follow...

—LETTER TO ALLAN ARBUS, JULY 19, 1962

...This place is so amazing. I am feverish with it. The not being able to drive is the worst. Trying to solve these things. Spent two glorious days wandering photographing around Venice and Santa Monica Pier and between and in an amusement park, overexposing and all that but free again and able to use the camera which on one black bleak day driving around with Bob [Brown] sightseeing (which is so something else from photog. that my heart was drowning) I thought I would never be able to do again...I only wish I could leave everyone alone. They need it and so do I. It's too luxurious and emotional here for me. Like a house full of children playing with matches. Triangles, scenes, flirtation, passion. Terrible. And I have lots of energy which gets wasted going to fancy restaurants or parties...

—LETTER TO ALLAN ARBUS, AUGUST 1962

With Bunny's help as driver, companion, and note-taker, she investigates the fortune-tellers—each of whom has his or her specialty, from astrology to tarot cards to crystal balls, and each his or her devoted movie stars.[148] They also go to the Laguna Beach Art Festival together but Diane is forbidden to photograph because the people enacting the living pictures are naked.[149] Her friend and former Fieldston classmate, screenwriter Stewart Stern, arranges to take her to the Universal backlot at dawn and to Forest Lawn Cemetery, Disneyland, and other Pseudo Places.

When she returns to New York near the end of August, financial pressures are weighing heavily on Allan and, as a result, on her. Amy—who had been attending The Little Red School House in Greenwich Village—enrolls that fall in third grade at Public School 41, *which fascinates her*, Diane says.[150] Diane begins to explore the possibility of obtaining a grant in photography from the Guggenheim Foundation, seeking advice and help from several former recipients, including Robert Frank and Lee Friedlander.[151] She writes Model, asking her to *sponsor me or recommend me or vouch for me or whatever it is called*.[152]

I am fine if a little precarious, I mean it all depends on how I look at it and there are bad moments when that depends much too much on the way someone else does, like a tightrope walker who might fall if somebody screamed. but mostly tightening my belt is exhilarating for me...I had to make it clear to myself that I had to at least try to become self supporting. So I am trying to work for money, even childrens fashions which is a little like an old nightmare but I got through it, and to apply for a guggenheim and to find a cheaper place to live, Sometimes these things are awful but other times they are fun. I mean I am terribly proud to make money for something I do except when I feel I would give anything not to have done it.

—LETTER TO LISETTE MODEL, SEPTEMBER 25, 1962

She contacts a number of other people in connection with the Guggenheim grant, including Edward Steichen and Grace Mayer in the photography department of The Museum of Modern Art,[153] and Walker Evans, whom she meets through Marvin Israel.[154] In late September, following an afternoon with Evans, she writes to thank him *for your generosity and the pleasures of this afternoon, for your counsel and conversation and for your worldliness* and encloses a copy of *Infinity* and caption material for the Horror pictures and the female impersonators, which she has apparently shown him.[155] In early October, shortly before the deadline, she sends Evans a copy of her Guggenheim project proposal, "American Rites, Manners and Customs," for his criticism or approval. Somewhat daunted by the application form, she adds in a postscript: *The application itself is going to be pretty barren or pristine because I never went to college or won an award or had a position with an organization or joined a learned or artistic society and though I speak a little French that will hardly be much help in the project.*[156]

Her Guggenheim project statement begins as follows: *I want to photograph the considerable ceremonies of our present...* Judging by the contents of her appointment books and notebooks, the topic has been brewing in her mind for more than a year. These are some notes from October 4, 1961: *the stuff of dreams, ritual, aristocracy, imposters, fame, anonymity, figments, real visions, american dreams, daily dreams, walking dreams, american hallucinations, real mirage.* And from November 22: *through the looking glass, legends of the here and now, shades of the here and now.* In accordance with the application instruction to supply a list *of the works of artistic creation you already have accomplished,*[157] she includes Psuedo Places and Portraits in Central Park as 1962 projects and Contests, Seers (for *Harper's Bazaar*), Silver Spoon (for *Harper's Bazaar*), and Winners as ongoing ones.

John Szarkowski—who had come to The Museum of Modern Art that summer to head the photography department—also receives a letter from Diane, dated September 23: *Walker Evans and Robert Frank and Lisette Model and Lee Friedlander have each said that they would speak for me and sponsor my request for a Guggenheim Fellowship for Photography. Each of them has suggested that I show you my work because your recommendation, if you could give it, would be so significant.*[158] Due to his schedule, however—as his secretary informs her—he is unable to see her work until after the October 15 Guggenheim deadline.[159]

She has already made a number of her important early 2¼ Rolleiflex pictures by this time [notably, Child with a toy hand grenade, Two boys smoking, Man and boy on a bench, A castle in Disneyland]. Given her standard practice, she would surely have printed them as well but there is no evidence that they are included in the portfolio she submits. Szarkowski recalls his reaction to the work he sees and to his subsequent meeting with her:

She sent in her portfolio, you know the way photographers do, and I didn't like it very much...They were a lot of the early freak pictures and the early eccentric pictures. There was one that I loved of the man and woman arguing on the walk at Coney Island. I didn't really like them but they were very forceful and you really felt somebody who was just enormously ambitious, really ambitious. Not in any cheap way. In the most serious way. Someone who was going to stand for no minor successes. And that feeling colored all our relationship because if you feel that it automatically sets up a kind of distance that you've got to respect no matter how well you may come to know each other. There's something untouchable about that kind of ambition. You can't manhandle it...I think she wanted every word she said, every picture she took, everything she did, I think she wanted it to be just perfect—for some great revelation to come through. Terrifying.[160]

Szarkowski recalls showing her *This Was Logging*, a 1954 book of photographs by Darius Kinsey, as well as the 1929 August Sander book, *Antlitz der Zeit*.[161] *She was floored*, he reports and, based on her response, has the impression that this is the first time she has seen Sander's work. In a note dated January 2, 1963, Diane follows up on their meeting: *That was nice, that little time I saw you a couple of months ago*. She goes on to ask for the title of the Darius Kinsey book and for August Sander's address *because there is something I would like to write him about.*[162]

1963

A month or so following the Guggenheim application deadline, the Foundation requests examples of the applicants' work. There appears to be no record of the photographs Diane chooses to submit for review by the Foundation's Advisory Jury. At any rate, a few days after delivering her prints to the offices in person, she sends Model a postcard, to remind her that the sponsors' recommendations are due.[163]

Dear Lisette, the g'gg'nh'm have summoned all photos and plan to keep them only until Jan 15 so I guess now is the time when they (whoever they are) make up their collective mind. I brought them there and it's so odd: just a small series of offices like judgement day in a bad dream.

—POSTCARD TO LISETTE MODEL, JANUARY 2, 1963

Model's letter of recommendation, dated January 4, begins as follows: *Photographers can be good, bad, excellent, first rate, or tops, but there are hardly any artists among them. Here is an exception.*[164]

In the meantime, Diane has proposed her Silver Spoon project (Children of Good Fortune) to *Harper's Bazaar* editor-in-chief, Nancy White. *I want to...discover the thousand ways they inhabit their rare and marvelous habitats...in a predicament as poignant as it is pretty*, she writes.[165] White encourages her to proceed with it. In a letter to a friend Diane says, *I am beginning the work of photographing rich children and the climb upwards appears to be a very long one. I mean I think I have found a whole new hidden hierarchy within the upper class and I am determined to get to the top of it, although I think it makes me uneasier than the bottom.*[166]

She is accumulating a list of qualified parents and their children, about three dozen in all, most of whom she visits and takes notes on: *Juan Carlos...darling ears, doesn't speak much english but smiles; Cecile has short hair, cross eyes slight, piquant, whimsical, sweet; Christopher...* [with whom, according to her notebook, she has the following exchange, *I hope to see more of you. There isn't any more.*] *is kind of darling funny typical spoiled looking, english hair; Elisabeth...beautifully pale blond bangs wide jowls wondrously sour like a Shirley T ugly doll.* About Penelope Tree, the thirteen-year-old daughter of Ronald and Marietta Tree, Diane writes simply, *Wonderful.*[167]

With the exception of the Silver Spoon (another project that, as it turns out, is never published), her magazine assignments in this period—for *Show*, *Harper's Bazaar*, and *Esquire*—consist of occasional portraits of writers, performers, directors.[168] They are of little interest to her beyond the professional challenge they present. On the other hand, many of the subjects and ideas she has been pursuing on her own are coming to fruition. These include a portrait of Andrew Ratoucheff—the Russian midget she first photographed for "The Vertical Journey"—with his friends in their living room, the widow Betty Blanc Glassbury, National President of Composers, Authors and Artists of America, and the 1963 winning couple of the Junior Interstate Ballroom Dance Championships, an event she has been attending for several years.[169]

Marvin Israel is fired from *Harper's Bazaar*. Some later suggest that he deliberately engineers his own firing because he is fed up with the bureaucracy, longs to devote himself to his painting full-time, and also wants to ensure his severance pay.[170] In a sense, however, his influence on the magazine persists even in his absence. Bea Feitler, a former student of Israel's at Parsons School of Design, and Ruth Ansel—both of whom he had hired as his assistants in the art department—succeed him as co–art directors and remain in that position for almost a decade.

On April 15 Diane receives a special-delivery letter from Henry Allen Moe, president of the Guggenheim Foundation: *Dear Mrs. Arbus: I have the honor to inform you that the Foundation has awarded you the Fellowship you requested.* The grant is for "photographic studies of American rites, manners and customs" in the amount of $5,000, covering a twelve-month period that commences in June 1963. He asks her for a written acknowledgment, Diane replies: *Dear Mr. Moe, Along with my acknowledgement, my profoundest thanks.* To which he answers: *Yours is the shortest acknowledgement and there is none better.*[171]

She sends a note to Walker Evans: *Dear Walker, I called to tell you I got it (Guggenheim), and to thank you. It is dizzying and if you have further counsel I will gladly listen.*[172] And to Model: *Dear Lisette, My father told me to thank you but your eloquence is your own and your friendship is mine so I cannot.*[173]

Around this time her father is hospitalized in New York, suffering from lung cancer. The family is resigned to the fact that he is dying.[174] *He would hallucinate when he was dying*, Diane recalls. *Businessman's hallucinations. He had an imaginary pocket with imaginary papers and he would keep stashing them away in a gesture that was familiar to him.*[175] Beneath the words "my father" in one of her 1963 notebooks (No. 13) she records two statements of his, followed by a question: *this message is paid for in advance; I cant get into the ceremony without it (piece of paper, breast pocket);* and *who made the moon?*

It's true I didn't really adore him [but]...I was really sort of awful when he died in the way that I watched. I stood in the corner of the room almost like a creep...I was just spellbound by the whole process. The gradual diminishment was fantastic. People really get to look like nobody, or just like somebody, you know what I mean?...All his lineaments changed. And I photographed him then which was really tremendously cold. But I suppose there is something somewhat cold in me. Although I resent that implication.

—1968 RADIO INTERVIEW WITH STUDS TERKEL ON THE DEPRESSION

David Nemerov dies on May 23. On that date Diane writes at the top of the page in her appointment book: *Daddy's death.*

Her enthusiasm for photography frequently extends to images produced by pragmatic, unselfconscious practitioners of the medium, in which the purpose is primarily to record information. In a 1962 notebook (No. 9) under the title "Photographers—The Double Image" she makes a list: *daily news, coney is or bway, wedding, baby, family, pony, graduation, theatrical, spirit, portrait, bachrach, itinerant, amateur, chinese-spanish school, passport or taxi, machine, lineup, banquet, postcard, candid, girlie, funeral, animal, nightclub, publicity.*

It is not clear how she becomes aware of James Vanderzee, a seventy-three-year-old studio portrait photographer, whose work is virtually unknown outside of the Harlem community where he has spent his entire career.[176] She seeks him out, buys some of his photographs, and later attempts to interest Szarkowski in his work. In a 1963 notebook (No. 11) she quotes what appears to be one of Vanderzee's principles of portraiture: *full length shows your shape, half shows your character, your type.*[177]

She spends the first week of July at Sunshine Park, a family nudist camp in New Jersey.[178] *I had always wanted to go but I sort of didn't dare tell anybody*, she says later. *It was a terrific subject for me.*[179] A year or two later, in an attempt to secure an assignment from *Esquire* on the topic, she writes a text largely based on her notes from this visit. It begins: *There is not much to it, you might say. It's like walking into an hallucination without being quite sure whose it is.*[180]

Some ladies wear beach hats or sunglasses or wedgies and curlers or earrings and pocketbooks. In the cafeteria the teenage waitresses wear organdy demi-aprons. Some men have on only a wrist-watch, or shoes and socks with their cigarettes and money tucked into their socks for safekeeping. Sometimes you see someone wearing nothing but a bandaid or a pencil behind their ear or walking a dog on a leash. Nudists aren't purists. Occasionally they even feel the impulse to slip into something more comfortable.

—"Notes on the Nudist Camp," unpublished 1965 article for *Esquire*[181]

Sometimes you begin to wonder. There is an empty pop bottle or a rusty bobby pin underfoot, the lake bottom oozes mud in a particularly nasty way...some guy asks, "What kind of bees give milk?" and answers, "boobies," the outhouse smells, the woods look mangy. It is as if way back in the Garden of Eden, after the Fall, Adam and Eve had begged the Lord to forgive them; and God, in his boundless exasperation, had said, "All right, then. STAY. Stay in the Garden. Get civilized. Procreate. Muck it up." And they did.

—"Notes on the Nudist Camp," unpublished 1965 article for *Esquire*[182]

When Doon leaves to attend Reed College in Oregon, Suzanne (Sudie) Victor, a student of Howard Nemerov's and recent graduate of Hollins College in Virginia, moves into Doon's old room. Sudie Victor is working as a copy editor at Random House and the plan is for her to live with the family and be available when needed to take care of nine-year-old Amy.[183]

Before the end of the year, Robert Benton resigns from *Esquire*.

1964

Diane's 1964 magazine projects and her own personal projects overlap and merge and evolve into and out of one another throughout the year. For *Harper's Bazaar*, she embarks on two assignments simultaneously: photographs of "young heiresses" that will appear in a regular feature of the magazine, "Fashion Independents,"[184] and "Affinities," portraits of creative partners. In the case of the latter, the lists of possible subjects in the early pages of her 1964 appointment book are soon narrowed down to four couples: the musicians Pearl Bailey and Louis Bellson, the ballet dancers Erik Bruhn and Rudolf Nureyev, the poets W. H. Auden and Marianne Moore, and the silent film star sisters, Lillian and Dorothy Gish.[185]

Accompanied by *Harper's Bazaar* feature editor Geri Trotta, who will write the article, she meets with the Gish sisters on January 13 and photographs them in Central Park in the snow. On that day in her appointment book she records these fragments of conversation: *D: [Dorothy] Lillian's face is in every museum in the world. L: [Lillian] Dorothy is the dearest sweetest funniest creature in the world. Always sees something odd. D: Lillian and Garbo had that something-plus, I can't say what it is. L: Come Dorothy—follow in my footsteps (snow).*[186]

In late January, she begins planning a trip to New Orleans for the February 11 Mardi Gras celebration. When she leaves on February 5 she has obtained from friends and through research the names and addresses of people to contact. She already has the address of photographer Clarence John Laughlin,[187] whose work interests her and with whom she has corresponded. It also includes—probably thanks to Lee Friedlander—the name of Lorenz (Larry) Borenstein. (It is from Borenstein and his partner, Al Rose, that Friedlander purchases the eighty-nine E. J. Bellocq glass plate negatives, which he prints and The Museum of Modern Art exhibits and publishes in 1970 as *E. J. Bellocq: Storyville Portraits.*)[188] Curiously enough, as far as Diane's own photographs are concerned, the New Orleans trip results in only one picture she chooses to print.

On her way home, she stops in Baltimore on assignment for *Esquire* to photograph Blaze Starr, known in many quarters as the Queen of Burlesque. This is her second collaboration with writer Thomas B. Morgan, whose article "Blaze Starr in Nighttown" appears in *Esquire*'s July 1964 issue accompanied by two of her pictures.[189]

Diane's relationships with many of the people she photographs continue long after the pictures have been taken. Her 1963 portrait of the Triplets in their bedroom is a prelude to a subsequent encounter with the family at a triplets convention in Palisades Park. She makes regular visits to Hubert's Museum and stays in touch with a number of the individual performers she has come to know, goes to a party for Prince Robert de Rohan Courtenay, or a performance by Stormé de Larverie, and keeps note of Michael Lerner's ensuing birthdays. Bishop Ethel Predonzan, whom she has been in contact with since 1960, is now living in Santa Barbara, and when Diane goes to California in August, meeting with the Bishop is one of the items on her agenda.

She stays again, for at least part of the time, with Bunny Sellers and Robert Brown in their home at 14 Malibu Road. Bunny goes with her on her visit to see the Bishop and describes the experience as "heartbreaking." *This perfectly together wedgie, neon lady living in Santa Barbara. The whole question of what's sane and what's insane, what's real and what's unreal.* And yet, as Bunny observes: *Diane was very caring* [with the Bishop] *and she was also terrifically persistent because she wanted her. In a sense she wooed her in the same sense as a lover would woo...One of the glories of it was that Diane had won her by that time. They were terrifically jolly together. But that was also an extraordinary thing about Diane. It was always like she knew exactly where she was headed—to the absolute inside of the inside. I never knew if she had a plan—I don't mean a plan—a device or technique for getting there. But she always seemed to arrive.*[190]

In an earlier letter to Marvin Israel on an unrelated subject, Diane remarks on her ability to elicit from people, sometimes without even wanting to, the revelation of their own unabashed images of themselves: *I think I must have been brought up to be a sort of magic mirror who reflects what anyone wants to believe because I can't believe they believe it, like atlas holding up a bubble and groaning.*[191]

On a cliff overlooking the Pacific, in a cemetery in the sun, a small lady in damask robes with hair of phosphorescent pink holds aloft a styrofoam cross encrusted with smaller crosses and raises her eyes till they pale at the vision of Jesus Christ. She is called Bishop Ethel Predonzan of The Cathedral of the Creator, Omnipresence, Inc. Christ, she declares, has summoned her there to Santa Barbara, California, all the way from Astoria, Queens, to await His Second Coming on December 4th of this year.

—"The Bishop's Charisma," unpublished text, 1964

According to the text, the Bishop acknowledges that Christ was scheduled to come once before, in 1957, but as she goes on to explain, *Everything depends on cadence and vibration. Conditions were too negative.* And, in the words of the final sentence of the piece, *if Christ does not come this time no doubt she* [the Bishop] *will wait till He does.*[192] On the December 3rd and 4th pages of her 1964 appointment book Diane makes a note for herself: *Call the Bishop.*

An echo of the Bishop's spiritual fervor occurs in Diane's text on Mae West, a story assigned to her by *Show* editor Nicky Haslam, which she has been planning and researching for months.[193] At the appointed time Robert Brown drives her to West's home (*a fortress...almost as impregnable as Sleeping Beauty's*[194]) and by prearrangement leaves her there.[195] Diane writes of her encounter with the seventy-two-year-old "original Sex Symbol": *She is imperious, adorable, magnanimous, genteel and girlish, almost simultaneously. There is even, forgive me, a kind of innocence about her.*[196] The article, published in the January 1965 issue of the magazine along with three photographs,[197] concludes:

But the world of Mae West is not entirely physical. Her psychic eye has been opened. She has seen visions...And she has heard voices...a deep rich masculine voice in her solar plexus uttering phrases from another century like THEE and THOU. "I don't know what He was talking about," she says, but she knew who He was. "I knew that in some marvelous way I had touched the hem of the unknown. And being me, I wanted to lift that hemline a bit more."

—"Mae West: Emotion in Motion," *Show*, January 1965[198]

During the month or so that she remains in California, Diane also photographs the eighty-two-year-old pioneer of modern dance, Ruth St. Denis;[199] several residents of a home for retired actors in their private rooms; and the children of movie stars, a new and far less happy incarnation of the Silver Spoon (probably for *Show*).[200] After returning to New York, she writes Stewart Stern:

...I am still stricken with good fortune and basking in it, a little frivolous, maybe a trifle smug but something like serene which is in itself therapeutic. If my cup doesn't run over it is only because I am always drinking. Autumn was here today which reminds me of when I was little...There are an awful lot of beggars around. Many of them sitting on the street and one with pink wooden legs. The city is like a terrible hallucination...You don't think, like the bishop does, that God has gone to california?

—LETTER TO STEWART STERN, CIRCA OCTOBER 1964[201]

Throughout the rest of the year, her projects continue to overlap. People and Their Pets, an idea that must have been intended originally as a magazine story, results instead in at least two photographs of carnival performers: Tattooed lady with her dog and Circus fat lady.

An acquaintance with the disc jockey, Murray Kaufman (known professionally as Murray the K), organizer and emcee for the rock 'n roll shows at the Brooklyn Fox Theater, enables her to get in touch with some of the girl groups (the Orlons, the Dixie Cups, and the Ronettes). The individual portrait sessions with Estelle Bennett and Ronnie Spector of the Ronettes resemble, both in style and content, a project she has been working on—variously entitled Ethnic Beauties, Racial Pin-ups, Minority Pin-ups—which she continues to pursue for several years.[202] Her extensive notes on each of the subjects indicate she intends to write an accompanying text.

A *Harper's Bazaar* fashion assignment on underwear (never published) provides her an opportunity to photograph several women who interest her. One is her friend Carlotta Marshall (*My, she is pretty. Like the paintings of a certain art nouveauish period I can't remember the name of*).[203] Another is a call girl she has come to know whose comments she records in one of her notebooks (No. 15): *I'm in love with love. I love to please. I could smother someone with love.*[204]

The list that appears on the November 6th page of her appointment book under the heading Plans to Do, reiterates a list in one of the 1964 notebooks (No. 15): *racial pinups (Jill and Gina); teenagers (April, Barry and other, Betty Berry), family (Ed Carmel), gangster (Scavullo), homosexual (Monti), wedding prep. (Nick P.) whores, pimps (China Monti Ida Puente), roxcknroll group, old people's club).*[205] At various times during the year, she attempts to interest editors in one or another of these projects.

In the case of *Harper's Bazaar*, sometimes she approaches Ruth Ansel with an idea, sometimes Bea Feitler, sometimes the two of them together.

Richard Avedon's second book, *Nothing Personal*, with a text by his former DeWitt Clinton High School classmate James Baldwin, is published by Atheneum.[206] The book, which is designed by Marvin Israel, renews his collaboration with Avedon and is the first of many photographic books Israel edits and designs.

Around mid-October, The Museum of Modern Art acquires seven Diane Arbus prints, six by purchase, one as a gift of the photographer. The MoMA records and Diane's own notes identify the following images as those selected: Child, night, Greenwich Street, Miss Venice Beach, Child with a toy hand grenade, A widow in her bedroom, Two female impersonators backstage, Retired man and his wife, and A husband and wife in the woods.[207] These are the first photographs of hers included in a museum collection. In the Artist's Record, dated October 5, 1964, which she fills out in connection with the acquisition, Diane describes her "Special Field of Interest in Photography" as *a kind of contemporary anthropology*.[208]

1965

Once again, commercial work dominates the first few months of the year. The *Harper's Bazaar* assignment "On Marriage" (published in the "Fashion Independents" feature in the May 1965 issue), happens to echo an idea Diane outlined five years earlier in a 1960 notebook (No. 3): *Marriage: the sort of why or wherefore of it with a text by anybody like B.Russell* [Bertrand Russell] *or MM* [Marilyn Monroe] *or Ashley Montagu or by a lot of people who do or don't believe in it, or what is becoming of it or anybody's quotes on the subj. like the inq. rep.* [the inquiring reporter] *asked people last week if they were better off married or single and pics of people who have chosen each other...*[209]

The couples she is asked to photograph for *Harper's Bazaar* constitute a less eclectic group than those she had envisioned doing earlier, but she records their observations and epigrams on the subject all the same. Elizabeth Oxenberg, married to Howard Oxenberg for five years, remarks: *mystery in a marriage helps preserve an otherwise impossible relationship*; the Gilbert Millers, married thirty-eight years, concur that *having the same interests is really the most important thing*.[210] The list of names on the March 10th page of her appointment book suggests that she photographs about twenty couples for the project. Nine portraits appear in the magazine.[211]

"Familial Colloquies," a simultaneous and somewhat parallel assignment for *Esquire* (July 1965) also consists of photographs of two people together, in this case a renowned parent with his or her adolescent child. Included are portraits of sculptor Richard Lippold and his daughter, Taina; politician Ogden Reid and his son, Stewart; sociologist Jane Jacobs and her son, Ned; and actress Jayne Mansfield and her daughter, Jayne Marie.[212] The four published photographs are accompanied by captions she writes, which consist almost exclusively of quotes from the parent and child portrayed.[213]

Her continuing fascination with self-enclosed communities, their customs and practices, leads her in a number of different directions at the same time. She investigates motorcycle rallies as well as Kerista, a free love society that occupies a commune in the East Village.[214] Many of these avenues prove to be dead ends, at least as far as her photography is concerned.

Beginning in May and throughout a good portion of the summer, she spends a lot of time working in and around Washington Square Park, photographing the people who hang out there. Curiously enough, she seems to find it one of the more intimidating and impenetrable worlds she has yet attempted to explore, although it also proves to be among the more productive.[215] Speaking of the experience several years later, she describes the park in terms of a kind of complex hierarchical social geography:

...One summer I worked a lot in Washington Square Park...The park was divided. It has these walks, sort of like a sunburst, and there were these territories staked out. There were young hippie junkies down one row. There were lesbians down another, really tough amazingly hard-core lesbians. And in the middle were winos. They were like the first echelon and the girls who came from the Bronx to become hippies would have to sleep with the winos to get to sit on the other part with the junkie hippies...I got to know a few of them. I hung around a lot. They were a lot like sculptures in a funny way. I was very keen to get close to them, so I had to ask to photograph them. You can't get that close to somebody and not say a word, although I have done that.

—*Diane Arbus*, Aperture, 1972[216]

Two typewritten pages, dated September 20, 1965, and included in a folder of hers that contains drafts of most of her writings,[217] tell the tale of a series of chance encounters with some of the members of this impromptu community she has come to know.

I had seen Jamie once and he had said sure that he would be photographed and we had trundled off, very motley him and Dexter who looks like Mick Jagger and has probably very accurately since been described by Jamie as a mad dog, and a number of peripheral characters, one of them a blooming insistent photographer. Someone who never showed up was looking for someone's pad for me to photograph them in but someone yet else had made off with the key and Dexter was so far gone out of his head that he kept sliding unseemly to the sidewalk and everyone's interest started to wane. But not before Jamie looking...seedy and Edwardian, pimply and ardent, delicate and messianic with the uncanny blue eyes of a child who will be forgiven anything, told me he was fifteen years old and could save people. Had in fact saved an old drunk that yesterday simply by looking him in the eye or saying a few words or something but the only trouble was that then the old guy wanted to stick around and be Jamie's friend and keep right on being saved or some such thing which wasn't it at all. Well the party broke up because some other messiah I knew passed by across the street and came over to tell me a great deal of unparalleled importance for the next eleven hours.

—UNPUBLISHED TEXT, 1965[218]

Then last night I was wandering around looking for Theresa with her plain pop eyes, her formidable boots and arrogant devotions. Her kiss seals a thousand small bargains like a bank presidents signature, almost the more so because she is ugly...The sort of girl who in high school would have suffered her ugliness in isolation, she had turned it to advantage and thrust her face full into the mouth of every boy and inflicted tongues mutually, or put her arms round everyone in vast tenderness and conspiracy and a sort of ready friendship which was by definition valuable.

—UNPUBLISHED TEXT, 1965

Later Andy turned up, shy as a boy at dancing class with the wrong pants on, solemn, enormous-nosed with his hair combed down in a great wave over his eye, like Barbra Streisand before anyone believed in her.

—UNPUBLISHED TEXT, 1965

Marty appeared on W. 3rd St looking odd and in a different costume from usual. He is very like a weasel and in the oddest way I find him trustworthy as if he were a REAL weasel. He was wearing an oversize apricot corduroy shirt. His eyes look hung like dark chandeliers and he appeared to be hiding something which is not unusual. He started a story about how he had got in a fight...with three guys who had jumped him but he hadn't begun the story with any urgency...so I was listening mildly when quietly...he opened his mouth not very wide but I guess he rarely opens it at all and there was a space so large it seemed as if it could accommodate 6 or 8 teeth which weren't there at all. They knocked 'em out was all he said about it...so I broke one guy's kneecap which is the worst thing you can do to anybody, he said portentously. So now the cops are looking for ME he said with heavy sarcasm, for a guy with a black t shirt and a red bandana, that's why I'm wearing this, fingering it contemptuously (the big shirt).

—UNPUBLISHED TEXT, 1965

That's the way it is, Diane writes in a kind of wistful summary about these young people midway through the piece. *You figure they are lying to you and they do indeed lie a lot and exaggerate and dramatize and allude and whatnot, but suddenly you will look into the mouth of the veritable brink they live on and it is truly the black pit you have only just ever imagined.*[219]

Since 1962 when she first adopted the 2¼ format, she has been printing her square pictures on 11x14 paper in the usual manner, with a clean, sharp edge framing the image. At some point in 1965—although it remains unclear precisely when—she makes what appears to be a radical change and begins printing her photographs with thick, irregular black borders. Whatever the genesis of this new method—whether it is conceived deliberately or happened upon initially by chance—it obviously strikes her as important. All the prints she makes of the Washington Square pictures are done this way, as are those of all the photographs that follow. For the next several years the black border continues to be a distinctive feature of the way her prints look.[220]

The Washington Square project is punctuated in early July by a trip she has been planning to Sunnyrest, a nudist camp in Pennsylvania.[221] Several months later, she sends John Szarkowski at MoMA a note asking him to refrain *just for the present* from showing one of the nudist pictures. She explains: *I am now for one thing a member of the movement and following where it leads in civilian life and I don't want any tiny blunder to betray me. This may sound nutty but I have discovered that life really is a melodrama.*[222]

The Ethnic Beauties project that she has been pursuing on her own for a few years—and for which she has already made a number of pictures—finally results in an assignment from *Esquire*. In a letter dated August 9, 1965, and signed *Sincerely, and ever your friend,* Harold Hayes writes: *For an acceptable story—hereafter referred to as "Minority Pin-ups,"—we will pay you at the rate of $250 per page, regardless of the amount of text or photography on the page…If for any reason this story fails to work out, we will pay you a spread guarantee of $400—twice the usual amount for an unsuccessful story, since you are submitting both text and photographs.* She continues to work on this project for at least the next six months, jotting down brief descriptions of prospective subjects she encounters. Several photographs appear to have come out of it, as well as the draft of a text intended to accompany one of them. As a story, however, it is never published.[223]

In accordance with arrangements made the previous spring—probably at Marvin Israel's suggestion and maybe with some help from him as well[224]—she begins teaching a photography course in the fall at Parsons School of Design on Tuesday afternoons. The class includes about twelve students and, although she has access to the Parsons darkroom for teaching purposes, it focuses primarily on photographic assignments and critiques.

The Museum of Modern Art includes two of the seven prints acquired from her the year before—Retired man and his wife at home in a nudist camp one morning, N.J. 1963 and Female impersonators, N.Y.C. 1961—in its Fall group show, *Recent Acquisitions: Photography*.[225] In applying to the Guggenheim Foundation for a renewal of her 1963 fellowship grant, she cites this exhibition, along with an earlier group show at the University of Wisconsin,[226] in a list of work accomplished. The list cites twenty-four of her photographic subjects as well, including: *Evangelist, Faith Healer; Nudists (convention, portraits, family groups, homes); Burlesque Show (stars, strippers, comics, the performance); Masquerade (Mardi Gras, Beaux Arts Ball, Halloween Party); Games (Canasta, Baseball, Jump-Rope);... Parlor (rooming house, widow, midgets)...Carnival; Beggars; Rock'nRoll groups; Triplets (portraits, club, convention).*[227]

As requested, she summarizes the title of her present position, current salary, marital status, and the number and ages of her children: *I am a photographer (freelance) and I have undertaken to teach photography part-time at the Parsons School of Design. Altogether I earn about $4000 a yr. I am married, but separated, and have two children, aged eleven and twenty.*

Her project is entitled The Interior Landscape and is described in the following four sentences: *The Fellowship enabled me to go far enough to find the way to go further. I have learned to get past the door, from the outside to the inside. One milieu leads to another. I want to be able to follow.* On the same page, as a footnote, she adds: *For example, to photograph: a certain group of young nihilists, a variety of menages, a retirement town in the Southwest, a new kind of Messiah, a particular Utopian cult who plan to establish themselves on a nearby island, Beauties of different ethnic groups, certain criminal types, a minority elite.*[228]

Reading her brother Howard Nemerov's memoir, *Journal of the Fictive Life* (Rutgers University Press, 1965)—a kind of tapestry composed of unfinished fiction; meditations on writing fiction or the inability to do so; recollections of his childhood and his family; dreams and his interpretations of them; puns and jokes and other fragments—elicits the following response from Diane:

hdearh I awoke with such an urgent necessity to write you not my last word about it, but it hits me with a kind of contagion, not precisely as though it were my book but I recognize so nearly everything in it, like I am possessed...it is as if our dreams people each others and endlessly like offshoots of branches the book is multiplying in my head...[I] have also stopped photographing a week or so...[and] have believed in both the guilt and innocence of photographing (which I privately call the butterfly collection), there are these thousand things...[and] that incredible place where it says Mommy, where do images come fr...[229] I am embarrassed even to write it. I havent ever read anything I so believed...

—LETTER TO HOWARD NEMEROV, CIRCA NOVEMBER 1965[230]

Nemerov's book also contains musings on the nature of images and image-making, and a surprising number of references to photography, including this one: *My vocation as a grownup has to do with making images, but I have never much cared for photographs. The same sister* [Diane] *is a professional photographer, whose pictures are spectacular, shocking, dramatic, and concentrate on subjects perverse and queer (freaks, professional transvestites, strong men, tattooed men, the children of the very rich). Thou shalt make no graven image.*[231] In the same letter to him Diane replies to this as well:

The only thing that I took personally in the way of feeling sort of pointed at was the list of my photogr subject matters which read like a dirty catalogue and perhaps the temporary exemption you grant me from what you say about photography, which because it is only temporary makes a sort of hilarious sense...[well not so hilarious, she writes in the margin]...the silent dialogue we have had all our lives on these matters is the more extraordinary for what we seem to have heard.

—LETTER TO HOWARD NEMEROV, CIRCA NOVEMBER 1965[232]

She invites him to stay at her place if he can when he is in town on the 12th and adds as a postscript, *There is a great deal more to say as well as not to.*[233]

Hubert's Museum is scheduled to close its doors forever in November. For weeks prior to its last day, Diane arranges sessions with the individual performers and does a few group portraits of them in the vacant basement space. She writes a text entitled "Hubert's Obituary," which she hopes to persuade one of the magazines to publish along with some of her photographs as a kind of requiem for the establishment, but her efforts prove unsuccessful.

It used to be that if, as your mother would say, you didn't know what to do with yourself, you would do it at Hubert's Museum. You'd...descend, somewhat like Orpheus or Alice or Virgil, into the cellar which was where Hubert's Museum was...Coming into the unholy fluorescent glare of it you'd see yourself dwarfed and fattened and stretched in several distorting mirrors and all around you like flowers a thousand souvenirs of human aberrations, as if the world had quite literally stashed away down there everything it didn't need.

—"Hubert's Obituary," *Diane Arbus: Magazine Work*, 1984[234]

She goes on to describe the show, which *was circular like the seasons or the stars* and each one of the performers: Charlie, the impresario Mr. R.C. Lucas, *he of the glittering eye, who talked like a spider, so sweet and scary at once in his old fez ringed round with a beaded snake...;* and Woogie *who was really Charlie's wife as Princess Wago, the African Dancing Venus,* [who] *undulated in the awful rosy darkness under her pythons and boa constrictors;* and Albert-Alberta, *a creature half man and half woman, seductive as a nightmare, a veritable French psychological novel...flirtatiously revealing a powdered perfumed sequined female left breast with a rugged muscular hairy male right hand while our mouths fell open in disbelief;* and Estelline, *such a pleasant motherly sword-swallower who taught us how we could swallow a bent wire coat hanger if we didn't happen to have any swords around the house;* and Presto, *a magician who looked like a rabbit himself* *("I don't really do this," he'd say. "It just looks like it.");* and Ramon Batiste, *a legless man...*[who] *did the twist with his torso, for that was all there was of him, poised on the bottom end of an upside down Pepsi-Cola bottle...*[235]

And naturally she also mentions Professor Heckler and His Trained Fleas; and Andy Potatochips, who is really the multilingual Russian midget Andrew Ratoucheff; and the water glass musician, Harold Smith; and, of course, Congo the Jungle Creep. *We had our awe and our shame in one gulp,* she adds. *What if we couldn't always tell a trick from a miracle? If you've ever talked to somebody with two heads you know they know something you don't.*[236]

Medical Science being what it is they don't hardly make 'em like that anymore and the laws prevent pretending or people are rich enough nowadays to hide their relatives away instead of selling them to the Carnival like they used to...If you feel like it you can go on over to Hubert's tonight, anyway...No one is there except the pictures on the walls of all the people who used to be there. As Mr. Schaefer the owner points out: prices being what they are these days, at a dime, even if you just want to go to the bathroom it's worth it.

—"Hubert's Obituary," *Diane Arbus: Magazine Work*, 1984

1966

In connection with her pending application, she delivers fifty-five prints to the Guggenheim Foundation prior to January 10 for review by the Advisory Jury. Although many of the photographs presumably involve subjects mentioned in her list of accomplishments (*Evangelists, Nudists, Burlesque, Masquerade, Parlor, Carnival, Triplets*) there is apparently no record of the specific images she selects.[237]

She resumes teaching at Parsons on Tuesday afternoons. The first class of the semester meets at The Museum of Modern Art on February 1 and the corresponding page in her appointment book contains some reminders for the occasion: *2 monitors, new people, strictness, new assignment.*[238]

On March 16 she receives notification from James Mathias of her second Guggenheim award (in the amount of the $7,500 she requested) and asking once again for her acknowledgment. She writes: *Dear Mr. Mathias, (This is my acknowledgement). With it my joy, my thanks, a little awe and that wee small voice that says to myself be quiet and get to work.*[239]

During the early part of the year she completes two magazine assignments. For *Esquire*'s July 1966 issue, she does a portrait of Brenda Diana Duff Frazier (Mrs. Chatfield Taylor), the 1938 debutante of the year, at her home in Medfield, Massachusetts.[240] For Clay Felker's *New York*, she photographs James Brown, "the hardest working man in show business." Two of these pictures are published in the March 20, 1966, issue of the magazine along with the article "James Brown Is Out of Sight," by her twenty-one-year-old daughter, Doon.[241] James Brown is scheduled to appear at Madison Square Garden in March and the idea for an article about him originates with Diane, who has seen him in performance at the Apollo Theater in Harlem.[242] This is the first of four magazine pieces she collaborates on with Doon.

Her work on the Guggenheim project is postponed for the month of April by her biggest magazine assignment to date, in terms of the number of portraits published. *Harper's Bazaar* co–art director Ruth Ansel is probably responsible, at least in part, for the assignment "The American Art Scene," which concerns an area of special interest to Ansel. Diane appears to have some degree of input in choosing the subjects for the piece. In the ensuing weeks she photographs the following artists: James Rosenquist; Charles Hinman; Larry Bell; Agnes Martin; Tom Wesselmann; Frank Stella; Roy Lichtenstein; Lucas Samaras;[243] Richard Lindner; Claes Oldenburg; Kenneth Noland; Lee Bontecou; and Marvin Israel (whose first New York exhibition of paintings opened at Cordier & Ekstrom Gallery on March 1).[244]

On the weekend of April 22, she joins Doon at Billy Hitchcock's Millbrook estate, the home of Dr. Timothy Leary's League for Spiritual Discovery (LSD). Doon has been there for about a week working on an article about Leary for Clay Felker's *New York* and Diane is assigned to do the photographs. The article is delayed and finally abandoned after G. Gordon Liddy, Assistant District Attorney of Dutchess County, organizes a drug raid on the mansion that results in the arrest of a number of residents and guests (including Leary, his future wife, Rosemary Woodruff, his eighteen-year-old daughter, Susan, and his colleague, Dr. Ralph Metzner).[245]

In addition to her continuing interest in twins and triplets—especially adult twins or elderly twins, who seem more difficult to find than the children—she is pursuing another project. Her appointment book reflects a number of attempts to investigate the science of sexual research. She contacts the Institute for Sex Research at Indiana University, which was founded by Alfred Kinsey in 1947. She makes some phone calls about Dr. Hans Lehfeldt, an influential German doctor living in New York, who is an early advocate of birth control, founder of the *Journal of Sexual Research*, and a member of the Society for the Scientific Study of Sex.[246] She gets in touch with Dr. Albert Ellis, author of *Sex Without Guilt*, and his Institute for Rational Living.

But the subject does not merely interest her as *a kind of contemporary anthropology*. It is one of the *Secret Rites* she hopes to photograph. She goes in search of willing couples among her friends and acquaintances.[247] (Ruth Ansel recalls being asked— and declining—to pose naked with her husband, sculptor Paolo Buggiani. *Too uncomfortable with my body*, Ansel later explains.[248]) She photographs orgies in which she is a participant and some of her own individual sex partners posing naked in the aftermath. The challenge of rendering in a photograph something akin to the experience of being there intrigues her. Although she prints a number of these pictures, she regards the majority of them as failures in the terms she prescribes herself, for what she perceives as their lack of eroticism and authenticity.[249]

Among her acquaintances within the community of documentary photographers of her era, in addition to Walker Evans, Robert Frank, and Lee Friedlander, are Garry Winogrand, Bruce Davidson, Larry Fink, Ben Fernandez, Danny Lyon, Duane Michals, and Joel Meyerowitz.[250] Although she is not part of a community—and there may in fact be no community to be a part of—she often attends a colleague's exhibition, visits a class or workshop as a guest, or meets up with one of them while roaming the streets or attending public events in which they happen to share an interest. Meyerowitz's description of his encounters with her may be typical: *We would meet on these infrequent occasions by chance and then spend an hour or two with each other just drifting, until she had had enough or until she found something she wanted to do...A few times we all went down to her house to see work. But that was it.*[251]

Her bed at the Charles Street carriage house occupies a far corner of the living room and is separated from the rest of the room by a screen of irregular weather-beaten wooden planks hinged together. Pinned to both sides of the screen are clippings, postcards, and a number of her own, mostly recent, rough prints on torn curling sheets of photographic paper. Other prints are stored in boxes in the adjacent closet under a staircase. On those occasions when she shows someone her work, she usually does so here.

John Szarkowski is in the process of planning an exhibition, scheduled for February of the following year, which will be called *New Documents*. *In the past decade a new generation of photographers has directed the documentary approach toward more personal ends*, he writes in the exhibition brochure. *Their aim has been not to reform life, but to know it.*[252] He has selected three photographers as independent manifestations of this development: Lee Friedlander, Garry Winogrand, and Diane Arbus. During the next several months Szarkowski works individually with each of the three photographers, selecting the pictures to be included in the show.

Szarkowski later summarizes the nature of his friendship and working relationship with Diane. *I did not really know...*[her] *well, although she was a cherished friend for...years. There was a large area of private thought and feeling that our friendship did not attempt to enter, except perhaps occasionally through jokes or other elliptical codes. She had about her an almost ceremonial sensitivity to roles—not only her own role, but the roles of others, defined according to her own subtly demanding intuitions. This made friendship with her rather like a measured dance at a masked ball—more exciting and more challenging and less spontaneous, than real life. This careful self-discipline, with its suggestion of reticence, was I think required by her work. She had assigned herself the task of photographing mysteries so shy, fugitive, and terrific that they, or she, might have been frightened off, had the issues been openly stated.*[253]

A letter from Diane to James Mathias dated June 9, 1966, reports that she plans to begin her Guggenheim project on July 1, requests a To Whom It May Concern letter, confirms payment arrangements, and refers in a postscript to the enclosed doctor's *good word*: a note from Theodore J. Edlich, M.D., dated June 7, stating that he has examined Diane Arbus and has found her to be *in good physical and mental health and free from communicable disease*. A subsequent notation at the bottom of the letter, probably written by Mathias, records the fact that *Diane Arbus called today 6-13-66 to say she has hepatitis.*[254]

On July 5, almost a month later, Diane writes to Mathias again: *I am considerably better and though it means proceeding more slowly than I would have liked I think I know some ways and means of doing that. So would you go ahead in accordance with my letter of ~~several weeks~~ a month ago.*[255] Mathias replies the following day: *Dear Diane: It's no go! And I won't budge until I get a release from your doctor. I am about to have my own check-up and intend to ask mine whether I can come to see you.*[256]

It is not until July 29 that she is able to satisfy his medical requirement. Mathias writes: *I am delighted to know that you are up and about and that your doctor has given his o.k...* The date for the commencement of her project is officially given as July 15, probably in order to facilitate the desired schedule of payments.[257] Judging by the scant entries in her appointment book for July and August, she seems in fact to have spent almost the entire three months recuperating. As she later summarizes the experience in a note to Stewart Stern: *I was horribly sick with hepatitis last summer which reduced me to despair for three months but when I found myself I was so happy to be happy I could hardly contain myself.*[258]

After resuming work in the fall, she encounters someone she comes to know *pretty well* and whom she photographs several times during the course of the next few years:[259]

...I just saw her on the street one day. I was riding my bicycle on Third Avenue and she was with a friend of hers.[260] They were enormous, both of them, almost six feet tall, and fat. I thought they were big lesbians. They went into a diner and I followed them and asked if I could photograph them. They said, "Yes, tomorrow morning." Subsequently they were apparently arrested and spent the night in jail being booked. So the next morning I got to their house around eleven and they were just coming up the stairs after me. The first thing they said was, "I think we should tell you"—I don't know why they felt so obligated—"we're men."

—*Diane Arbus*, Aperture, 1972[261]

Obtaining releases from the people she photographs has always been an issue— *sometimes I've gotten a release without even taking a picture*, she says on one occasion[262]— but the prospect of the exhibition makes it more pressing. She visits many of the people she has photographed in the past to tell them about the show and the possible inclusion of their portrait. In a letter to Stewart Stern she writes: *Saw Shirley* [Fingerhood, a lawyer, friend, and former Fieldston classmate] *who has given me legal advice because my photographs are becoming more and more questionable...*[263] On another occasion she writes Szarkowski: *I forgot to get back from you the release for the nudist couple you were going to xerox. Would you keep it for me or send it to me because it begins to strike me as having a value of its own.*[264]

By early November she and Szarkowski seem to have made an initial selection of pictures to include in the show, but she is having second thoughts:

Dear John I looked in the box and maybe I was still sick that first time or something but I don't like a lot of the pictures so...[could we meet] please for dinner (or breakfast or lunch) so we can come to an understanding. I am in no particular hurry though because I fancy that what I am doing now is better than most of what I have done but it's true I haven't even seen it yet.

—Postcard to John Szarkowski, November 8, 1966

In spite of her apparent dissatisfaction with some of the choices for the show at this stage, she has already begun printing. For the first time, she is making 16x20 prints of some of the photographs—the largest she has yet attempted—probably in consideration of the effect she wants the images to have when they are seen on the exhibition wall.[265]

She makes several references to her eagerness to give Szarkowski a print as a present. In a postcard about his book *The Photographer's Eye* (The Museum of Modern Art, 1966), she refers to his essay as not only *lucid but encouraging too* and adds *while I am printing, anything you want an extra of, just tell me.*[266] In another instance, she writes: *It would please me to give you a photograph so if you think of one you'd like or perhaps you should see some of the more recent ones you haven't seen or you might like to wait for one of the ones I haven't made yet. Tell me.*[267]

Her progress on the exhibition is briefly interrupted by an assignment that takes her to Kingston, Jamaica. On December 28, she and Amy leave with *New York Times* editor Patricia Peterson and Peterson's son, Jan, to work on the newspaper's upcoming spring children's fashion supplement. The goal is to use the children they happen to find there as models. The four of them spend the next several days or so traveling around in a rented car filled with clothes, on the lookout for potential subjects.[268] "Children in the Sun" is published the following spring and consists of the magazine cover and eleven color and black-and-white photographs by Diane Arbus.[269]

1967

She has recently learned to drive, has a license and has purchased a 1962 Renault for $200, which she describes to a friend as *famous for being no good but it is fine for me to learn bklyn and N.J.*[270] Responding to an inquiry from her brother as to whether she has a picture that might serve as the cover of his next book of poems (*The Blue Swallows*, Chicago University Press, 1967), she offers this incidental description of her photographs:

Dear H. Cannot think what I have. It is all so specific. The only landscape is one of a photomural of a landscape with an electric socket in it. Is that too something or other? Anyway its got no swallows but it might have. Can you wait and look when you are here but no—I can't see what else there is that is lyrical or allusive or elusive. It's all people who are right there...

—POSTCARD TO HOWARD NEMEROV, CIRCA JANUARY 1967[271]

She notes on the January 27 page of her appointment book that this is the day Szarkowski is framing the 16x20 prints for the show. There are four out of the thirty images involved: Puerto Rican woman, Young man in curlers, A family one evening, and Identical twins. All her prints are framed unmatted in Kulicke plastic boxes the same size as the prints themeslves.[272]

The exhibition space designated for *New Documents* is on the ground floor of the museum and consists of one discrete room and a contiguous long hall that opens onto a second room about twice the size of the first. Early on it is decided that Diane's work will occupy the first room, while Lee Friedlander's and Garry Winogrand's photographs are to be hung in separate areas of the larger one.

According to Szarkowski, this decision is partially a response to the difference in format, style, and subject matter of Diane's work, which would look strange paired with the work of either Friedlander or Winogrand.[273] There may also be a desire to exhibit her photographs in the more sequestered of the two available spaces. Szarkowski recalls a mild, subtly expressed, but persistent disagreement he has with the director of the museum, Rene d'Harnoncourt, on the subject of the hanging of Diane's pictures: *We walked through the gallery and Rene said, "I've never liked that gallery. It's always been such an unsatisfactory space. Wouldn't it make the space more interesting if we put up a wall here." He knew that I knew what he was trying to say: Segregate the transvestites in a nook of their own. And I said, "No, Rene, it's impossible. You can't divide these people up according to your private standard of morality because if you do, there are always those people who are going to fall between chairs. You have to put the respectable suburban matron right next to the transvestite..." But he wasn't altogether persuaded. He'd pretend he was persuaded and then he'd go at it again in some other round about Viennese way. So finally I said, "Look, Diane is coming in and why don't the two of you get together."*[274]

The meeting between them takes place at the museum on February 23, less than a week before the opening. Szarkowski describes it this way: [Rene] *was about six feet eight, this mountain of a man with a Viennese ceremony every bit as formidable as Diane's was...They met here in the office and it was one of the best confrontations I ever saw. I stood in the corner, smiling, and watched them. Absolutely polite. Absolutely gracious on both sides. Absolutely smiling. Both of them really understood and respected each other but finally Rene with great graciousness just gave up and bowed and retreated from the field.*[275]

Diane remains a little torn about the prospect of showing her photographs. As she puts it in an interview on the subject with *Newsweek*'s Ann Ray Martin after the fact: *I always thought I'd wait until I'm ninety to have a show or...*[do] *a book because I figured I was good for only one shot — that I wanted to wait until I had it all done.*[276] Her ambivalence is not lost on Szarkowski who later suggests some additional reasons for her hesitation. *Diane was not at all eager to exhibit her work...When* [the pictures] *were exhibited or published she wanted to be certain that it was at the right time and in the right way and under the right circumstances, so that the pictures were not in violation of her personal, moral commitment. In addition to that, she was conscious of the fact that what she was doing was quite different from what other photographers were doing, and she wanted a chance to complete it...before getting it out in public.*[277] On the other hand, he believes that *what was there* [in the *New Documents* show] *I think she found very satisfactory.*[278]

In anticipation of the opening, Diane supplies Szarkowski's secretary, Pat Walker, with a handwritten list on lined legal size yellow paper bearing the names and addresses of people she hopes will be invited on her behalf. This is followed soon after by a two-page typewritten list with additional names accompanied by marginal notes on some of the prospective guests. She includes the names and addresses of three editors *who have asked me about doing a book of photographs* and then adds in the margin *No, let's not invite them...more colorful people are more fun.* As she notes in conclusion: *I'm not greedy. I just want it to be a good party.*[279]

She makes uncharacteristically elaborate preparations for the evening: gets her hair cut, permed, and set at Vidal Sassoon, buys a new dress, and arranges for a friend to do her makeup especially for the occasion.[280] Szarkowski recalls her entrance the night of the opening: *Diane came in. Very fashionably late. Very elegant like a movie queen from the thirties. And Dick* [Avedon] *was there with a great big bouquet of yellow roses. She was very radiant. But studied...she did have split feelings about those kinds of public displays. She couldn't just come and have a good time. Like Lee or Garry.*[281]

Richard Avedon and Marvin Israel have organized a photographic workshop together that takes place once a week at Avedon's studio on East 58th Street. Among the young photographers participating in the class are Peter Hujar, Deborah Turbeville, and Chris von Wangenheim. Diane attends one of the sessions as a guest following the opening of *New Documents*.[282]

She makes her photograph of the twins into a postcard (inscribed on the back in pen *Identical twins Diane Arbus Postcard*) and sends it to a number of friends as an announcement. To Stewart Stern on March 5 she writes: *From now till June 7* [the show actually ends May 7 so this date is probably a misprint] *there's one third of a show of my photographs at the museum of modern art. I wish you could see it. It's just much more beautiful than I had ever seen it at home.*[283] And to the Meserveys: *Everything here is too overwhelming. The show I mean. I go from laughter to tears. I bought a $200 car and have braces on my teeth for four months.*[284] And to her friend the peace activist Paul Salstrom, who is living in Berkeley:

Now there is a show...30 of my photographs at the modern museum. I long for you to see it. It is so beautiful, all in a splendid room and people stare into them, hundreds of strangers as if they were reading. I stand there for hours watching people watch the pictures and listening to what they say.

—POSTCARD TO PAUL SALSTROM, MARCH 5, 1967[285]

The reviews of her portion of the exhibition—both positive and negative—focus almost exclusively on the issue of her subject matter. "Showing It Like It Is," John Gruen's review in *New York* [*The World Journal Tribune Sunday Magazine*] says: *Diane Arbus is the most shockingly alert to a human stratum most of us have little contact with...Her photographs are brutal, daring and revealing because she not only succeeded in invading closed territories, but obviously gained the confidence of subjects living on the peripheries of the accepted.*[286] In *The New York Times* review entitled "People Seen as Curiosity," Jacob Deschin writes: [She] *seems to respond to the grotesque in life...there is occasionally a subtle suggestion of pathos, now and then diluted slightly with a vague sense of humor. Sometimes it must be added, the picture borders close to poor taste.*[287] And in the March 20, 1967, issue of *Newsweek*, Ann Ray Martin—who interviewed Diane on March 6 at the museum—summarizes her work this way: *With the sharp crystal-clear generous vision of a poet, Mrs. Arbus turns her lens on the margins of society.*[288]

By the end of March, she is planning a trip to Florida that she seems to regard at least in part as an escape from the heady atmosphere engendered by the show. She responds to a letter from Stewart Stern:

You sound edgy and wild and miserable and I don't know but you made me feel good...I am going to Florida for 10 days to Ft. Lauderdale and Miami and I dunno wherever the travel brochures tell me. Just to photograph. With the Guggenheim money. The show was splendid but too many calls and letters and people thinking I am an expert or incredibly lovable. I need to be forlorn and anonymous in order to be truly happy. Get edgier yet and try to visit NY. It's a nice place to visit.

—POSTCARD TO STEWART STERN, CIRCA MARCH 1967[289]

She leaves for Ft. Lauderdale on March 25 and sends Marvin Israel a postcard from Miami recounting in brief her failed attempt to meet with *the World's Greatest Female Pinup Photographer,* Bunny Yaeger,[290] who fascinates her but who when they spoke *was wary if not downright hostile and very snobbish. Just because I have heard of her it does not follow that she has heard of me.* She concludes with this summary of the place, *Ionesco would be pleased here but my hotel is for Beckett* and then adds as an afterthought, *It cannot be anti-Semitism but they do not accept me here.*[291]

A few days later she sends him a second postcard, this time with one of Yaeger's photographs on it that bears the credit line *color by Bunny Yaeger.* She writes underneath *blk & wht by Diane.*

There is kind of a bad smell here like God cooking chicken soup in the sky. And the language is full of money. There is a word called condominium something to do with real estate. It is written everywhere. And high-rise means skyscraper. When my mother says she realized [something] she doesn't mean an insight she means profit on an investment. Ask me about Oedipus when I come home because I think I realized something...There is a law here against miniskirts but they are too embarrassed to invoke it...It is as if I am a bottomless waitress...How will we be when we are old? A thousand times D.

—POSTCARD TO MARVIN ISRAEL, CIRCA MARCH 1967[292]

Ruth Ansel gets a postcard from Florida, too: ...*I'm in the land of our ancestors. They look at me very oddly...It is like a dream. (My car is a turqouise air conditioned nightmare Mustang). yours till retirement.*[293] Ansel recalls several conversations with Diane about *photographing the Fontainbleau Hotel in all its Miami glory,*[294] an assignment that Ansel, Bea Feitler, and Diane continue to hope will be forthcoming from *Harper's Bazaar*. But as Ansel later explains, *It was too "downmarket unglamorous" for the editors. A real loss.*[295]

Following Diane's return to New York in early April, her interests as a photographer prompt her to attend an unusual number of public events, both political and social.[296] These include the Rouge et Noir Ball at the New York Hilton, the Heart Association Ball at the Waldorf Hotel, the Spring Mobilization to End the War in Vietnam on April 15, the march to "Support Our Men in Vietnam" on May 13, and a Human Be-In in Central Park's Sheep's Meadow in June.[297] She begins considering a trip to San Francisco and asks Paul Salstrom's advice.

Dear Paul, would it be a good thing if I was to come to San F. in the beginning of July? I would come in no official capacity. Are there too many photographers. Could you be my guide...

—POSTCARD TO PAUL SALSTROM, CIRCA JUNE 1967[298]

Apparently his response persuades her. She travels on American Airlines, arriving July 6 as scheduled. She stays in a house at 591 Waller Street in the Haight-Ashbury, where Salstrom is living with a group of war resisters. She finds San Francisco—with its glut of hippies, tourists, and journalists—oppressive. In a letter to her brother she confesses: *California...made me queasy and repudiated. Probably I took it personally.* She blames her failure to meet with writer Kay Boyle—a friend of Nemerov's whom she knows and who is a resident of San Francisco—on the fact that she *couldn't bear to see anyone who felt comfortable being there.*[299]

She and Salstrom leave the city and drive to Southern California together, then head back East. They part in Oklahoma City, where Salstrom decides to stay a while. After her return to New York, Diane writes him about the rest of her trip:

...The bus began to hearten me and I read McLuhan [*Understanding Media* (New York: Mentor/Penguin, 1964)] and lots of sh. Stories. But on the last lap the stench and filth and tragic aspect of all those abandoned sleeping creatures was nearly too much. Arrived at 5:00 A.M. and walked N.Y. all day, exhausted, refreshed, elated. Even met a gypsy who asked me (unprecedented!) to photograph her. I will not apologize or thank you. It is all too mysterious. Diane.

—POSTCARD TO PAUL SALSTROM, JULY 28, 1967[300]

She gives Amy, who is away at camp in upstate New York, this account of the summer's progress:

dear amy I have been strange as anything, curioser and curioser as alice said. Last night I dreamed you had taken all the pictures off my wall "because you needed the tape" (!)...today it seems to have turned blessedly cool...The other night I went to Times Sq and suddenly there is a parking lot smack in the middle of Broadway a Whole Block Sq. I guess it is where the Astor Hotel used to be. It looked the way it would if someone you knew awfully well but hadn't seen very recently had lost two front teeth...We miss you. You are somehow the backbone or the lifeblood of this house. It is oddly random without you. I hope the people look promising. I hope you have enough pants. I love you beloved (Amy)...your ma.

—LETTER TO AMY ARBUS, SUMMER 1967

On August 16 she goes to Palisades Amusement Park in New Jersey for the 30th annual Diaper Derby contest to photograph the event as well as the winner and losers. The experience seems connected in her mind to some incipient change she believes is occurring in the pictures. She writes her brother in the fall about her recent photographic projects: *The subjects are terribly odd—dogs and babies—but that pleases me. It is like starting over again.*[301] And in a letter to her friend Carlotta Marshall: *I have been photographing babies which is odd and absorbing. Also the pictures are getting bigger. Some are lifesize or more. That is fun. Like making people instead of photographs.*[302] To Amy she puts it this way: *I suddenly realized that when I photograph people I don't anymore want them to look at me. (I used nearly always to wait for them to look me in the eye but now its as if I think I will see them more clearly if they are not watching me watching them.*[303])

The magazine assignments she works on in 1967 are not published until the following year. These include a portrait of Gloria Vanderbilt and Wyatt Cooper's infant son, Anderson, for *Harper's Bazaar*;[304] folk singer/prophet Mel Lyman for *Esquire*;[305] and a project of her own on a camp for overweight girls.[306] She also has several assignments from a new magazine, *Cheetah*.[307]

Stewart Stern has written the screenplay for *Rachel, Rachel*, a movie that marks Paul Newman's directorial debut, with his wife, Joanne Woodward, in the lead.

Stern, a friend of the Newmans, introduces the notion of hiring Diane as the still photographer on the set, which is seriously considered for a while. By September, however, to Stern's chagrin, the prospect has fallen through, probably for financial reasons.[308] She writes to him at the Danbury Motor Inn in Connecticut where the movie is being shot.

I don't know quite how it happened that I'm not doing it. I miss you and would have liked just doing it for you. I may have asked too much money...Dunno. I am working on two marvelous assignments. Feel much stronger. One is on prophets.[309] Don't bother to answer. I know you are at the grindstone. Will see you afterwards. Try to save an evening...Till then...

—LETTER TO STEWART STERN, SEPTEMBER 27, 1967

Following publication of his book *The Blue Swallows*, Howard Nemerov inquires as to whether Diane was paid for the use of her picture on the cover. She answers: *Yes yes I got pd. And when I saw it I didn't feel any sort of twinge. It is an odd red but I didn't take it personally.* She goes on:

I've been jumpy. Going in fits and starts since the show...But suddenly I have a lot of work, an odd combination of public and private work and probably that will be good.

—LETTER TO HOWARD NEMEROV, CIRCA OCTOBER 1967[310]

Responding to news of the recent birth of Carlotta Marshall's first child (a son named Jamie, born October 18) Diane writes to her in Holland where she has been living with her husband, Louis Berger. *Dear Carlotta we are so glad to picture it. your parenthood. tell us more than we can picture.* She adds:

The first breath of cold frightened me into staying home today to write you as I ought to have long ago. My popularity or success or whatever it was has ebbed somewhat which has its compensations and now it is time to get back to a sort of obscurity and see what I come up with...I have wangled a weekly ride in a radio car with a press photographer. This is more adventure than photography but perhaps eventually some of it will become photographable. I would like to make a sort of news photographs.

—LETTER TO CARLOTTA MARSHALL, CIRCA NOVEMBER 1967[311]

During the summer, Diane has been in touch with two editors from *The London Sunday Times Magazine*, Michael Rand and Peter Crookston, and with one of the magazine's writers, Pauline Peters. In late October, when Crookston comes to New York, she meets with him several times and invites him to Charles Street to see her work.[312] Among the pictures she shows him are Widow in her bedroom and a number of images from the Diaper Derby (both of which inspire stories written by Pauline Peters and published in the magazine the following year accompanied by Diane's photographs).[313] On November 30 she writes Crookston a follow-up letter consisting of eleven short, hand-numbered paragraphs with asterisks indicating those items that require answers or actions.

(1)YES I will send the photographs of the lady poet tomorrow (friday) evening. Must print the new ones first. They amaze me.[314] (2) *Would you give me a special Big Credit Line because I really love that photograph...saying PHOTOGRAPHED BY DIANE ARBUS... thanks (3) I will also send the Diaper Derby photographs and the ones you chose of women for possible use. Some of the prints are crude and not for reproduction but I will send what you want when you do. (4) *Please when you have finished with the ones you do not need would you send them back and the stats you borrowed as well. Thanks... (7) *If you have any sort of press credentials that look nice and professional would you send them. (8) *If there is some way of getting me some money for these three stories we worked on please do Either by paying me a daily rate or some sort of arrangement for the ideas...

—LETTER TO PETER CROOKSTON, NOVEMBER 30, 1967[315]

She says she expects to be coming to London around January 5—*The man I spoke about* [a reference to Marvin Israel] *has asked me to go with him*—and suggests Crookston think of something she might photograph for the magazine while there. She concludes with this:

I am so happy and the strangest things have been happening as if someone had turned my life around for me and showed it to me in a whole different light. It makes me giddy. If all goes well I will see you soon how truly nice diane.

—LETTER TO PETER CROOKSTON, NOVEMBER 30, 1967

The imminent expiration of her lease at Charles Street and the threat of a substantial rent increase as a result compel her to look for another place to live. A couple of weeks later, in answer to what she describes as *a happy headlong letter* from Crookston, she writes him again:

It is raining endlessly and I have been apt [apartment] hunting ceaselessly so I have developed a cold and a dislike for all dwelling places and a sort of blankness about christmas which even surpasses my normal scroogeness. Thanks for your painstaking replies and reactions to every one of my queries and requests. I could not be in better hands...We never mention... London, marvin and me, (the man who asked me to go). partly out of superstition or discretion or prudence or the plain old sense that so much has to be cleaned out of the Augean stables first that one had best not speak of it at all so that it will come in the nature of a surprise if it comes and not a disappointment if...oh well we'll see...

—LETTER TO PETER CROOKSTON, DECEMBER 12, 1967[316]

On December 15 Allan goes with her to look at an apartment she is considering renting at 120 East 10th Street between Second and Third avenues in the East Village.[317] *Might have found an apt*, she says when she writes Crookston a few days later to let him know that she won't be coming to London after all.

I'm not disappointed really. I couldn't have taken more in. The changes I've embarked on like moving and some odd new thing I think I see ahead in the photographs are either necessary or exciting and I must do one thing at a time...I want to make order and begin again.

—LETTER TO PETER CROOKSTON, DECEMBER 19, 1967[318]

1968

The apartment at 120 East 10th Street is actually two separate apartments on the top floors of a five-story brownstone walk-up, connected to one another only by the building's public staircase. The apartment on the lower floor consists of three small bedrooms (for Diane, Doon, and Amy), an entrance hall, and bathroom; the one on the upper floor is a living room, open kitchen, and second bathroom. In early January, just before the move, Diane sends Crookston some prints she had promised him for the magazine, accompanied by a note:

I am in the midst of cleaning and packing and moving—haven't worked for so long it makes me queasy and strange to myself. But it is fun. I have thrown out and given away more than I have kept it seems. I am pure housewife and I hate that it is so barren and obsessive but I look forward to the new beginning like a bride.

—NOTE TO PETER CROOKSTON, CIRCA JANUARY 1968[319]

The move takes place on January 15. *Fell into a terrible funk, moving. The old house fell apart and the new won't fall in. My incompetence looms like a middle name*, she reports a few weeks later in responding to a proposed assignment from Crookston to photograph the Republican presidential hopefuls. *Yes I've wanted to do those baroque Republicans. Can someone make all arrangements for me? Or would I go with a writer.*[320] The January 29 page of her appointment book includes a list of names (*Reagan, Rockefeller, Nixon, Percy, Romney*) but the magazine's attempts to organize this project apparently fail.[321]

On February 14 she travels to South Carolina for several days on assignment for *Esquire* to accompany crusading country doctor Donald Gatch on his rounds and photograph him and his patients.[322] Dr. Gatch is in the midst of a campaign to call attention to widespread malnutrition and discriminatory medical practice in poverty-stricken rural Beaufort County. Diane describes the experience to Studs Terkel a few months later when he interviews her about the Great Depression of the 1930s: *I never saw poverty like that. I have never been in homes like that. There was one family with fourteen children. One of the children had one eye. One was a hydrocephalic... The doctor...told me an incredible story of a mother with an illegitimate mentally defective boy who, because she couldn't get welfare, had to go to work and since she had no one to take care of the boy she chained him to the bed for her eight hours of working.*[323] Bynum Shaw's article "Let Us Now Praise Dr. Gatch," accompanied by three Diane Arbus photographs, is published in *Esquire* in June.

Of the six previous 1968 magazine pieces in which her pictures appear, three are published by *The London Sunday Times Magazine*, all using photographs she made independently the year before or earlier: "Pauline Peters on People: Dr. Glassbury's Widow" (January 7, 1968); "Pauline Peters on People: How to Train a Derby Winner" (March 21, 1968); and "Please Don't Feed Me," by Hunter Davies, about a camp for overweight girls (April 14, 1968).[324] The only new assignment she receives in this period is from *New York* magazine, recently inaugurated as an independent entity following the demise of its parent newspaper, *The World Journal Tribune*.[325] In March editor Clay Felker assigns her to photograph the underground movie actress Viva, star of several Andy Warhol films including *Blue Movie, aka Fuck*. Diane visits Viva on several occasions and describes the results to Crookston following publication of the April 29 issue: *The article* [by Barbara Goldsmith] *is harsh and humorless, but there are lots of fascinating pictures. It was something of a cause celebre, much mail and cancelled subscriptions and pro and con phone calls and whatnot, even a threatened lawsuit.*[326]

She continues to research and explore possible photographic projects for *Esquire*, *New York*, *Harper's Bazaar*, *The London Sunday Times*, and for herself. On the March 5 page of her appointment book, under the heading *Dandies*, are five names of possible subjects and some additional topics—*chic beauties and generation gap*—apparently as suggestions for *New York*. The May 17 page reiterates these ideas and adds others: *activist youth leaders abbie H.* [Abbie Hoffman], *richest and poorest, pot proliferation, and heroes of the underground: Marcuse, Taylor Mead, Abbie* [Hoffman, again]. She gives Crookston this summary of things:

My new apartment is cozier than I had imagined. Work goes along oddly and obsessively...Lots is happening here and I live two blocks away from St. Marks Pl which has become one of the great corners in the city where just standing still you feel in the heart of the maelstrom. The underground has a whole bunch of new heroes. There are some amazing flamboyant bewigged and empurpled whores who hang out on one particular place on Broadway...I am also trying to do something on criminals, and maybe on returned runaways.

—LETTER TO PETER CROOKSTON, MAY 18, 1968

The project on criminals leads her to the books of Dr. Frederick Wertham: *Dark Legend: A Study in Murder, Show of Violence,* and *A Sign for Cain: An Exploration of Human Violence.*[327] She also obtains Wertham's phone number,[328] although it is possible that the two never actually speak. She is anything but single-minded, however, about what she intends to pursue. Around the same time, in a message written sequentially on two separate postcards, she adds this:

One more thing, perhaps too exotic...I know a Jewish giant who lives in Washington Heights or the Bronx with his little parents. He is tragic with a curious bitter somewhat stupid wit. The parents are orthodox and repressive and classic and disapprove of his carnival career...Once many years ago I photographed them but I don't know where it is[329]...They are a truly metaphorical family...Also. I know an incredible set of triplets. And an association of twins in New Jersey some of whom are identical...

—POSTCARD TO PETER CROOKSTON, CIRCA MAY 1968

The same communication goes on to mention *the largest family* and *an association who pick the mother of the yr,* and concludes, *You can see I've got suddenly more energy than I can use. I need a dam...I hope I can really do something, not just feel elated.*[330] In response to a subsequent suggestion by Crookston that she come to London to work on an issue the magazine is planning to devote exclusively to the subject of the family, she responds:

I have been wanting to do families. I stopped two elderly sisters the other day and three generations of jewish women from Bklyn whom I am to visit soon...the youngest is pregnant. And especially there is a woman I stopped in a Bookstore[331] who lives in Westchester which is Upper Suburbia. She is about 35 with terribly blonde hair and enormously eyelashed and booted and probably married to a dress manufacturer or restaurateur and I said I wanted to photograph her with husband and children so she suggested I wait till warm weather so I can do it around the pool!...They are a fascinating family. I think all families are creepy in a way.

—LETTER TO PETER CROOKSTON, CIRCA JUNE 1968[332]

In the same letter she notes, not altogether parenthetically: (*my mother* [widowed since 1963] *is getting married again this month!!!! I have only a photograph of her fiance. It is so odd. He looks like a dentist...*[333]) She details the financial and logistical impracticality of her making a trip to London for this purpose, suggesting Crookston *think about American Families I might provide you with at this end,* and adding, *I don't think I can come unless I can make a little money to bring home. I am so behind in work. Reams to print.*[334] She is also reluctant to leave home because of her own pending photographic projects:

Someone is getting me permission they swear, from someone at the head of the New Jersey prisons and mental hospitals to photograph in them, just for me.[335] Meanwhile I still have the opportunity to ride in a radio car for crimes in the long hot summer nights...I havent done returned Runaways, only thought of it as part of my Families...Of all these possibilities two thirds will fall through. (there is also sex clubs still and country clubs and vigilante women but these are only notions.)

—LETTER TO PETER CROOKSTON, CIRCA JUNE 1968

In a marginal note scrawled in pen at the end of this two-page letter which she refers to as *all in haste, like a waterfall*, she returns once more to the word *family*:

The working title if you can call it that for my book which I keep postponing is Family Album. I mean I am not working on it except to photograph like I would anyway so all I have is a title and a publisher[336] and a sort of sweet lust for things I want in it like picking flowers or Noah's Ark. I can hardly bear to leave any animal out...

—LETTER TO PETER CROOKSTON, CIRCA JUNE 1968

Running parallel to the torrent of ideas that constitute the bulk of her correspondence with Crookston is an equally persistent series of pleas and complaints about payments from the magazine. On May 18, following publication of the three Diaper Derby photographs, she writes: *I've received an unaccountable check for $166.93 for the How to train a Derby winner photos. I haven't cashed it because it isn't at all the right amount...*She proceeds to defend her arithmetic for this story (*Even figured at the ASMP minimum daily rate which is $150 per day that comes to $750*) and for the other two stories she has worked on and delivered, all of which, as she points out, were her suggestions. *I think the fee...should come to $900. Let me know how to bill it and what to do with the check I received which doesn't seem to signify anything at all.*[337]

This letter is followed soon after by one that begins *I don't mean to quibble but I will*, in which—responding to a cable from Crookston—she rehashes earlier discussions about the $150 page rate she agreed upon with the magazine. *We all seemed satisfied with this arrangement for the fat girls,* she notes in the margin, *and I assumed it was the precedent for all future assignments with the possible exception of a future alteration upwards rather than down...I don't see why it has to suddenly dip down to $120 like it says in your cable. or the mysterious dribbly payments on the diaper derby.* Then, somewhat apologetically, she adds near the end: *Thirty dollars is unimportant but multiplied by the real and happy possibilities of our working together as much as we* *might it shld be considered...I like to work for you because you are daring dashing fair decisive formidable and even rather wise but those are the Financial Expectations Michael* [Rand] *himself had led me to. are they too Great? (my enthusiasm alone should be worth it.)*[338] A subsequent letter from her offers this explanation:

If I sounded sharp or irate it was only trying to get into a sort of efficiency about my financial state which is confusingly and delightfully wed to my husbands and he seems to be perhaps planning to marry a very nice girl [actress Mariclare Costello] although I may be over anticipating. Anyway I just wanted to gather everything together because part of my snobbery is to act excessively casual about money as if I didn't care if I ever got any and if I am to be supporting my small self soon I should know something about how much I make.

—LETTER TO PETER CROOKSTON, CIRCA JUNE 1968[339]

The matter remains unresolved and in a letter dated July 4 she writes: *please lets settle this because I do not want to feel that I am impractical and imprudent to the point of idiocy and since I have only so far recd 300 actual dollars for working for you, I might easily feel that.* The letter also contains, buried amid a slew of proposed ideas, the following casually prophetic sentence: *I seem to be undergoing some subterranean revolution in which the surface hardly stirs but I sleep and dream a lot and once in a while signs erupt that seem portentous to me at least.*[340]

A week or so later she writes to Amy at camp, apologizing for her failure to be as prolific a correspondent as she'd intended to be and explaining what happened: *I told you I had been feeling lousy and I went to a doctor and he said there wasnt anything wrong but altho that was nice I still felt rotten and he just looked at me like I was imagining things...*[341] She later gives Carlotta Marshall the following, somewhat more detailed, account:

For months...doctors kept reassuring me I didn't have hepatitis all over again like I kept thinking and that it was purely psychosomatic or menopausal or just old age itself which scared the shit out of me and theyd prescribe some little bunch of pills and I would 'plunge myself into my work' feeling lousier and lousier till it got so that I couldn't walk up the stairs to my own apartment without resting halfway up and collapsing onto my bed for 15 minutes at the top. Finally these symptoms erupted into whatever sort of reality...is the opposite of psychosomatic and I crawled into the hospital.

—LETTER TO CARLOTTA MARSHALL, AUGUST 4 OR 5, 1968

The Thursday July 18 page of her appointment book records in Allan's handwriting: *into hospital period began.* Other than childbirth, this is her first experience as a hospitalized patient.

I am having a terrific time in the hospital where I have gone to get all sorts of tests made on my liver and all the rest of my inner workings. It is really fun. They give me enemas and take my temperature and blood pressure and give me marvelous baths in bed. I have a marvelous room with an air conditioner and a TV which I work with a pushbutton from my bed and every time I pee or shit they ask me to save a sample of it. I am starting to feel much better...

—LETTER TO AMY ARBUS, CIRCA JULY 1968[342]

In a typewritten letter on Doctors Hospital stationery, Diane responds to Carlotta—who at this point is unaware of their parallel circumstances—and to Carlotta's news that she has been hospitalized in Holland with some mysterious and as yet undiagnosed disease of her own: *I was so touched and saddened by your letter. The only good thing is that I have been undergoing some of that myself and have come through the other side and the difference between sickness and health is so extraordinary and absorbing I must just see if I can shed any light at all for you.*[343] She recounts a few of her recent comically nightmarish adventures in the land of medical care:

One day the Dr would come in and say I was progressing just fine and the next day he would explain squeamishly that...they might have to remove my gall bladder or see if I had TB and it wasn't that they suspected cancer...etc etc. and I would start to cry partly out of the snobbish feeling that I shouldn't be a sick person...So they took out a piece of my liver...It was a strange Dr. and to show him I wasn't scared I said brightly what is the liver for? well, he answered let's put it this way: you couldn't liver without it...Then I couldn't move for a day and had to be fed by an aide who stuffed such big pieces sideways into my mouth that the gravy or remains would dribble down my chin. I was a 45 yr old infant and angry to boot.

—LETTER TO CARLOTTA MARSHALL, AUGUST 4 OR 5, 1968

But she is primarily intent on describing to Carlotta some of what she believes she has figured out during her three-week hospital stay, while going through so many changes:

...I have learned to see that no state of being is intrinsic or autonomous. Oneself is dispensable and so are a whole bunch of one's most precious attributes...but they come back when you can afford the luxury of them again. When I was most sick and scared I was no longer a photographer (I still am not and something about realizing that I don't Have to Photograph was terribly good for me) or a mother and I lost my curiosity and most of what humor I've got, but I learned that is OK....Life continually gets better and worse and better. Demand your share.

—LETTER TO CARLOTTA MARSHALL, AUGUST 4 OR 5, 1968

She says she is *scheduled to go home the following day and then to the country to recuperate and I am not allowed to do too much or to have any responsibilities which is just dandy as far as I'm concerned.*[344] From her friend Tina Fredericks's home in East Hampton, a frequent place of refuge, she writes to Amy, attempting to provide some reassurance about things: *I have to eat a pound of red meat a day and take endless vitamins...but I am quite OK and apparently if I...do just as I am told I will be better than new in a few months.*[345] At the same time, however, she is obliged to break the news of the recent death of their seven-year-old cat, Ishmael, whom Allan had discovered to be seriously ill on the day before Diane's release from the hospital.[346] *Pa felt you should know now so you wouldn't come home and suddenly find out and feel we had been lying to you,*[347] she writes. This is how she describes her recuperation to Carlotta:

It is so pretty and calm here. Rabbits and pheasants and chipmunks alternately appear and disappear on the lawn in front of me and I am learning such serenity... Once in a while I feel a vague anxiety about what is happening around where I am supposed to be but then I remember that I am 'not supposed to have any responsibilities.' So I look once more out upon the lawn and see who is chasing whom and hope for the best.

—LETTER TO CARLOTTA MARSHALL, CIRCA MID-AUGUST 1968

Shortly before her return to New York, she learns from her hostess, Tina Fredericks—and relays to Marvin Israel—that Rene d'Harnoncourt, former director of The Museum of Modern Art, *died OUT HERE last week, run over while crossing the street, reading the morning paper.*[348] That night she has a dream which she recounts to Israel the following day in a detailed four-page handwritten letter:

I dreamed that Rene d'Harnoncourt was my doctor...looking for all the world like Bela Lugosi...He was 9 ft tall. I could never reach him. I summoned the courage to face him, saying unequivocally in a ringing voice... "Please Doctor tell me what is wrong with me and how you propose to cure it," but he affected not to hear me and strode off...looking elated like a mad scientist who has discovered a cure that kills people... I pursued him to Times Square...even though he kept outdistancing me because I was sick and not supposed to EXERCISE...He was starting to change (metamorphose) to elude me...growing absolutely flat (2 dimensional) and utterly black like a silhouette and then at 45th St...as he was stepping off the curb... he suddenly split into lots of silhouetted little men scurrying off in different directions so there was no way of knowing whom to pursue and I realized you are dead when you ask the doctor why you are sick and he doesn't hear you... This morning I am quiet and nice again like Mr. Hyde but tired because I have been exorcised all night and the doctor said not to, (Dr. Jekyll I presume.) Smile when you meet me at Max's [referring to Max's Kansas City, one of their regular Manhattan hangouts]. Love, D.

On August 25, about a week after her return to New York, she attends a screening of the Stewart Stern, Paul Newman, Joanne Woodward movie *Rachel, Rachel* but doesn't stay for the event that follows. In a letter to Stern she explains: *I wouldn't have left so fast except it was hepatitis that I had, a sort of relapse and it was my first public event since. I lost energy quite suddenly which left me feeling very shy. But illness is terrific for taking you back to the beginning like bankruptcy. I think its better to start from scratch than anywhere.* About the movie she adds: *I'm glad about Rachel. I'd know you in it anywhere...You left none of your old stones unturned.*[349]

In response to Carlotta's latest news of her progress, medical and otherwise— which includes an operation on her brain that has left her bald with two holes in her head and temporarily seeing double—Diane writes: *Dear Carlotta, Wow, you really do things gloriously. My illness looks positively anemic beside yours...and my romance with death ludicruously onesided.*[350] Of her own recovery she has this to say:

Convalescence is rather extraordinary...I think it seemed to me for a while as if I had the option of being any of a number of things and I couldn't bear to be merely me but now I am glad to have somewhere to begin...some history, some attitudes because I am back in the city and here it's hard being as faceless as I felt. I dread work a little and sometimes pretend I am an imposter but last week I put the camera around my neck although I didn't use it and I was grateful just to wear it.

A week or so later she writes to Crookston:

I have started to work. In a way I miss being sick but during convalescence a strange rage developed in me. It especially appears every night around 4AM like a werewolf. I don't know if it can be made to make something but it feels like raw wild power. I don't yet know how to make it energy.

Somewhat reluctantly she begins to teach again at Cooper Union.[351] *They called me one day before the Semester and we are too poor for me to have refused*, she tells Carlotta.[352] Around the same time she receives a tantalizing offer that will require her to spend several months away from home, in California, Mexico, and Rome. She later describes it to her brother this way:

...I have been asked, via Mike Nichols who will direct it, to photograph stills on the set of Catch 22 which films for 5 mos, mostly in Mexico and a little in

Rome. It all started out terribly grandiose with long distance calls from Hllywd and considerable insertions of flattering words like genius and I could bring my child along and come and go as I pleased. Meanwhile on the best advice (Avedon) I asked for 3000 dollars a wk, which they found rather high and so did I but I wd easily dwindle. They just havent given me a chance. I alternately think what thehelldoiwanttodo thatfor and then realize we are so flat broke that there is simply no question but that I must and then think it would be fun and amazing to see a million Hollywood people at work and play and at least in the original offer there were to be no restrictions or demands on What I shd photograph... just anything I want. Occasionally I feel enormous zest for it and also know it is a much more intelligent way to make money that will let me do what I want for a yr or so than my current way of dashing off everywhere for $100 at a time which leaves me a little frazzled altho the variety is nice.

—LETTER TO HOWARD NEMEROV, NOVEMBER 10, 1968 [353]

The London Sunday Times Magazine's upcoming issue on the family is still on her mind. She has already sent Crookston her 1966 photograph of A young Brooklyn family and provided what information she could about them based on her notes at the time. (*They live in the Bronx. I think he was a garage mechanic. Their first child was born when she was sixteen...*[354]) She follows up with another newly discovered possibility.

If your material on The Family is not utterly signed and sealed, I have one of the upper middle class suburban family on their lawn, just two parents and a child [adds in the margin, the ones I told you I would do and was going back] which I did before I was sick[355] and just printed and its so odd, nearly like Pinter but not quite, it might just serve to introduce the whole thing along with that quotation you sent me of...("the family with its narrow somethingorother and its etc etc might be the source of all our woes"...I've forgotten it, but in the picture the parents seem to be dreaming the child and the child seems to be inventing them, Maybe its more like Charles Addams.) Anyway I have a print so if you could use it you could get it fast.

—LETTER TO PETER CROOKSTON, CIRCA SEPTEMBER 1968

She has a couple of assignments from *Harper's Bazaar* in this period, including a trip to Atlanta to photograph the widow of Dr. Martin Luther King, Jr. (*awful photos, but glorious fun hanging around and peering at everything. I have decided photography is a sort of private sin of mine. As a virtue I find it really hard to sustain.*[356]) *Esquire* sends her to do a portrait of Democratic presidential nominee Eugene McCarthy on election eve,[357] an adventure she later recounts to her brother, who turns out to have been unwittingly instrumental in the success of it.

The night before Sudie [Trazoff, née Victor] told me that he read poetry and wrote some etc. and that he would know and care about you. Well the minute I was ushered into the office and introduced in a mumble by the press secretary... McCarthy looked as pained as if I was a dentist and began that curious gesture of looking like he was about to give me his face to photograph managing all the while to avoid inhabiting it. Well right then and there I knew I would have to stoop to it and I did... said my schoolgirl piece about my brother the Howard Nemerov and the whole climate changed...Finally by the end of the day when he came to sit in the chair in front of me he was terribly open and curiously willing, although in the photograph he looks haunted. Anyway I'd never have been able to do it without you. I needed that kind of attention from him and he gave it on the assumption that any sister of yours must be an artist instead of a reporter.

—LETTER TO HOWARD NEMEROV, NOVEMBER 10, 1968[358]

She is also assigned by *Esquire* to photograph Tokyo Rose in Chicago,[359] and by *The London Sunday Times Magazine* to photograph a Weight Watcher's success story, Alice Madeiros, the heroine of an article written by Doon which Crookston plans to republish.[360] These jobs, however, appear to provide her little reassurance about either money or work. She makes the following observation about her situation:

...Editors appear to be putting me off...It is partly that my reputation has gotten enormous and...somehow people decide either that I am too big for my britches or temperamental or simply that I need taking down a peg. It is a terribly familiar syndrome...I am not as good a photographer as people think except sometimes and in my head. And somehow they don't like it that I am no good or too good. I will never be just right.

—LETTER TO CARLOTTA MARSHALL, CIRCA NOVEMBER 1968

A few weeks after the opening of a Brassaï exhibition at The Museum of Modern Art, she attends an event that takes place there in honor of the photographer. (About his work and its impact on her she later says: *He taught me something terrific about obscurity, that obscurity could be as thrilling as clarity, which for a long time I didn't realize because I had been moving more and more towards clarity for years.*)[361] The event itself however turns out to be something of a disappointment.

I've been meaning to say I'm sorry I (or we for as much as I can speak for the others) flubbed the Brassai occasion. My essential question seemed to me by turns banal, vulgar, vague or simply unanswerable, like how do you do it Monsieur? And some of the people who took the bull by the horns made it seem more than ever that we were in a china shop. But it would be really nice to have a robust dialogue, a bit less frantically polite or sycophantish.

—LETTER TO JOHN SZARKOWSKI, CIRCA MID-NOVEMBER 1968

On November 10 *The London Sunday Times Magazine* publishes its special issue on the family which includes, under the title "Two American Families," the Diane Arbus photographs Family on their lawn one Sunday in Westchester, N.Y. 1968 and A young Brooklyn family going for a Sunday outing, N.Y.C. 1966. The pictures are accompanied by extended captions credited to Diane but actually fashioned by the editors from the contents of her letters about them. The publication prompts this reply from her to Crookston: *The family on the lawn looked good I think but let me next time write it so it makes more sense. Wish I had photographed more. Would love to have done a family tree.*[362]

She is still pursuing her attempts to obtain permission to photograph at institutions and has received considerable help from Carlotta's friend Adrian Condon and Condon's cousin by marriage, Mary Stevens Baird, who is a member of the New Jersey State Board of Control of Institutions and Agencies. She writes Crookston:

I would like to photograph mentally retarded people, idiots, imbeciles and morons (morons are the smartest of the three): especially the cheerful ones. And I am looking for elderly twins. I have heard of a source. And there is an old retired actors home in NJ I want to visit if I can get permission. And I wonder about plastic surgery and Beauty Queens.

—LETTER TO PETER CROOKSTON, CIRCA DECEMBER 1968

She is also preoccupied with the idea of another project she has so far been wary of pursuing: *I begin to think about a book or rather about a book I might do with someone before I get to doing The Book which I know Im not ready for although some people refuse to believe that*, she says in a letter to Carlotta.[363] And to Crookston: *I think I am going to do a book, not The Book but a book of all new things, a book About something.*[364] A few weeks before Christmas—when she leaves with Amy for two weeks in St. Croix to work on her second job for *The New York Times Magazine Children's Fashions* supplement with Patricia Peterson[365]—she sends Paul Salstrom a letter in response to his request that she do the illustrations for his new book of poetry.

...I must begin at whatever pace is possible, to work on the book of my own that i vaguely keep assuming lies at the end of the rainbow. It is after all my rainbow and if I don't do it no one else will. So I musn't photograph with/for your poems or with or for anyone else except when it is absolutely necessary to make a living at...Survival is the secret so you really can't afford to doubt yourself for long because you are all you've got. The only thing to do is to go the limit with it. Exceed. thats whats nice. We go in different directions...godspeed...Diane

—LETTER TO PAUL SALSTROM, DECEMBER 5, 1968[366]

1969

She returns from St. Croix with Amy around January 10. Museums are beginning to evidence a growing interest in acquiring and exhibiting her photographs which—encouraging as it may be—requires her spending more time than usual in the darkroom. (*I have taken to printing 16x20 which somehow takes lots more time than doing smaller prints*, she notes in response to the request of one curator.[367]) Meanwhile, many of the projects she is most eager to pursue for herself entail a lot of red tape, both official and personal. The result is that she keeps encountering obstacles that stand between her and the work she wants to be doing.

In February Peter Crookston is appointed editor of the British magazine *Nova*, and in his new capacity suggests she come to London for a few weeks to work on some assignments for the magazine, including the Wives of Famous Men and a portrait of the rock group The Who.[368] *Of course I'll come over*, she replies in a letter congratulating him on the new job and proposing a few other possible notions:

In August there are two National Baton Twirling competitions in the south which sound marvelous. I am checking on it. Enclosed is a Terry Southern story about one of the schools. It is an enormous Passion and they absolutely Have to retire at the age of 21.

—LETTER TO PETER CROOKSTON, CIRCA FEBRUARY 1969

And in a follow-up letter that includes a number of additional ideas[369] as well as a drawing of a *Nova* press pass she hopes he can provide her with, she adds:

...Ive been reading R. D. Laing (The divided Self [London: Tavistock, 1961] and I forget the name of the other more recent more popular one [*Sanity, Madness and the Family* (London: Tavistock, 1964)] I read a while ago). He seems so extraordinary in his empathy for madness that it suddenly seemed he would be the most terrific guide.

—LETTER TO PETER CROOKSTON, CIRCA LATE FEBRUARY 1969

There is something to be done about Singles (here) but I don't yet see how to do it. In the Catskills there are entire weekends devoted to the procurement of people for people...For later [in the year]...there are extraordinary motels in the midwest, veritable oases like miamibeach in a desert or snowstorm.

—LETTER TO PETER CROOKSTON, CIRCA LATE FEBRUARY 1969

There is another thing which I dont remember whether I mentioned. Drs. Phyllis and Eberhard Kronhausen are sexologists and they edit collections of erotic art and promote sex causes and make movies and money and meanwhile have private patients whom they analyze by a technique of living in their homes and spending 24 hours at a time with them. They were very eager to be photographed by me…and to talk about everything and although they may well be self appointed apostles of sex they certainly have a lot of authentic information and an eagerness to divulge it. They love publicity but are also…quite straight.[370]

—LETTER TO PETER CROOKSTON, CIRCA LATE FEBRUARY 1969

Near the end of the letter she reneges on this last suggestion: *…I don't think I am really eager to do the Kronhausens after all. Its too verbal and it gives me a funny eerie sense of mutual exploitation which I don't like.*[371] She expresses her impatience and uneasiness about journalism (*the prospect that…*[it] *might expose its own privacy*) and reiterates a little wistfully: *I want to do something unfathomable like the family.*[372]

In a later report on the progress of an assignment for *Nova* to photograph defense attorney F. Lee Bailey (a portrait the magazine doesn't publish in the end)[373] and on the plans for her approaching trip to London, she updates Crookston on other news:

The main thing that has happened to me is that Allan is going to close the studio and move to California to become an actor in earnest. It is terrific for him and wildly adventurous. At moments though I feel like Little Orphan Annie. I must find a darkroom of my own and learn a thousand things I don't know. But I am not really abandoned and he will set me up and his ex assistant [Howard Harrison] will probably share the dkrm with me etc.

—LETTER TO PETER CROOKSTON, CIRCA LATE MARCH 1969

I have a bit of nasty advertising to do. but the money is too much to say no to. It is supposed to be a photograph of a camera by 'one of the greatest photographers in the world…' the others are avedon, penn, Bruce [Davidson] and I dunno who. it really gives me nightmares. Dick [Avedon] got me into it which was good of him but I keep wishing it was all a bad dream. The Agency man gave me carte blanche…you can even, he said brightly, photograph it (the camera) on the point of a knife to show how sharp it is…we want your interpretation, something creative and totally honest.[374]

—LETTER TO PETER CROOKSTON, CIRCA LATE MARCH 1969

Her reaction to jobs of this sort—and in fact to any assignment she doesn't actually originate—strikes her on occasion as a bit perverse. *I have never understood whether it is a certain intransigence in my nature that makes me inwardly partly sabotage anything anyone else wants me to do,* she muses in a letter to her goddaughter May Eliot. *It must be more complicated than that. But because I am so little rebellious I think it manifests unwittingly.*[375]

On April 2 she sends Crookston the following account of her itinerary in the weeks prior to her departure for London: *Going to Texas tomorrow to photograph a terrible Texan who owns the Astrodome.*[376] *Then to New Jersey* [to the April 7 Easter parade at one of the state's residential institutions for the mentally retarded[377]] *and then to you.*[378]

She arrives in London as scheduled on April 17 and begins work on a story she had proposed, "People Who Think They Look Like Other People."[379] *Nova* places the following ad in *The Times* and *The Evening Standard* which generates a tremendous response from prospective candidates:[380] *Have you ever been told you look the double of someone famous? Like Elizabeth Taylor…Twiggy, The Queen, Mick Jagger, Sir Winston Churchill? If you think you are the double of someone famous you could be famous too.*[381]

In connection with what might be considered a related theme—people or things that appear to be what they are not (a theme she has been exploring for years in all sorts of manifestations, from twins to transvestites)—she gains access to Madame Tussaud's Wax Museum on behalf of the magazine. *I got permission to go there at night when it was empty. I touched some of them,* she confesses in a letter to Amy.[382] But the *Nova* assignment that appears to provide her the greatest satisfaction is photographing Rockers, teenage motorcycle gang members in Brighton. A month or so later when she sends Crookston the pictures she writes, *I thought of the rockers as a sort of family album,*[383] and comments after seeing the story in the magazine, *I liked the way the rockers looked. Really more than any published thing in a long time.*[384]

On the other hand, the city of London itself (which she had once written Crookston she imagined as having *the dirtiest secrets in the world*[385]) she finds eerily antiseptic. In a postcard to Ruth Ansel, she observes: *Nobody seems miserable, drunk, crippled, mad, or desperate. I finally found a few vulgar things in the suburbs, but nothing sordid yet. Where have they hidden it?*[386] And in a postcard to Richard Avedon: *Its nice here but I think I'd have been a Pilgrim.*[387]

About a week after her return to New York on May 5 and a few days before Allan's scheduled departure *to someplace just across the mexican border to get our divorce which is so amicable that we cannot even divide the monies so we arent going to,*[388] she writes:

Things are in a state of flux, more subterranean than overt, well both I guess. Allan moved the darkroom and has taken over the hideous task of getting carpenter plumber etc to do what must be done…but he has designed it beautifully… all the film from England is undeveloped which makes me feel constipated and anxious as if there might be nothing there (did I leave the lens cap on or forget to adjust the whatchamacallit?) But Allan has gotten someone to do all 175 rolls in the specially mixed formula so I will know soon.

—LETTER TO MAY ELIOT, CIRCA MID-MAY 1969

She reports to Crookston around the same time: *I am marvelously exhausted by the trip...the splendid and the sleazy of it. My darkroom is heavenly...through an alley with its own anonymous door, like a secret house. It will be in working order soon I hope.*[389] Her next job is for the Social Security Administration's Office of Public Affairs. The Agency has hired several photographers, including Duane Michals and William Gedney, to take pictures of selected beneficiaries. Diane's assignment entails a trip to St. Petersburg, Florida, to photograph retirees and nursing home residents.[390] Among her subjects are Andrew Ratoucheff, the Russian midget she first photographed for *Esquire* in 1960, and his friend Al Krauze. A 1969 notebook—which dutifully records each of her Florida encounters in anticipation of the need to write them for the Agency—contains the following account of her visit with Ratoucheff and Krauze in their Tampa home:

Andrew Ratoucheff and Al Krauze were at home in their little house at 6319 Little River Dr. They have a new Evinrude outboard motor for their rowboat on the brackish creek out back and rifles for shooting rats. Andy says he is an inch and a half shorter than Al but Al says he is only an inch taller. They own the house together and have been friends since 1939...After that we went to the El Sol Retirement Motel to meet Mr. Maloney who is the oldest living softball player in the world...

—1969 NOTEBOOK (NO. 37)[391]

In retrospect the whole experience—as she describes it to former *Glamour* editor Marguerite Lamkin (now married to Mark Littman and living in London)— strikes her *as a little grim because everyone seemed to be the same age and they were so pink, so powdery so well behaved except a little petulant...I did the oldest living softball player in the World and the oldest Dance instructors in America and a lot of firsts or rather lasts like that.*[392] She adds this summary of her personal situation:

Allan has gone to California and we are divorced although I don't have any papers to prove it. Arent you supposed to have divorce papers. I've always heard of them and they sounded like the best part of it. Doon and I saw a psychiatrist on television saying that divorce is terribly good for everybody especially the children but that amicable divorce is no good...there should be total severance he said, using some image which had to do with surgery.

—LETTER TO MARGUERITE LAMKIN LITTMAN, CIRCA EARLY JUNE 1969

During the same trip she also goes to Palm Beach to photograph the bodybuilder Charles Atlas for *The London Sunday Times*[393] and to Gainesville to give a speech.[394] *My speech in Gainesville was lousy*, she says in a letter to Allan in early June, *but they gave me the 400 bucks anyway and I ran feeling I had done something fraudulent.*

Feels so good to be back. My next speech is to nuns.[395] She is not looking forward to her immediate prospects with much enthusiasm:

My mother is taking measures to Save Her Marriage [measures which soon prove unsuccessful]. The London Times wants me to go to LA to do a middleaged super fag Joan Crawford fan which would only be a day or two.[396] I put it off because I am really tired of travelling, but if I do it I will see you next month I guess. Meanwhile I have four pages to do for them on the Women's Liberation Movement which I have begun.[397] These vary from Revolutionaries to real nuts who think men are totally dispensable even for sex and reproduction. I do not feel in the mood for them but I guess a little sleep will change all that.

—TYPEWRITTEN LETTER TO ALLAN ARBUS, CIRCA EARLY JUNE 1969

I miss you. and this isnt exactly total divorce, she writes on one occasion. *I'll be OK. So will you.*[398] A subsequent letter the same month offers the following amendment: *If you want more total divorce lemme know.*[399] Their correspondence in this period consists largely of professional issues, both technical and strategic, punctuated by news about Doon and Amy, and about Mariclare Costello—who frequently joins them for Sunday breakfast, as she and Allan used to do when he was living in New York—and by domestic anecdotes: *The laundry has been losing all our clothes and giving us back other peoples clothes marked ARBUS and staunchly maintaining it is a sinister plot on our part to pretend they arent ours or that there is another arbus sneaking in his shirts. I don't get mad till I leave.*[400]

There is also, on both sides, a good deal of anxiety about money.[401] *I guess most of this panic is transitional,* she volunteers. *The rest is traditional.*[402] When he responds to her anxiety by sending her a check at one point, she answers: *Thanks for your response to my hysteria but I didn't mean it that way. You know me by now. I've torn up your check.*[403] A month or so later she tells him, *I have nearly 4000 if you need any.*[404] These acts of generosity on both sides continue with some regularity but it is not clear whether they result in any cash from their joint bank account actually changing hands.[405]

In the meantime, although the prospects of exhibitions and museum acquisitions persist, they hold out little hope of providing any financial solace. In January, prompted by Henry Geldzahler, curator of contemporary art, and by John McKendry, curator of prints and photography, The Metropolitan Museum of Art purchases three of her photographs.[406] In late June, however, having failed to pay for them as yet, the museum revisits the subject, asking *if it could buy Two Prints instead of the three they had bought because they were short of the money ($75!). So I guess being broke is no disgrace,* she remarks to Allan.[407] The Smithsonian Institution's

Division of Graphic Arts and Photography selects five prints for purchase at a total of $125.[408] Her work appears in a show called *Thirteeen Photographers* at the Pratt Institute[409] and in *Human Concern/Personal Torment: The Grotesque in American Art*, organized by Robert Doty for the Whitney Museum.[410] Ten of her photographs are included in The Museum of Modern Art's traveling exhibition *New Photography U.S.A.*[411] She is approached by Irving Blum, director of an eponymous Los Angeles gallery, about purchasing twenty prints on behalf of an anonymous collector who intends to donate them to the Pasadena Museum of Art. *(He* [Blum] *just called and wanted to do a show. I said no, not for a year or so, but when he came I said I needed money to work and somehow we arrived at this.*[412]*)* In spite of all this activity—or more precisely, because of it—she writes in a moment of exasperation:

I feel paranoid and besieged…Partly it is the goddam honors and people wanting to see me and show me pictures just like mine and museums wanting prints for no money. (I had a letter from the Bibliotheque Nationale de France asking for 20 prints.[413]) It all means I cant photograph. And most of what Ive been doing is such junk…I hate the world of photography and photographers. Everyone is turning to Rolleis and Portriga-[the photographic paper she uses] and printing with borders.

—LETTER TO ALLAN ARBUS, CIRCA MID-JUNE 1969

In reflecting on what he describes as her *great sense of privacy…and…pride of ownership about her work*, and on the changes that begin to take place in her photographs over the next couple of years, John Szarkowski later observes: *I'm sure in a lot of this last work she was intentionally reformulating so she could get out from under all those people she felt she was carrying on her back.*[414] She alludes to her restlessness and her desire to give up the 2¼ twin lens reflex and find herself a different camera in the following remark to Allan: *I think I am about to abandon the square* [format] *too. Which seems a great leap to me.*[415]

A series of ideas that began taking shape the previous year in the form of a list now reappear, clustered around the heading *stigma. Stigma: Notes on the Management of Spoiled Identity* (New York: Prentice Hall, 1963) is the title of a book by sociologist Erving Goffman that intrigues her.[416] In her own lexicon the word has a very broad reach. (Earlier in the year, for example, she suggests a story to Crookston on The Stigma of Beauty. *Think of this: That Beauty is itself an aberration, a burden, a mystery, even to itself.*[417]) The subjects listed in her current notebooks in connection with this heading include: *Beauty Queens, hypnosis, leper colony, little people of America…Stigma* [Daughters of] *Bilitis, x alcoholics, x follies… old, nude, Blind, Handicapped, clubs, S&M, Stratoliners {the club for tall people}…*

masks, shame…narrative photograph.[418] (There is also a persistent and somewhat incongruous reminder: *GO TO NIAGARA FALLS IN JUNE*—which she doesn't do.) Among the other books she investigates in this period are *Encyclopedia of Aberrations*, a 1953 psychiatric handbook, and Joanne Greenberg's fictionalized autobiographical account, *I Never Promised You a Rose Garden* (New York: Holt, Rinehart & Winston, 1964), about an adolescent confined to a mental institution, from which she copies out this passage:

> One had to choose or be chosen as a partner at camp, a seatmate at school, the member (in a certain order of importance) in all kinds of cliques and groups and classes…Deborah had found that she could meet the demands of this membership only with the tainted, the very poor, the crippled, the disfigured, the strange, the going-insane. These pairings off weren't planned or thought out, even secretly; they came about as naturally as the attraction of magnet and metal, yet many of the fragments which had been drawn together thus knew why in their hearts and hated themselves and their companions.

—FROM *I NEVER PROMISED YOU A ROSE GARDEN* (P. 143), 1969 NOTEBOOK (NO. 36)

In August she spends three days at a baton twirling contest in Syracuse, New York, a project she had proposed to Crookston earlier in the year to which he seems not to have responded. The following text on the subject is written in her notebook:

> Twirling is the only they say American art form…It is Icathian [meaning, like Icarus] in its extremity, its uselessness and the way that uselessness has been put to use creating minor industries, major sinecures, passions and tragedies, legends and at the least a kind of frenetic belief in itself… "Don't bend both knees at the same time or pump body up and down while marching. Dress tastefully. Be a doll."…The amazing thing about a roomful of them practicing is the frenetic movement which seems like it doubles back on itself and the smiles…Its like a most ascetic mystic moral discipline in the bobbysox and blond flip hairdo and sequins and feathers and diadems of middle class dreams. The parents and teachers seem strict and nostalgic because they can instruct what they can no longer do and because the childrens eminence is to be so short-lived, like raising butterflies, or training fleas.

—1969 NOTEBOOK (NO. 38)

In a curious way the above account echoes her response to a project she has been looking forward to with great anticipation for months. (*Something wonderful has happened in the way of a private project for some of the summer*, she says without further explanation in a letter to Crookston in late March. And on another occasion in equally opaque terms: *I am going to be working on a marvelous project in NJ sometime this summer when I can.*[419]) She has managed to secure the necessary permission to photograph at several state institutions—but other than attending a dance at one of them in March and an Easter parade at another in April, she is unable to really begin working on the project until the end of July.

darling amy, I went to New Jersey, to the retarded school. Some of the ladies are my age and look like they are 12. I will show you in the pictures. Others look older than they are. Some of them are perfectly rational, but simple and tend to repeat things. One lady said, "Oh God," every time she saw me. "You're cute," she'd say. "You're too much." ...She Could say more but those are the things she kept wanting to say over and over. And many of them just love to hug. Some of them are so small that their shoulder would fit right under my arm and I would pat them and their head would fall on my chest. They are the strangest combination of grownup and child I have ever seen...One lady kept saying over and over "I'm sorry, I'm sorry." After a while one of the staff said "That's all right but don't do it again" and she quieted down...I think you'd like them. Some of them are perturbed and miserable. One of them says over and over very earnestly, "Was I the only one born?"

—LETTER TO AMY ARBUS, CIRCA EARLY AUGUST 1969

Her record of the experience—which precedes the baton twirling contest in time, but follows it in her notebook—goes on for five pages and is marked by the following sorts of individual observations: *Pearl. Like Lennie* [in John Steinbeck's *Of Mice and Men*] *benign and violent. Could lift anyone as if they were a doll. Carried Kitty...Is Joanie the breathless one in the pale swimsuit...Rosalie has saucer eyes and the body of a doll you cant tumble. and humility...Phyllis is the one with glasses and large lips. Solemn intelligent mongoloid...Barbara is sweet and bright and modest. When I did her in her flowered nightgown she lowered her eyes before raising them...Their pocketbooks seem to keep them alive.*[420] And this:

Marlene Woodruff posed in the rose garden. I've got a boyfriend. He says I'm beautiful. I told him you haven't seen the pretty parts... Around her neck on a string was a key. Her girlfriend gave it to her before she died. It's good to remember people who die.

—1969 NOTEBOOK (NO. 38)

In a letter to Allan she describes the photographs made on this occasion with a mixture of exhilaration and bafflement, as if hovering on the verge of something new:

Some of the...pictures are exciting but I must go back a lot. I am plagued by mysterious technical problems, like trying to make my sharp pictures blurred but not too much so. Having great trouble balancing strobe and daylight when used together especially on gray days but sometimes this nutty method seems just beautiful to me. And very different. It is a little agonous. a thousand misses but when it all of a sudden works I recognize it is what I wanted without precisely knowing I wanted anything. I am like someone who gets excellent glasses because of a slight defect in eyesight and puts vaseline on them to make it look more like he normally sees. It doesn't Seem sensible. But somehow I think it will be right.[121]

—LETTER TO ALLAN ARBUS, CIRCA MID-AUGUST 1969

Although she has been making all her own prints for well over a decade, processing the negatives has remained a task left to Allan's assistants, one which she is only now attempting to master. Her gradual progress toward technical independence in the darkroom is a source of pride:

I have been in the darkroom all week. Learning to do negatives. Have done two batches with Howard [Harrison, Allan's former assistant who is currently sharing the darkroom with her.] He was very nice and patient. We will do another together. And then I'll be on my own...Its arduous but good to be learning. I feel like I am making my own shoes. Dunno how anyone ever became a photographer with having to do all this. Dunno how people can bear to do other peoples. Dunno how you did it. But I see I Can. and that's a great relief.

—LETTER TO ALLAN ARBUS, CIRCA MID-AUGUST 1969

In late November she reports on her achievement in this area: *I really like doing negatives. I mean its kind of nice and quiet and pleasant and lonely going there. and it's the only darkroom activity that when I go I know I will be done in roughly an hour and a half...I really like having the darkroom to myself.*[422] The same five-page letter contains the following account of another visit to one of the New Jersey institutions that has fueled her enthusiasm for the project:

...I took the most terrific pictures. the ones at Halloween in NJ of the retarded women. Somehow and I don't understand it at all, I mean I don't know if the strobe didn't fire or did or if it was just like a fill in but they are very blurred and variable, but some are gorgeous. FINALLY what I've been searching for. and I seem to have discovered sunlight, late afternoon early winter sun light. its just marvelous. In general I seem to have perverted your brilliant technique all the way round, bending it over backwards you might say till its JUST like snapshots but better. I think its going to be marvelous. (Doon says they look like if you blew on them they'd disappear. Like made of smoke. And Amy likes the retarded photos more than anything Ive ever done.)...They are so lyric and tender and pretty...I have developed this terrific method which is to proof hundreds of them on the machine instead of making rough 16x20s.[123] Gradually I will go backwards proofing to see what I turn up. I think about doing a book on the retarded. And maybe a folio of other prints. marvin suggested that.[424]

—LETTER TO ALLAN ARBUS, NOVEMBER 28, 1969

After several digressions, she returns to the subject once more in the same letter:

The book about the retarded ladies excites me. I could do it in a year...[425] it's the first time Ive encountered a subject where the multiplicity is the thing. I mean I am not just looking for the BEST picture of them. I want to do lots...And I ought to be able to write it because I really adore them.

—LETTER TO ALLAN ARBUS, NOVEMBER 28, 1969

She has secured another job with Patricia Peterson for *The New York Times Magazine Children's Fashions* supplement that entails a trip to Barbados over Christmas. *I THINK it'll be like last year, I mean that much work and money which is a godsend (5000).*[426] John Szarkowski has asked her to research and edit an exhibition of news photography he is planning to mount at MoMA, and after thinking it over for a while she replies: *I think Id really like to do that news photography show. February, March and April seems a good time because the weather is so rotten mostly then. (forgive me.)*[427] To Allan on the same topic she writes: *...sounds good to me. I love the subject and I'll get paid, not enormously but regularly*[428] and *I think it'll be fun and surely better than teaching.*[429] Her sense of independence is at least momentarily almost intoxicating. *I did my first job all by myself this week, negatives too. For NY, which I got by calling on a flimsy excuse. Dumb. Santa Claus. but its fine and I was wondrous calm.*[430] All of which in summary prompts her to say the following:

But look, try to get calmer about money. I have a feeling I can be making it more easily and I Want to do it and it makes sense for you to feel the leeway to let me do most of it for a while. You did it for me for years and I sense that I am in shape to do it for you. I have a hunch that this sense of form I feel is going to partly translate into a freedom to make money more easily with less fuss and guilt. I don't mean fortunes but enough to sustain us. We Do have a partnership and its my turn to do that part.

—LETTER TO ALLAN ARBUS, NOVEMBER 28, 1969

Even before the move to 10th Street she had investigated the possibility of applying for an apartment in Westbeth, the former Bell Laboratory building in the West Village, which was then in the process of being converted into living and working spaces for visual, performing, and literary artists.[431] The requirements for admission are stringent and complex and subject to the approval and annual review of the Federal Housing Administration. At times during the application process she despairs of being able to meet the qualifications, which among other things restrict her maximum income to $8,400. As she says to Allan at one point: *I feel a bit boxed in between not making enough and making too much.*[432] In the end, the fact that she and Allan maintain a partnership reduces her income enough to satisfy the financial requirements. *At any rate*, she writes, *I've decided it's all worth the risk. The people in the building look terrific and I know quite a lot of them.*[433] The move is scheduled to take place shortly after the end of the year. In a letter to Carlotta she reflects on things:

I suppose freedom is a bit eerie. Its what I want but something in me tries to pretend I can't. And there is so much work to working that there are moments, moments, where I stop and look around and it seems too arduous to go on. It isnt of course. But that is why people have jobs and pay checks…it helps keep you from unanswerable questions.

—LETTER TO CARLOTTA MARSHALL, CIRCA NOVEMBER 1969

1970

In the course of the ten days she spends in Barbados with Patricia Peterson working on *The New York Times Magazine Children's Fashions* supplement,[434] she sends Marvin Israel this description of her stay:

Birds fly indoors in these hotels, feasting on leftovers. I have been dreaming endlessly, domestic dreams in which I am a child or a mother. Its a very pretty island, rich, pastoral, rolling, wild, flat, by turns. Tiny houses with cotton curtains printed with fruits or roses and inside a glimpse of a Christmas tree and a chair, and hardly room for more…each one like a house in the woods where Snow White or Hansel and Gretel lived…We go blithely (sort of) from one hotel to another, no one questions us, Pat [Peterson] corners children and their parents and I am often free to idly photograph ladies on the beach or corners of lobbies…I really don't like the children. I long to be with you.[435]

—LETTER TO MARVIN ISRAEL, CIRCA EARLY JANUARY 1970

Although the account she gives Allan a few weeks later of the photographs themselves sounds relatively unperturbed, it reflects no enthusiasm for the results:

The [*New York*] Times pics were rather lousy and there was a bit of trouble, Pat said it was because the cover photo was of a black girl and a white boy about 4 years old, holding hands. Pat has been incredibly sweet. They wanted a retake which I think she has effectively blocked…I am pretty calm about the whole thing. She was full of appreciation for the most minor virtues of the photos. and believe me they were minor...[356] and as for the miscegenation, junior style, it may end up being regarded as a major civil rights breakthrough, if they finally let it pass.[357]

—LETTER TO ALLAN ARBUS, JANUARY 16, 1970

She, Amy, and Doon (who is searching, so far unsuccessfully, for her own place) move to the new apartment in Westbeth on January 22. A number of people Diane knows are—or are about to become—residents of the building, including the photographer Evelyn Hofer, writers Marion Magid and Edward Hoagland, and artist Mary Frank.[438] She promptly indulges in a binge of decorating. *I have discovered the joys of spray paint in silver and gold although not much skill at it yet*, she says in a letter to Allan.[439] And to Crookston, after what has apparently been a couple of months of silence between them:

I was away on a job and then moved, marvelously to...[she supplies her new address and phone] where there is a panorama out my window... and a blessed lot of sky. Best place I ever had. I have been buying somewhat insanely. An ant farm so I can watch them working when I am not...a desk made entirely of chrome, so shiny it is well nigh invisible. marvelous toys I have always wanted...fake worms, lady shaped ice cubes, a transparent plastic lady with all her organs and bones ready for a clever child to insert but it seems too difficult so I have left her as empty as she is naked....the plants which died in the moving because it was terribly cold have been reborn, and I suddenly like to cook.

—LETTER TO PETER CROOKSTON, CIRCA LATE JANUARY 1970

In anticipation of the stipend for researching the news photography show which has helped make her new home a reality, she writes Szarkowski to thank him and express her eagerness to begin: *This is a palace you got for me. even the fishermans wife would be pleased. I have never felt such homely bliss. Should we have lunch or something to talk over plans for our show? Come visit me and see what you have wrought...*[440]

A memorandum from John Szarkowski to Inez Garson dated January 19 regarding a proposed MoMA research fellowship for the projected exhibition tentatively titled *The Iconography of the Daily News*, reads as follows: *The exhibition is conceived as an investigation of the content and form of news photographs, with special attention to their traditional and ritualized nature. The project is based on the premise that much of what is in fact newsworthy is not photographable, and that what is photographable is generally concerned less with news than with the vicarious sharing of a few basic and constant human experiences...The force of many of these pictures on a visual and psychological level—as experience rather than information—is attested to by their affect on painters such as Francis Bacon, as well as on the awareness of other photographers.*[441]

Szarkowski requests a research stipend of $4,000 on Diane's behalf and an additional $2,000 for study prints and other documentation expenses. He adds: *I consider Diane Arbus to be an ideal person to do this work. Though she is an artist rather than a scholar, she has demonstrated through her own work a profound understanding of the central qualities of the news photography tradition. She is in addition a person of acute intelligence, and an excellent writer.*[442] The fact that the proposal does not receive final approval and funding until June delays commencement of the research.

The list of books in the front of her 1970 appointment book exemplifies the breadth of her current preoccupations. The list includes: *Prints and Visual Communication* by William Ivins (Cambridge: Harvard University Press, 1953; Boston: MIT Press, 1969) (related to her upcoming MoMA project); *Mental Deficiency of Different Origins: A Pictorial Survey by Hans Forssman and Hans Olof Akesson* (Copenhagen: Det Berlingske Bogtrykkeri, 1964); *Ghost Hunter: True Stories of Psychic Phenomena* by Hans Holzer (New York: Bobbs Merrill Co., 1963); *On Death and Dying* by Elisabeth Kübler-Ross (New York: Macmillan, 1969) (probably connected to an assignment for *Esquire* about dying people she is supposed to work on in Chicago in July,[443] which never actually takes place); *An Essay on the Causes of the Variety of Complexion and Figure in the Human Species* (1787; Cambridge: Harvard University Press, 1965); *Further Confessions of Zeno* (Berkeley: University of California Press, 1969), the sequel to a novel by Italo Svevo she describes as *funny and marvelous and heartening*[444] and recommends to a number of friends; and a book by Lancelot Law Whyte which she refers to as *something about the nature of man* (*The Next Development of Mankind*, London: The Cresset Press, 1944), apparently suggested by her psychiatrist Dr. Helen Boigon, whom she has been seeing on a regular basis since the previous September.[445]

Although she sounds a little dubious about Dr. Boigon in the summary she initially gives Allan of the first several sessions (*I still don't move but I begin to guess Dr. B may be OK. She threatens to make me work, I get mad.*[446]), her more recent accounts of their exchanges suggest an improvement.

Dr. B said a terrific thing to me…something like that human beings are obsessed with the question WHY which is really a very gratuitous meaningless question which attempts to remove or erase the subject of itself and the whole point (this is a graceless paraphrase) is in the experience of the Way It Is which WHY seeks to evade.[447] Anyway, she is endless fun, although I begin to get restless for the end to come in sight simply because it seems it could go on forever, and I feel slightly mollycoddled. I am learning something and her mind is fascinating. She translates my thoughts into her language and its terrific. She has put up the photo of the twins which I gave her and told me several stories of the reactions of patients.

—LETTER TO ALLAN ARBUS, JANUARY 16, 1970

Mariclare Costello, who is planning to leave New York later in the year and move to Los Angeles to join Allan, arranges for Doon to take over her studio apartment on West 68th Street in April. Diane has been working on the design (with Marvin Israel) and content of her limited-edition portfolio and seeking advice on ways to market it.[448] A single 20x24 sheet of vellum is entirely covered with her practice handwritten titles and commentary: *what is this? a box of photographs...not a book... by me. and who pray tell are you?...how many? ten. how much? 1000...marvin israel. gosh...this isnt half bad.* It indicates several alternate images (such as A family one evening in a nudist camp) originally under consideration. Of the ten images ultimately included in the portfolio, three are made in the spring of 1970: Lauro Morales (aka Cha Cha), the Mexican dwarf in his hotel room in March; Eddie Carmel, the Jewish giant at home with his parents in the Bronx in April; and The King and Queen of a Senior Citizens' Dance in May.[449]

Her production of the portfolio is plagued by technical difficulties, even down to some basic issues like ensuring that the prints dry flat. Allan apparently volunteers some suggestions, to which she replies: *Thanks about the 16x20s. Tried it on a print which had been dried already. better. will try it again on a fresh one. Its edge ripples I get.*[450] A few months later she reports success in addressing this problem:

Thanks again about the blotter roll. Ive done a dozen each of two prints. They look terrific. Very flat and fine. Ive eliminated the black borders, left an uneven edge. Nice I think. Ive worked it out so it only takes 3½– 4 hours so I am going in to dkrm at 6AM as often as I can so it will be done by mid July roughly.

—LETTER TO ALLAN ARBUS AND MARICLARE COSTELLO, CIRCA JUNE 1970

Amy leaves for the summer on a youth hostel trip through Europe at the end of June. *A bit of an inauspicious beginning for Amy*, Diane says in describing the scene of departure to Allan and Mariclare. *The kids looked rather frightful...The girls very lipsticked or eye shadowed and prissy and suburban—like they were off to the beach...The boys very misfit and bemused...She must have been appalled.*[451] She writes to Amy the next morning:

Its weird without you. So far very virtuous. I got up at 5:30 to the darkroom by 6:15 so Ive finished printing for the day already and Im just eating breakfast in a diner. Then to the newspaper library next door where I'll look at random Daily Newses of ancient vintage.

—LETTER TO AMY ARBUS, CIRCA LATE JUNE 1970

Between her acquaintances at United Press International, Associated Press, and other photo sources, and her investigation of the files of the *Daily News*, she constructs a list entitled *Subjects (mostly 1920–1955)* that has a curious resemblance to some of her own lists. It includes the following: *accident, grief, pain...death of pet animals; murder victims, murderers...corruption, people hiding* [their] *faces...kidnapping, execution, lynching; suicides, before, during, after...heroes, posthumous and otherwise, mouth to mouth resuscitation; revolution (Hungarian), riots, strikes...cyclone, tornado, overturned houses, flood, fire, dust storms; depression, breadlines, apples, hoovervilles...; child abuse, closeted children...people dying of mysterious disease; photographers being shot.* And further down the page, as if on the other, upbeat side of the ledger: *Contests, Winners, crying or otherwise, Beauty, Losers, Pieeating...Queens (Beauty, Publicity, as Donut Queen, etc.), pinups, starlets; Ceremonies, ribbon cutting, contract signing...Harmless nuts, Collectors, fads, cults, New Year Babies, child brides, May-Dec Marriages, Weddings of old people, mother of the year (lots of children), feats of strength, daredevils...Dance marathons.*[452]

I have been both lazy and industrious, she says in a letter to Crookston, after another lengthy silence. (*don't lets get guilty. Its been long but that's the way it is.*) She expresses some regret at having turned down a *Nova* assignment on political groupies. *I was deep in the midst of something and it seemed I'd have to give up one thing for the other and at that moment all my enthusiasm for that notion* [the political groupies] *had utterly left me.* She reports that *Harold* [Hayes at *Esquire*] *has given me a nice page rate increase and two assignments I suggested,*[453] and describes her progress on the portfolio[454] and on the show of news photographs for MoMA.[455]

She leaves on June 29 to attend the July 2 opening of Richard Avedon's retrospective exhibition at the Minneapolis Institute of Arts. Marvin Israel has designed the show as well as the catalogue and is overseeing the installation.[456] Doon—who has been working with Avedon (at Israel's suggestion) since the summer of 1969 on a long-term project of his—is there for the event too.[457] Everyone coming for the opening stays at the Ambassador Resort Motor Hotel. *Dick's show is terrific. And life is full of room service,* Diane says in a letter to Amy on hotel stationery. *The party is tonight. There are Avedon sheets and balloons and T-shirts and ash trays but Dick doesn't know at all I don't think.*[458] Her subsequent account of the event goes like this:

Minneapolis was so much fun. I loved the show and doing little tasks for it so that Doon and I felt very part of it, not just audience and Marvin was funny and splendid. Everyone felt it...The Party was a bit much at moments. The preparations were great, all the secrecy and conspiracy and everything Looked fantastic. The masks were unbelievable, a thousand Richard Avedons, the cake was Black and white with his face drawn on in icing, so good I couldnt believe it, in fact I didn't eat any. I mostly blew up 144 balloons of all colors with Dicks face on them and Doon and Marvin and Ginny [Heyman, Avedon's secretary] tied them to chairs and tables around the pool. But when Dick walked in the first moment, and there were these multiple imposters facing him and advancing towards him, he looked really shocked, "Oh no," he gasped faintly like someone in a nightmare. Then Marvin appeared in the old persons mask and then people began to take them off and Dick recovered and jumped in the pool with all his clothes on and we all swam a lot. Then lots of rowdy people, strangers, kids appeared and started cutting up a bit, swimming with clothes and taking all their clothes off. So marvin and me left for the nearby delicatessen and when we got back, mysteriously, all the strangers had dispersed, having been warned of a 10 o'clock curfew. And the rest were in Laura's [Kanelous, Avedon's agent] room and Dick was reading aloud the [phoney] telegrams and the little book [of his sayings]. He really loved it all. Then the greatest thing was that after it was all over and we were quietly swimming in little groups or some people were going to bed, there was this sudden enormous awesome thunderstorm like a benediction. It rained so hard that plastic dome leaked. so we swam under the clatter and crash. beautiful.

—LETTER TO AMY ARBUS, CIRCA EARLY JULY 1970

She returns home a little reluctantly. *The portriga* [photographic paper] *I ordered hasn't shown up which is enraging because I could have finished the box this week*, she says in a letter to Allan and Mariclare. *Anyway it'll be done in July and Dick said he'd buy the first one. and if nothing else they are flat.*[459] But, as she goes on to admit, the aftermath of Minneapolis leaves her wistful.

I'm a bit sad to be back. The show was beautiful and I loved working at menial tasks to get things done. The people were lovely and marvin was radiant and working at a fever pitch...In minneapolis the prints were enormous (some of them) BEAUTIFUL. One room had just maybe nine huge heads. Like presences. The pictures never looked so good. love. take care of each other.

—LETTER TO ALLAN ARBUS AND MARICLARE COSTELLO, CIRCA EARLY JULY 1970

At the end of July she heads for Hagerstown, Maryland, on an assignment she secured from *Esquire* to photograph at a carnival there. *A little dubious about it*, she says in a letter to Amy. *I am supposed to photograph girl shows for Esquire and I dunno how much of that they have.*[460] In spite of the fact that she turns out to be right about the girl shows—there don't appear to have been any—the trip proves very productive. She prints about six of the photographs—among them, Albino sword swallower, which she considers including in the portfolio—and *Esquire* plans to publish several of them as a feature story on carnivals.[461] A week later she sends Amy the following note from Florida:

Dearest Amy I came to see <u>my</u> mama. felt sort of lousy and NY was making even me scream. Like a crowded stuck elevator. Then our phone kept breaking so I'd go to call someone and couldn't or else if they called me they'd hear it ring but I wouldn't. And work felt like day old cereal every time I'd do something it'd get undone or have to be done over. Here its quiet and insulated. Marvin and Doon call...Mom's been sweet. Lets me drive half the time although I know she much prefers to do it herself.

—NOTE TO AMY ARBUS, AUGUST 11, 1970

Within a day or two of her return to New York from visiting her mother in Florida,[462] she escapes the city again on August 15—this time with Doon as a companion—for a long weekend at Avedon's summer house in Fire Island, which is temporarily unoccupied.[463]

For some time Amy has been unhappy—both socially and academically—at Elisabeth Irwin High School. With Sudie [Victor] Trazoff's help and advice and with Diane's somewhat cautious encouragement,[464] she is investigating alternative, "liberated" schools for her junior year commencing in the fall. After sifting through the options she chooses the Study, Travel, Community School in Maine, which Diane later refers to as *totally not a school*[465] and on another occasion as *a euphemism* for a school.[466] On August 29, Amy, Diane, and Doon go to Brattleboro, Vermont, to meet with the man who runs the program. In a hasty note to Allan just before the trip, Diane writes: *It's been bad...I hope this works this school. I fall apart so easy. I think its important to get Amy away.*[467] (She reports that her regular medical doctor *has taken lots of blood tests. Wants to give me an anti depressant but Dr. B doesn't believe in em. Don't know how I'll resolve that conflict.*[468]) Almost as an afterthought she adds: *The first box is done. Dick is giving it to Mike Nichols. It looks good. He was very moved.*[469]

Her first job for *The London Sunday Times Magazine* since June of 1969 takes her to Los Angeles near the end of September. Her assignment is to photograph two separate California leisure communities: the South Bay Singles Club near Marina del Ray and the Sun City Retirement Community,[470] a project somewhat akin to an idea she proposed to Crookston for *Nova* the previous year. During the trip she has a brief visit with Allan and returns home by way of Detroit, where she stops off to do a portrait of Reverend Albert B. Cleage, Jr., pastor of The Shrine of the Black Madonna, for *Essence*, an experience she refers to as *a nightmare*.[471] About a week later she writes Allan:

You took such incredible care of me. I was very moved...Your generosity to me had some effect, some enormous reassurance I cant explain. I don't think we are good for each other in the sense that we tend to remind each other of our own sadness, but there will always be something you do for me that nobody else in the world can. thanks forever, d.

—LETTER TO ALLAN ARBUS, CIRCA EARLY OCTOBER 1970

She acknowledges—almost as if it were an embarrassment—receiving something called The Robert Leavitt Award from the American Society of Magazine Photographers, which is recorded in the September 1970 issue of *Infinity*, the ASMP's magazine, in the following terms: *for her revelation of truth in the "found" individual, who might not be noticed, otherwise, by the less observant.*[472] The ceremony takes place on October 5 and, with considerable reluctance, she attends.

I got some award from the ASMP, and I didn't want to have to go through the acceptance or make a dumb speech, it just depressed me so. And then it turned out that Bruce [Davidson] got a better award, he is the Photographer of the year, and Gene Smith got on the Honor Roll[473] which is better too, so mine was a little like the Booby Prize, so I couldn't afford not to go because it wouldve looked unsportsmanlike. I told everyone not to come like Lisette [Model] and Dick [Avedon] and I didn't tell Marvin when it was going to be...I hadnt prepared a speech at all. I simply couldn't think of what to say and those finky others all said Oh no they werent making speeches, so up they get and talk for ten minutes...I said that I guessed I had my bunch of people that it wouldn't have been possible without but I had told them not to come and anyway what was most fun about it was that you had to do it all by yourself in the end. Then I kept working the slide machine wrong but it didn't distress me in the slightest and everyone was roaring with laughter and I talked about each picture, told funny stories (bruce had insisted on total silence: "the pictures should speak for themselves").

—LETTER TO ALLAN ARBUS, CIRCA EARLY OCTOBER 1970

Her triumph over this dreaded event appears to have buoyed her spirits. The same letter to Allan begins with this pronouncement: *things seem better, lots better. I just feel good. I have an odd hunch you helped.*[474] She is full of news. About the status of the portfolio: *Bea* [Feitler] *is buying a box too (and that's just Dick's public relations...I haven't begun to hussle them...in fact they still aren't done. the manufacturer made them wrong for about the fourth time.)*[475] (This goes on for months, prompting her to say at one point: *god youd think I wanted a glass house people could throw stones at.*[476]) And about her work on the MoMA show she reports: *John Szarkowski and I went over the photos I had chosen from the [Daily] News and it went smashingly, really fun, we narrowed those down to 200 (of which maybe 40 will be in the show) and we were both delighted with the way its going.*[477] About a week later the MoMA project leads her to a discovery that excites her even more.

The best thing this past week was the discovery of ALL Weegee's work in the house of an old lady he lived with, a charming lady...She is a social worker, cultivated, midwestern, sterling, thoroughly his opposite, plain looking, even a bit prim, fascinating...We went through about 8000 prints of which I chose 383, some for the news show, some for a Weegee show which seems inevitable to me. He was SO good when he was good. Extraordinary! I came across a photograph of Lisette at about my age. Wish you could see 'em. Such wild dynamics make everybody [else] look like an academician. People pushing, shoving, screaming, bits of extraneous events thrust into the main one. When he was bad he was pretty terrible, but I borrowed some of the distortions too, and a few of his utterly vulgar ones...There are among everything about 1500 photos of himself.

—LETTER TO ALLAN ARBUS AND MARICLARE COSTELLO, CIRCA LATE OCTOBER 1970

This is followed immediately by a sentence that seems a complete non sequitur: *What if I am no longer a photographer.* She says she is due to leave in a few days to be with her mother who is about to go into the hospital for an operation. *Its for removal of something in the colon. I don't mind* [going]. *I seem to feel grim when I am free to do anything I want and less so when I am obliged to do something I don't. (!)*[478] Just before her scheduled departure on this mission, she sends Allan another brief letter that ends with a description of the advent of winter.

It is getting colder and that weird 4 oclock evening is setting in, people look so sad and hurry home in the bleakest light imaginable, but I guess it is a change that I feel sad for them.

—LETTER TO ALLAN ARBUS, CIRCA EARLY NOVEMBER 1970

It has been months since her last reply to Carlotta Marshall's letters. *Dear Carlotta, I have been perfectly terrible, not answering over and over. I fell into a most terrible funk from which I have emerged into a funny limbo, a bit frivolous, pleasant, lazy and somewhat apprehensive. But not bad.*[479] She volunteers this summary to make up for the silence:

I am going to a woman doctor who seems to be teaching me a lot. I am really learning to live alone...I guess it was oddly enough the finality of Allans leaving (for Calif) that so shook me. He had been gone somewhat for a hundred years but suddenly it was no more pretending. This was it...I am learning all over again it seems how to live, how to make a living how to do what I want and what I don't, all sorts of common sensical things I have tended to make a big deal about. Partly it seems a matter of severing connections in my head. Like if I do this that will happen, because sometimes it does and sometimes it doesn't and I have spent a lot of energy exercising non-existent magical controls.

—LETTER TO CARLOTTA MARSHALL, CIRCA NOVEMBER 1970

In answer to Carlotta's inquiry, she also adds the following account of what has been going on with Amy:

Amy is in Maine in a school which is totally not a school, I mean they have spent all fall digging a well, building a kitchen and bath and communal building and now she is building her own dwelling place [a yurt] BY HERSELF. She sounds happier than in years. There isnt a book in sight just woods and sky and of course it must be damn cold but she seems to be a lot closer to what she wants. She has guts.

—LETTER TO CARLOTTA MARSHALL, CIRCA NOVEMBER 1970

Since the summer of 1969 and her work on the Untitled series (which continues in the form of visits to one of the institutions every couple of months for special events) she has been in turmoil over something she is searching for—and remains uncertain how to achieve—in the quality of her photographs. This yearning for an alternative approach is exacerbated by persistent technical problems. *My strobe broke and I discovered it was the gun part so I got a new one, but I begin to suspect I am sick of strobe,*[480] she reports to Allan in November. And again a few weeks later: *Im a bit sick of the strobe outdoors. Suddenly started to look at the real light and its so various and pretty.*[481]

At the same time there is film trouble: *Avedons asst. says they use panatomic x and some faster film, either plus or tri, I will try em both because it looks like Eastman* [Kodak] *is squeezing out all competition. I hope Portriga* [paper] *doesn't go too.*[482] And subsequent frustrations about it: *I still have film trouble, hate plusx. trying panatomic. Would a cold light head on the enlarger help? Hiro has a very nice assistant* [Neil Selkirk] *who has suggested some things. There is an Ilford film I can try but so far its out of stock.*[483] At one point she writes, as if it shouldn't be too much to ask: *I just want less grain, more speed. softness, roundness.*[484]

By early December, she has narrowed this complex dilemma down to a single primary issue:

...Have gotten obsessed with buying a new camera. Utterly smitten with the new 6x7 pentax. (2¼ x 2¾). Its just like a big Nikon, which is what Ive always wanted, but there are problems...what speed short of a 250th can it be hand held at? and it only synchs at a 30th...I am borrowing Hiro's and must try all sorts of things, mainly sharpness at slow speeds. It makes an enormous difference in the pictures, Of course they arent very good. Its hard to get used to a new shape. It looks like a greater degree of reality and I havent yet learned How to use that. A little like when I switched from Nikon to Rollei. I wake at night with the excitement of it, or alternately with dread and confusion and worry and abhorrence...At some moments I have wanted it so bad and felt so positive that I thought, hell I'd give a class to pay for it, no problem. Then the next day I think, do I really want it, maybe its dumb and frivolous, maybe it wont work, maybe its just pretentious, maybe I'll never learn to take as good pictures with it as with the Mamiya. Then I think, Gamble. Then: what with? and again: Why?

—LETTER TO ALLAN ARBUS AND MARICLARE COSTELLO, DECEMBER 6, 1970

96

At this point she writes in the margin, *One day I nearly went in and just BOUGHT it*, and continues her account of the internal argument:

What it could do is make the pictures more narrative and temporal, less fixed and single and complete and isolated, more dynamics, more things happening. Id like that. The difference knocks me out. Of course it's not to the good, not yet anyway, and probably it wouldn't be so apparent to anybody else, I mean nobody else gives a shit, but that's OK...The pentax has such a Gorgeous ground glass. This marvelous shape (exactly 11x14, 8x10 proportions) and clarity, focusing is fun. And turning it for horizontal or vertical is delightful, like any 35, just heavier.

—LETTER TO ALLAN ARBUS AND MARICLARE COSTELLO, DECEMBER 6, 1970

Even after she seals the envelope she can't stop thinking about it. She scrawls on the outside before mailing it: *This camera controversy in my head is like the mini and the midi.* A subsequent letter to Allan and Mariclare in mid-December begins: *its pretty good here. I mean I just feel good.* She sounds undaunted—possibly even elated—in her litany of what has failed to come to pass:

I didn't win the Life contest, not even the booby prize, although I must say I'm glad not to have got one of the 25 or so Honorable Mentions which yielded some Encyclopedia as a prize. I also didn't get the [New York] Times [children's fashions] job. So something must be done...I think I'll give a course from home (or try to borrow some space in this bldg once a week so as not to have students in snooping and hanging about like they're fond of doing but at any rate I'll give it myself. That'll give me some money and I'll get to keep it all and it need only be 6 or 8 weeks long in the middle of winter, so nothing much will be lost. Also will apply for a grant...Mainly the damn boxes had better get done and I had better peddle them in real earnest.

—LETTER TO ALLAN ARBUS AND MARICLARE COSTELLO, CIRCA MID-DECEMBER, 1970

She makes a flyer to send out for the portfolio that includes two strips of 35mm copy contacts of each of the ten prints pinned on a sheet of paper beside the following typewritten text: *...there is a portfolio of ten photographs by Diane Arbus dating from nineteen sixty-two to nineteen seventy in an edition of fifty, printed, signed, numbered, annotated by the photographer, sixteen by twenty inches in a nearly invisible box which is also a frame, designed by Marvin Israel. Available from Diane Arbus, four sixty-three West Street, New York City, for one thousand dollars.*

She responds to a series of questions from a Georgia State University student she has never met expressing interest in her and her work. She writes: *Dear Gail, yes, a lecture would be fine. I don't have a show, but I could talk and show things and look at things if the Dept has funds for that. I like doing that, talking to strangers, I mean...And it'll all come out in the talking, all the rest...never used a view camera except a couple of times about the first pictures I ever took...I'd like to see Georgia and there is a camera I want which costs more than I've got so try to arrange it.*[485]

In the midst of a series of postscripts at the conclusion of a December letter to Allan and Mariclare, she reiterates almost verbatim something she said to Carlotta the month before: *I have so much to learn about how to live...what have I been doing lo these 47 years.*[486]

1971

She places an ad in the newspaper for the class she has decided to teach, posts a notice about it on the bulletin board of The Museum of Modern Art, and mentions the prospect to friends and acquaintances. Among those interested in joining the class are several people she already knows. They include Neil Selkirk, Paul Corlett (both assistants of Hiro's), Susan Brockman (a filmmaker she originally met more than ten years earlier through Robert Brown), Ann Tucker (a New York State Council for the Arts curatorial intern in the photography department at MoMA), Cosmos Savage (a photographer living at Westbeth), and Deborah Turbeville (a former *Harper's Bazaar* fashion editor—who quits after the first class). The afternoon of January 7 is set aside for interviewing prospective students in a vacant room in the Southeast Gallery at Westbeth. Almost two dozen applicants show up, more than twice as many as she had originally anticipated or intended to accept.

...I did the class interviews last thurs. a bit grim. it had been a lousy day waiting for the telephone co. to fix my fone and I felt frazzled and like Not Talking so one after another would parade into this empty room like as if I was a burlesque producer or a pimp or sumpn. I just felt confused. their pictures mostly bored me and I had a slight feeling like I didn't know what was wrong with 'em, they werent after all so wildly different from Good pictures, except there was that mysterious thing...I didn't want to look at them, as if it might be catching and I would end up learning from the students how to take just such boring pix as those. Then there was how to choose between em. it all seemed so arbitrary. this one I didn't like the way she talked, that one seemed funny, another sad etc. so I decided to take em all. let it be 22 or 3 or 4. more money for the same amount of singing and dancing on my part...

—LETTER TO ALLAN ARBUS AND MARICLARE COSTELLO, JANUARY 11, 1971

The class takes place in a vacant room at Westbeth on Thursday evenings, starting January 14 and continuing—with an occasional interruption—for ten sessions. She appears to find the teaching alternately exhilarating and draining. After a few sessions she reports to Crookston: *I am swimmingly. Giving a class. piles of students. 28 at last count. sometimes its fun. last week was a dud.*[487] In general, she is distressed by her inability to remain sufficiently interested in the photographs the students are producing.

I've been jittery. waking at 4 AM which is damned annoying talking to myself endlessly (because of the class, I all of a sudden find I hardly stop talking... exhausting.) The third class was pretty good but its like a performance, and with no script. I all but sing and dance...29 students at last count. The main trouble is I don't really know, understand, care about each ones work enough. And I work too hard at it. after each class I think, whew...but that's a hard act to follow.

—LETTER TO ALLAN ARBUS AND MARICLARE COSTELLO, CIRCA LATE JANUARY 1971

Although she has been unenthusiastic about the photographs she made the previous September for *The London Sunday Times Magazine* on "The Affluent Ghetto," she likes them better when published than she had anticipated. She acknowledges as much in a letter to Crookston: *Several people called about the pictures. It did look rather endearing, specially the schoolteacher on the bed in the bikini. What do you do about sending copies to them. I think both Ann* [Leslie, author of the accompanying article] *and I rather promised they wd see themselves become famous.*[488] The same letter refers in glowing terms to her new Pentax camera, even though she doesn't have it yet:

Its coming from Japan. Borrowed one from Hiro for several weeks and I adore it. It will change things. I am awkward with it at first. But its very thrilling. Nobody understands but me what a difference it might make. It looks hilarious like an Enormous Alice in Wonderland 35mm, a little fake as if a bird might pop out instead of a picture.

—LETTER TO PETER CROOKSTON, JANUARY 25, 1971

The job that has been occupying most of her attention for more than a month is an assignment for Time-Life Books, *which doesn't pay all that much, only $500,* she tells Allan and Mariclare, *but...its more than worth it.*[489] This is the way she describes it to Crookston:

I've been working on an assignment which has opened a lot of doors I wanted open and has got me going at a great old pace. (a little like your Family assignment.) Its dumber...Its about LOVE and its for Time-Life bks so nearly nobody says no. I have found some 60 yr old twins who have always lived together and dress alike, a lady in NJ with a pet monkey who wears a snow suit and a bonnet, an incredible heart-stopping handicapped couple. He is retarded and terribly tall and thin and she is radiant, maybe three and a half feet tall with curly red hair like Maureen O'Hara (and tiny limbs and crutches). I saw them dancing at a dance for handicapped people. Never saw anything like that. I danced with a 60 yr old man who was very shy and spoke like a 9 yr old. He sells good humors in the summer.[490] There were people dancing who could only move their arms. There is also a lady with a houseful of 150 cats I think...havent seen her yet but I will soon...Every day nearly there is a fresh delight.

—LETTER TO PETER CROOKSTON, JANUARY 25, 1971

I will be working on things I have found in the course of it long after it is forgotten,[491] she adds in a letter to Allan and Mariclare after recounting the following momentarily appalling discovery which nonetheless appears to have left her undaunted.

I was at a gallery opning and met a photog I know who said in the usual way, what areyouworkinon? I was vague in my usual way and he said eagerly, "I've got this assignmt from TimeLife Bks, a stupid assgnmt, but its gotten me going again, to photograph LOVE"...(I turned white)..." and I've been photographing blind couples and deaf ones and all the most terrific things." I was so mad at this tricky game [on the part of Time-Life Books]. But oh well...I'm off to do a blind couple in Wantagh.

—LETTER TO ALLAN ARBUS AND MARICLARE COSTELLO, CIRCA LATE JANUARY 1971

The *LOVE* assignment is not her sole preoccupation. In addition to a number of earlier projects she continues to pursue, including the Untitled series, new prospects are on the horizon. Among those she mentions to Crookston is this:

I met a man who is one of the leading figures of the local sado-masochistic community.[492] He has one arm only (lost in an auto accident not masochistically he assured me) although he said most people suspect otherwise and it lends him a certain glamour. It is also, he explained a potent phallic symbol (the stump that is). He is terribly articulate and described his year in jail marvelously, and is going to inquire of his friends about my photographing one of his parties. So, so far it is a good winter. and you?

—LETTER TO PETER CROOKSTON, JANUARY 25, 1971

On January 26, a Walker Evans retrospective exhibition opens at The Museum of Modern Art, followed by a dinner in his honor. Earlier in the week Diane has a meeting with Davis Pratt, curator of photography at Harvard University's Fogg Art Museum, to select a group of her prints for inclusion in his upcoming spring show, *Contemporary Photographs I*. They are both present at the dinner for Evans, although apparently seated at separate tables with little opportunity to speak to one another. A few days later, when Pratt writes to identify the photographs he has chosen, he says: *Marvelous to see you the other night. Your dress was really swinging!*[493] To which she replies: *You looked very good, too. At one of the most painful of the dinner moments I looked across the room at you and was cheered.*[494] (Pratt later volunteers, *We were both bored by the endless words of praise for Walker.*[495])

Diane's response to the Evans retrospective—which she returns to see on several occasions—leaves her somewhat baffled, as she attempts to describe both to her class[496] and in a letter to Allan and Mariclare: *First I was totally whammied by it. Like THERE is a photographer, it was so endless and pristine. Then by the third time I saw it I realized how it really bores me. Cant bear most of what he photographs. Cant explain that confusion.*[497] Her admiration for Evans—whom she describes as *a fantastically honest photographer*[498] compared to those whose work moves her much more, like Brandt or Brassaï or Lartigue—is tempered by a kind of indifference to both his subject matter and something about his approach to it, ironically the very quality she admires in him.[499] Evans has produced a portfolio as well.[500] Not surprisingly, this confronts her with further evidence of the gulf between their respective sensibilities.

He has done a box too, and this (I quote from the prospectus) just gave me the willies: 'the prints were made on bla bla bla polycontrast F paper. Glycine developer was used to give desired print color and long (8-10) min developing times so that large groups of prints bla bla. Fresh developer was used for each batch of prints to minimize any variations. to insure minimum carry over of developer in to the first hypo, prints remained for two minutes in the stop bath, which was mixed fresh for each batch etc Three baths were used, the first with hardener, the second two plain. then on and on about the selenium toning and the air drying and godknows what all.' I read it in a cold sweat, with images of those people buying my box and calling me up in a year to ask about the brown spots.

—LETTER TO ALLAN ARBUS AND MARICLARE COSTELLO, JANUARY 31, 1971

She finds her progress stalled, both on the portfolio and in other areas. *I still don't have either the boxes Or the camera Hiro sent to Japan for…All this month I thought I was working so hard and don't have anything hardly to show for it. I can make such lousy pictures.*[501] Even the film problem remains an unresolved dilemma: *Panatomic Is so hideously hard. just makes me sick… isopan is no longer made…The panatomic x doesn't look like it has anywhere near enough details in the blacks.* She has been hoarding Adox, which has been discontinued and is the only film she knows that really suits her needs. At this point she has only two rolls of it left. *I can tell just by the contacts which is adox,* she reports wistfully. *It looks so gentle.*[502] As a kind of comic relief after this litany of woes, she concludes by recounting an incident between her and Dr. Boigon that amounts to a classic tale of psychiatrist and patient noncommunication:

Had a hilarious, ridiculous fight with Boigon. Went yesterday morning. My Saturday appt is annoyingly early (8:30) which means leaving home about 7:40. Ive asked her to change it but she cant yet. well that's OK...When I arrived her door was locked (rare but not totally unprecedented) so I rang and her son opened it. He is a funny fat boy about 10 yrs old and he sat down to talk to me, more than he ever has. It was great fun...and [then] he went off somewhere. I noted it was 9 and thought in a joke that Boigon might be testing me to see if I would get mad...A few minutes later Boigon appeared in deshabille, a robe, nightgown, no makeup, saying, "Who let you in?" I told her Seth had and she disappeared again... [then] came back into the office and started SCOLDING ME FOR NOT HAVING KNOCKED ON HER DOOR OR ASKED SETH TO MAKE SURE SHE KNEW I WAS HERE, for in short so failing to take care of my own interests, quite as if her understandable oversleeping was a symptom of MY illness. I was so furious. I burst into tears. Couldn't make her understand. SHE NEVER APOLOGIZED, not even a little. and what little time there was was taken up with that stupid controversy in the light of what it showed about ME. Everything is really fine though.

—LETTER TO ALLAN ARBUS AND MARICLARE COSTELLO, JANUARY 31, 1971

And in fact within days of the letter above, several of the nagging issues cited in it have either evaporated or been successfully addressed. A long overdue check for a thousand dollars she has been unable to extract from *Essence* arrives in the mail thanks to Jay Gold, a lawyer and a friend of hers and of Marvin Israel's, who intercedes with the magazine on her behalf. Her new Pentax camera finally arrives at Hiro's studio from Japan. She receives two summer teaching job offers for one week each, both in New England with room and board and cars available. (*What a racket*, she remarks.[503]) And she finishes *the LOVE thing* [for Time-Life Books,] *which was very good, and has left me lots to follow up with. They are using one of a lady with a baby monkey in her lap all dressed up in a bonnet and shirt and panties. She looks very grave.*[504] Around the same time she mentions the unanticipated prospect of a new, even more ambitious, assignment she had almost inadvertently initiated.

Just got a call from Eng (London Times) I had written complaining about being paid too little and to make the letter sound better suggested a few ideas—one about the LOSS OF POWER. They are all breathless about it. Want to send me to do Kruschev, Eden, de Gaulle, Nkrumah, Truman, Johnson!!! a spread on each. They will arrange it all. I said I'd do it in July so I don't have to leave Amy.

—LETTER TO ALLAN ARBUS, CIRCA FEBRUARY 1971

She is eager to start on the prints she needs to make for the Fogg Museum exhibition in hopes of finishing them before the end of February when she expects to be away for about a week. She writes to Davis Pratt for clarification of one item—identified by him merely as *Vicki (version 1?)* in the list of seven images he sent her[505]—and offers this description of the two transvestite pictures in question:

> Which picture of Vicki? One is pretty close up, very rounded, nearly classical, with a torn stocking, her cleavage line showing, something in her face both dire and delicate [which turns out to be the one Pratt has chosen]. The other shows more of her room, funny oblique angle, two nails somewhere on the wall, a coffee table with her magazines and comic books on it, she lies there, sort of wanton and childish and terrible. remember?…Let me know soon so I can get to work on it.
>
> —LETTER TO DAVIS PRATT, FEBRUARY 4, 1971

She sends the prints off on February 22: *Here they are. Seven prints. Titles and dates on back of each. value: $150 ea.* Pratt has indicated the Fogg Museum would like to buy them for its collection should funds become available, and in that event she tells him she intends to reprint three of the images. *The other four are good, archival prints. Just made 'em specially for you.*[506]

Her anticipated absence at the end of February entails a trip to Germany with Marvin Israel, which she has been looking forward to since January with mixed feelings. He is having a show of his paintings at Brusberg Gallery in Hannover and has asked her to come with him. *So I got a tiny assignment.(Schmeling.)gosh*, she says in a letter to Allan and Mariclare.[507] The approaching date of departure does nothing to alleviate her ambivalence about going. *Nearly have cold feet*, she writes.[508] And then: *Well it looks like we are going. wednesday evening* [meaning the 24th, although they do not actually leave until the 27th] *to Germany. Gulp. feel all jittery.* The Schmeling assignment has fallen through at this point and for a while she considers not even bringing a camera, *but yesterday I felt suddenly that maybe I wanted to do at least one little thing, so I called around and I think Günter Grass for the Bzah is it.*[509]

As it turns out, a sitting with Günter Grass doesn't take place either. Instead, while she and Israel are in Berlin, she is assigned to do a portrait of Bertolt Brecht's widow, Helene Weigel, director of the Berlin Ensemble, for the magazine. Following their return home on March 8 Israel sends her a handmade postcard of one of the works from his exhibition with this message: *Dear Diane—It sure sounds like you had a terrific time in Germany. Boy, are you lucky. It is difficult not to be extremely envious of you. As ever, Marvin.*[510] The Westbeth class resumes on March 8 as well and continues through March 25. *The class is pretty good, exhausting. will give them a party at the end*, she writes in a letter to Allan and Mariclare. *I'll be glad.*[511]

Immediately before her departure for Germany she had dutifully applied for a grant from the Ingram Merrill Foundation *(a little grant, only one I know of at the moment*[512]*)* and requested recommendations from a few people, including Henry Geldzahler and John Szarkowski. In a note to the latter, she says: *I would rather have you speak for me than anyone. If that's okay and if you know me well enough to just write... The description of the project is enclosed. There is lots to do and I really want to do it.*[513]

Szarkowski's ensuing letter of recommendation reads as follows: *Dear Sir, Mrs. Arbus has asked me to send a reference for her application for an Ingram Merrill Fellowship. I have known Diane Arbus professionally for ten years and I consider her a photographer of exceptional talent and achievement...She is in addition a person with a very high sense of responsibility, and I am confident that she would complete her project in a way that would be creditable to herself and the Foundation. I recommend her without reservation for the Fellowship.*[514]

Geldzahler's recommendation is brief and to the point: *To me Diane Arbus' photographs are as sensitively original and heartbreaking as anything in the field. I highly recommend her to your attention. Her work speaks for itself. I know she needs the assistance.*[515]

What she writes about her intended Ingram Merrill project—entitled "The Quiet Minorities"[516]—seems to have been inspired at least in part by three quotations that appear on a single typewritten sheet of paper in one of her binders next to the draft project statement. They consist of these lines from Gerard Manley Hopkins' poem "Pied Beauty": *All things counter, original, spare, strange; Whatever is fickle, freckled (who knows how?)*; an unattributed statement: *Only minorities effect change*; and a paragraph from Norman Mailer that begins: *I refuse resolutely to lump them all together. I think that's the beginning of totalitarianism. The essence of totalitarianism is that all people are alike.*[517] Her project description itself reads as follows:

The sign of a minority is The Difference. Those of birth, accident, choice, belief, predilection, inertia. (Some are irrevocable: people are fat, freckled, handicapped, ethnic, of a certain age, class, attitude, profession, enthusiasm.) Every Difference is a Likeness too. There are associations, groups, clubs, alliances, milieus for every one of them. And each milieu is a small world, a subculture with a slightly other set of rules for the game. Not to ignore them, not to lump them all together, but to watch them, to take notice, to pay attention...towards a book of photographs.

—"The Quiet Minorities," Ingram Merrill Foundation project description, 1971

She is not awarded the grant. Since around 1969, she has been in contact with Lee Witkin of the Witkin Gallery, one of the first successful photography galleries, and on occasion he has purchased prints from her for clients or for the gallery.

From time to time she has also sold prints through other dealers as well and through The Museum of Modern Art's Lending Service. For the most part, however, sales of her prints have been dependent upon her direct contact with museum curators, friends, or private collectors.[518] Now that the first dozen sets of the portfolio are nearing completion and the problem with the manufacture of the boxes appears to be solved, she is looking for ways to promote it in addition to the flyer she is sending out.

The box looks very good I guess, it'll be in Art forum in May and New York will do two pps I think. Liberman [editor of *Vogue*, whom she and Allan used to work for years ago] nearly did something on it but I played my cards wrong. no matter. Fun to see him. He just looks like Dracula has been at him. a little grayer, not really old, just brittle. And he is just the same. Same unbelievable enthusiasm and gallantry. Could I work for Vogue? Was I under contract to the Bazaar? It was really fun. because it was just a sentimental journey and I knew I had nothing to lose and even less to gain.

—LETTER TO ALLAN ARBUS AND MARICLARE COSTELLO, CIRCA LATE APRIL 1971

She concludes with a report of plans and bits of news, delivered in uncharacteristically short staccato sentences, as if in haste. *I'm going up to visit Amy in a week or two, and photograph the yurts*[519]*...I bought a new strobe. very good. the [Pentax] camera is somewhat difficult. but absorbing. look for Art Forum. Bea is buying a box. They are at Dick's studio. havent seen em. Doon says they look good...Spring is not very pretty here yet. lots of rain and denseness.* And finally: *one fascinating thing I am beginning to get through my thick head from Boigon is that it doesn't matter what you do... except to yourself. I am always answering to someone who isnt even asking.*[520]

The photograph, Boy with a straw hat waiting to march in a pro-war parade, N.Y.C. 1967, appears on the cover of *Artforum*'s May 1971 issue. In addition, five of the remaining nine images from the portfolio are reproduced, one per page, in the magazine under the title "Five Photographs by Diane Arbus,"[521] accompanied by a brief text she writes for the occasion.

Once I dreamed I was on a gorgeous ocean liner, all pale, gilded, cupid-encrusted, rococo as a wedding cake. There was smoke in the air, people were drinking and gambling. I knew the ship was on fire and we were sinking, slowly. They knew it too, but they were very gay, dancing and singing and kissing, a little delirious. There was no hope. I was terribly elated. I could photograph anything I wanted to.

Nothing is ever the same as they said it was. It's what I've never seen before that I recognize.

There is an old joke about a man who goes into a bar and he sees that the bartender has a banana in his ear so he says, Hey, you have a banana in your ear; and the bartender says, Speak louder please, I can't hear you because I've got a banana in my ear.[522]

Nothing is ever alike. The best thing is the difference. I get to keep what nobody needs.

A photograph is a secret about a secret. The more it tells you the less you know.
— "FIVE PHOTOGRAPHS BY DIANE ARBUS," *ARTFORUM*, MAY 1971

The opening paragraph of this text is the retelling of a dream she had in 1959 that is first recorded in one of her notebooks (No. 1). This recent version is apparently recounted from memory since, although the essential features remain intact, several significant details have been altered or omitted: the original *ornate white gorgeous hotel* has become a sinking ship, the obstacles to photographing have vanished. *Artforum* had initially agreed to run an announcement about the sale of the portfolio along with the piece but, having inadvertently failed to do so, the magazine agrees to publish a separate announcement for it in the June issue.

In answer to a very enthusiastic response from Allan about the *Artforum* piece she writes: *what a good note (about artforum) yesterday on the heels of all sorts of small and nasty things…Im really glad you liked the writing. I sweated and Doon was a help and suddenly it fell into place.* About the future promotional prospects for the portfolio she adds: *It'll be in NY mag next week reduced from two pps to one with a terribly dumb interview (a girl called and said 'I don't know the first thing about you I must confess; tell me what you've done. 'uggh.)*[523]

The small and nasty things she enumerates include the fact that *Harper's Bazaar* is refusing to pay her expenses in Germany for the Helene Weigel photograph she was assigned to do *meaning that for a $200 photo I was to have spent 165+film etc. I was so mad and in tears and they were all polite…Ruth disavowing all knowledge and responsibility, clucking sympathetically about how rotten they are but refusing any real help and at one moment having the gall to say Geri* [Trotta, editor] *had given me the assignment as a favor!* This last allegation which Diane confides to Marvin Israel so outrages him that he promptly intercedes with Ruth Ansel about the matter.[524] The paucity of the sum involved only seems to make the whole thing worse. *I have a hunch I'll get the money. Ill go to Nancy White* [editor in chief] *if necessary, there is absolutely nothing to lose. I don't even ever work for them.* She also mentions, with a certain equanimity, doing *a lousy page for a terrible new magazine called NEW WOMAN, of Germaine Greer* [author of *The Female Eunuch* (London: MacGibbon and Kee, 1970)] *who was fun and is terrific looking but I managed to make otherwise.*[525]

Still, it isn't all bad, not by any means. The same letter contains this: *Spoke to Amy who is superb with a million plans for the summer, none of them fixed, but with a totally instructive sense of no worry and rich possibilities…She is so freewheeling but practical and she has developed so many means of being self determining and has access to this vast network of her generation, so that she literally doesn't feel alone in an alien world the way we always have.*[526] As she once said of Amy with a mixture of admiration and relief: *she seems so capable and so clear that it is Her responsibility and mine is mine.*[527]

There is also, to her apparent delight, interest in the portfolio from an unexpected, unsolicited source. *I had a call from some art dealer to say that jasper johns wanted a box. how terrific. first one who doesn't know me.* She adds this note in the margin: *four are sold, 2½ pd for. the owners are out of who's who. my confidence is absurdly on a roller coaster.* And trails off at the end of the letter with a summary, not unlike some observations she has made before: *There is so much to learn. mainly it is never as good as you hope or as bad as you dread.*[528]

The disposition of the completed portfolios, each with its own individually handwritten cover and title sheets accompanying the ten annotated, signed prints appears to be as follows: The first in the edition of fifty—on which the number *ten* in the title *A box of ten photographs* is crossed out and replaced by *eleven** with a note that says **especially for RA*—is purchased by Richard Avedon and includes an additional print she made for him, Masked woman in a wheelchair. The second is also purchased by Avedon as a present for his friend Mike Nichols. The portfolio purchased by Bea Feitler is numbered 5/50 and also includes an additional print, Woman with her baby monkey. The portfolio purchased by Jasper Johns is numbered 6/50. Each of these four portfolios, including the one for Johns, is delivered by her to the purchaser in person. Evidence suggests that these are the only editions of the portfolio distributed during her lifetime.[529]

Another letter to Allan, written around the same time as the previous one quoted above, makes it clear how pervasive and haunting the issue of money continues to be for her, even as she readily acknowledges that her assessment of her financial situation may be somewhat inaccurate.

Sudden money panic and as you say I always do this…will probably have to borrow and get work. The London Times job [on loss of power] looks dubious. They don't seem to have been able to round up enough heavyweights…I owe 1800 not counting normal next month bills and taxes…This is the point at which I usually get sick but I wont this time… [in a handwritten note at the bottom of the page she adds] I overreact both ways. A month ago I thought I was on easy street and today I think I am one of the neediest cases. love from the middle of the road, d

—LETTER TO ALLAN ARBUS, CIRCA MID-MAY 1971[530]

On May 21 Davis Pratt returns the eight prints[531] she had loaned to the Fogg Museum for the *Contemporary Photographs I* exhibition, noting that one of them, Boy in a straw hat waiting to march in a pro-war parade—which he refers to as *Bomb Hanoi*—was damaged. He confirms that a claim for $150 will be paid and goes on to say: *We still do not have news of the grant we have applied for so we cannot buy these prints…thanks for your brochure about your portfolio. I still hope we may buy individual prints that we particularly want.*[532]

Meanwhile, the unfulfilled *London Times* assignment on loss of power is soon replaced by another equally unlikely one that takes her to Washington, D.C., in the middle of June. The magazine sends her to cover the White House wedding of President Richard Nixon's younger daughter, Tricia—whom she describes as *very pretty really but something like a paper doll*[533]—to fiancé, Edward Cox. Immediately following her return home, Diane sends Peter Crookston this detailed account of her experience at the event:

It is funnier in retrospect. I don't know what you and Michael [Rand, *London Sunday Times Magazine* editor] pictured but what flitted through my head was quite different from what was. I had thought to myself that mobility was the key. That I was to infiltrate at the Arrival, The Departure, The Descent into The Rose Garden. I had thought that Billy Graham might whisper something to J. Edgar Hoover and there I'd be, amid all the clothes rustling and the eyelashes flitting. Miss Wilson told me to come down friday so I weasled out of a picture of (mafia) Joe Columbo for Harpers which didn't matter to me. As soon as I arrived and Miss W showed me the Maps and Lists, like battle plans, I began to realize how remote it was going to be. There were lists of positions, all taken by newsmen and wire services. I acted irate, but nobody cared. All the positions had been filled on Wednesday…Well then saturday morning after being searched by the FBI which was great fun because you knew you were innocent, there we were in the press tent, rubbery, soggy, humid, like a shower stall the size of an airplane hangar, several hundreds of us, more than the wedding guests, and ladies, minor press attaches, would step to the microphone to explain, while a thousand reporters scribbled notes, that Tricia had risen at 8:02 and breakfasted with the President and Mrs N on orange juice and cereal. What kind of cereal, some enterprising reporter queried. Hot, she said, cream of wheat it turned out to be. And endless reports of what Ron Ziegler said the president said as well as explanations of what that meant and why it was funny…Finally (no food all day) it was near arrival time and we were taken to the East Gate in the rain. The real old time newsmen who knew the score were working in teams with lenses the length of my arm and great enormous tripods and a kind of general unfriendliness which only meant that if they had to slit your throat later they didn't want to pal around too much in advance. They had ponchos and sandwiches and entrenched themselves in pre-marked positions, like assassins. We were roped in and every time you wandered off so much as a foot, the FBI or whoever they were pushed you back. So every time you clicked your shutter you heard a hundred or so other clicks and sometimes when you didn't. Meanwhile the reporters and the photographers were bickering because every time a guest ran the gauntlet, the society reporters would call them by name and ask what their dress was made of so they would turn their heads away from the photographers at the crucial moment. There was only one crucial moment because you couldn't move out of this position you'd wangled, even though someone's elbow and someone else's umbrella were poking at you, because if you moved your space would get swallowed up and the radio people were droning on about how lovely it was and what a shame about the rain...Then back to the Tent for more reports about Billy Grahams witticism about trying to stop the rain. What felt best was the end, THE DEPARTURE, I was up on a kind of column, where only a few photographers were, and there were the front steps of the White House. Inside you could see guests and lights and something going on and suddenly they piled out, guests like movie extras, and a man with a trumpet and maybe bits more of a band and fifty of the photographers straining against the ropes and Secret Service and the Pres and the Mrs and the Cox family, incredibly hometown looking and cozy...illuminated sort of unearthly by the TV lights. (Why Did Tricia Leave In Her Wedding Gown?) anyway she did and each one kissed all the others, like a midwestern small town celebration scene in the movies, endearing, exaggerated with everyone playing their part with enthusiasm. and that black limousine waiting for them.[534]

—LETTER TO PETER CROOKSTON, CIRCA MID-JUNE 1971

She encloses a bill for the expenses and requests an advance for the upcoming Twins Convention assignment which, in her own words, *sounds better and better. There will be Kings and Queens, four of em and Double Twins...(Twins who've married Twins)* [an idea she originally proposed to Crookston in 1968] *so at last we will get that story, and yes I'll do captions, twin lore, twin jokes, whatnot. Looking forward a lot.*[535]

It is not clear when the Twins Convention she is referring to is scheduled to take place, especially since she has recently returned from one held in Grand Rapids, Michigan, on June 4, 5, and 6. She photographed there and spoke with many sets of twins, whose stories appear, somewhat hastily transcribed, in her 1971 Notebook (No. 39). Among these is the first-person account by an unnamed identical twin of a shopping expedition she went on with her twin sister Martha.

As they were trying things on, *Martha wandered away*. Moments later the narrator looked up, thought Martha was there and asked her whether or not she liked the dress but it wasn't Martha she was talking to, *It was me in the mirror.*[536]

Diane spends the last week of June at Hampshire College in Amherst, Massachusetts, on a teaching assignment—one of the two summer teaching jobs she'd been offered and accepted earlier in the year—organized by the program's director, Jerry Liebling.[537] Amy is nearby attending Woolman Hill, a former Quaker Center in Deerfield, which is now functioning as a "free" school, and she comes to Hampshire College briefly for a visit. Some time after her return home, Diane goes to see Lisette Model, who later describes her on this occasion as *so beautiful and so strong coming from the beach. She looked like I've never seen her before in my life. Not one wrinkle. Brown. Young-looking.*[538] All the same, she says she is dreading her next teaching stint and refers to the Hampshire College experience as *horrible.*[539]

She remains in regular contact with many of the people and places she has photographed in the past, including Eddie Carmel, several sets of adult twins, and the homes for the retarded she continues to visit. A letter from one such state facility, dated June 14 and sent by mistake to her former East 10th Street address, thanks her for the camera she arranged to give them as a gift: *Just a note to let you know we received either the repaired camera or a new camera from Willoughby's today and it seems to be operating well. Again, we appreciate your thoughtfulness in donating the camera and the Recreation Division will be able to take snapshots which they were not able to do before your donation.*[540]

An announcement and reservation form for the Federation of the Handicapped annual picnic is stapled to the July 10 page of her appointment book. *Dear Member, Summer is just around the corner and it won't be long before everyone's mind will be turning to thoughts of the Great Outdoors, picnics and picnicking. With this thought in our minds, we cordially invite you to attend the 1971 Annual Picnic sponsored by the Entertainment Committee of the Federation of the Handicapped.* She is among those in attendance and she brings her camera along and takes pictures at the event.[541]

For some of June and the first half of July, Carlotta is in town on one of her regular trips back to New York and they see each other on several occasions during this period. On the evening of July 16, just before Carlotta's scheduled departure, Diane arrives on her bicycle for a visit and the two of them spend a long time talking in much the same way and about many of the same subjects as they have so often in the past.[542] This is the way Diane once described to Carlotta the unpredictable fluctuations in her state of mind between exhilaration and gloom.

I go up and down a lot. Maybe Ive always been like that. Partly what happens though is I get filled with energy and joy and I begin lots of things or think about what I want to do and get all breathless with excitement and then quite suddenly either through tiredness or a disappointment or something more mysterious the energy vanishes, leaving me harassed, swamped, distraught, frightened by the very things I thought I was so eager for! I'm sure this is quite classic.

—LETTER TO CARLOTTA MARSHALL, CIRCA NOVEMBER 1968

Or, as she wrote on another occasion, *the worst is I am literally scared of getting depressed...And it is so goddamn chemical, Im convinced. Energy, some special kind of energy, just leaks out and I am left lacking the confidence even to cross the street.*[543]

Carlotta Marshall leaves on July 17 to return to Holland. Amy Arbus is in summer school at Woolman Hill in Deerfield, Massachusetts. Doon Arbus is in Paris completing the text of an upcoming book, *Alice in Wonderland: The Forming of a Company and the Making of a Play.* Marvin Israel and his wife, Margie, are spending a long weekend at Richard Avedon's house on Fire Island. Allan Arbus is in Santa Fe filming the Robert Downey movie *Greaser's Palace,* in which he plays a zoot-suited aspiring singer-dancer-actor-Christ-figure in the Old West. Diane Arbus is home.

I used to think consciousness itself was a virtue, so I tried to keep it all in my head at the same time, past, future etc. tried even to feel the bad when I felt good and vice versa as if any unawareness was a marie-antoinette sort of sin. its like throwing ballast overboard to only do what there is to do NOW. a kind of confidence that later will bring its own now...It makes Sunday more Sunday and even Monday is better...

—LETTER TO ALLAN ARBUS AND MARICLARE COSTELLO, JANUARY 11, 1971

Her suicide seems neither inevitable nor spontaneous, neither perplexing nor intelligible. On the evening of July 28, having been unable to reach her by phone for two days, Marvin Israel lets himself into the apartment where, according to the medical investigator's subsequent report, he *found her dead...crunched up in bath tub, on left side...wearing red shirt, blue denim shorts, no socks.* Israel gets in touch with three friends, Larry Shainberg, Jay Gold, and Richard Avedon. They each come to help in whatever way they can. The police are notified. The medical investigator arrives on the scene at 9:45 p.m., about two and a half hours after official notification, and leaves at 10:15 p.m. The body is removed to the mortuary of the Office of the Chief Medical Examiner of the City of New York. Three items are listed in the investigator's report as having been submitted separately for study: *Razor blade, "Last Supper" note, medications.*

The item referred to as *"Last Supper" note* is actually an entry on the July 26 page of her 1971 appointment book, but this page (along with those of July 27 and July 28) have since been meticulously excised from the appointment book, presumably by the medical investigator or by someone else in authority. The appointment book appears perfectly intact, but the pages in question are no longer in it and have never been recovered.

Diane's uncle, Harold Russek, Gertrude Nemerov's younger brother, assumes the responsibility of making the official identification of the body at the Medical Examiner's Office and states that his niece had *a history of depression*. As required by law under the circumstances, an autopsy is performed. The medical examiner is Dr. Yong-Myun Rho and the complete report of his findings, dated July 29, 1971, reads as follows:

EXTERNAL EXAMINATION

The body is that of a white adult female appearing the stated age of 48 years, well-developed, well-nourished, measuring 5'6 1/2" in length and weighing 100 lbs. Rigidity is absent. Dark greenish post-mortem discoloration is present over the face, the left side of trunk and anterior aspects of the lower legs.

The epidermis of the skin of the face has been sloughed off, due to decomposition. Hair can be pulled out readily.

Networks of vascular markings can be visualized on these greenish discoloration areas. The anterior aspects of the right and left wrists have been cut transversely. There are three such cuts on the left side and two cuts on the right side. These cuts are deep and have severed many tendons of the muscular insertion. The radial arteries and veins on both sides, however, are intact. The hands are covered by a large amount of dried blood and the anterior aspects of the lower legs, below the knees, are also covered by a large amount of dried

blood. There is no other evidence of external violence to the body surface.

HEAD & NECK: The head is symmetrical and is covered by abundant dark brown long hair. The conjunctivi are congested; the cornea are cloudy. Pupils are round. Irides are brown. Sclerae are decomposed. The external ears and nose are not remarkable. Natural teeth are present. The neck is symmetrical.

CHEST AND ABDOMEN WALLS: Not remarkable.

GENITALIA: The external genitalia show no evidence of external violence.

EXTREMITIES: Apart from the cuts on both wrists, the extremities are not remarkable. Back is natural.

INTERNAL EXAMINATION

PRIMARY INCISION: The body is opened by a Y-shaped incision.

BODY CAVITIES: A small amount of blood-stained liquid is present in both pleural cavities and the peritoneal cavity. This is presumably due to post-mortem decomposition. There are no adhesions in the body cavities.

NECK ORGANS: There is no evidence of trauma or obstruction to the neck organs.

CARDIOVASCULAR SYSTEM: The heart lies within the sac and weighs 320 grams. The coronary arteries are widely patent. The mural endocardium, valves, and myocardium are not remarkable. The aorta and its major branches are not remarkable.

RESPIRATORY TRACT: The trachea and the large bronchi contain a moderate amount of reddish mucus. The lungs are not remarkable and they together weigh 600 grams. The pulmonary vessels are patent.

LIVER: The liver weighs 1400 grams. It is congested.

SPLEEN: Weighs 110 grams. Not remarkable.

URINARY TRACT: Each kidney weighs 125 grams. They are not remarkable. Urinary bladder is empty. The bladder wall is not remarkable.

GENITALIA: The vagina is not remarkable. The cervix is not remarkable. The uterine cavity contains a whitish plastic twisted contraceptive device. The mucosal surface of the uterus is not remarkable. The tubes and ovaries are not remarkable.

ADRENALS: Not remarkable.

PANCREAS: Not remarkable.

GASTROINTESTINAL TRACT: The esophagus is patent. The stomach contains approximately 100 cc. of greenish-brown liquid material. No unusual material can be detected, in the stomach. The gastric wall is not remarkable. Small intestine, appendix and large intestine are not remarkable.

HEAD: The scalp is incised by an intermastoid incision. A segment of calvarium is removed and dura incised. There is no evidence of trauma. The brain weighs 1380 grams. The leptomeninges are slightly congested. On serial section the brain shows nothing remarkable. The pituitary is not remarkable.

OSSEOUS SYSTEM: Not remarkable.

ANATOMICAL DIAGNOSES:

1. Post-mortem decomposition of body.

2. Deep scars on anterior aspects of both wrists.

3. External hemorrhage.

4. Congestion of organs.

5. Diary suggestive of suicidal intent, taken on July 26th, noted.

6. History of depresssion, given by deceased's uncle.

LABORATORY FINDINGS: Brain: Amobarbital present, Secobarbitol: present; Liver: Barbiturates present 3.45 mg %

Final cause of death (9/14/71) Incised wounds of wrists with external hemorrhage. Acute barbiturate poisoning. Suicidal.

They are the proof that something was there and no longer is.

Like a stain. And the stillness of them is boggling.

You can turn away but when you

come back they'll still be there looking at you.

—FROM A LETTER TO DAVIS PRATT, FOGG MUSEUM, CAMBRIDGE, MARCH 15, 1971,

IN RESPONSE TO REQUEST FOR A BRIEF STATEMENT ABOUT PHOTOGRAPHS

ENDNOTES

Unless otherwise stated, the originals of the material cited are currently in the possession of the initial recipient or his or her estate. The Archive of The Estate of Diane Arbus retains letters, photographs, and documents from Gertrude Nemerov's collection, letters from Diane Arbus to Marvin Israel, letters from Diane Arbus to Carlotta Marshall, letters from Diane Arbus to Peter Crookston, and letters from Diane Arbus to Allan Arbus, Amy Arbus, and Doon Arbus. All other original material, unless otherwise stated, is in The Archive of The Estate of Diane Arbus. The Archive of The Estate of Diane Arbus is a promised gift to The Metropolitan Museum of Art.

[1] Frank Russek obituary, 1948, Collection of Gertrude Nemerov, Archive of The Estate of Diane Arbus.

[2] Diane Arbus 1934 autobiography, seventh-grade class assignment, Fieldston School. Original given by Elbert Lenrow to Howard Nemerov, Howard Nemerov Collection, Washington University Libraries, Department of Special Collections, St. Louis, Mo.

[3] Diane Arbus 1940 autobiography, senior class assignment, Fieldston School, original given by Elbert Lenrow to Howard Nemerov, Howard Nemerov Collection, Washington University Libraries, Department of Special Collections, St. Louis, Mo.

[4] Frank Russek obituary, 1948.

[5] New York City telephone directory, 1924; also Diane Arbus 1934 autobiography.

[6] Diane Arbus 1934 autobiography.

[7] Howard Nemerov, *Journal of the Fictive Life* (Chicago: University of Chicago Press, 1965), p. 74.

[8] Gertrude Nemerov note on verso of photograph taken in St. Mark's Place, and notation on photo of Gertrude with children in La Touquet, 1927, Collection of Gertrude Nemerov, Archive of The Estate of Diane Arbus.

[9] Handbook of the Ethical Culture Fieldston School, 2001.

[10] Elisabeth Sussman interview with Stewart Stern, February 2, 2002.

[11] New York City telephone directory, winter 1929–summer 1930; also Diane Arbus 1934 autobiography.

[12] Studs Terkel, *Hard Times: An Oral History of the Great Depression* (New York: Pantheon, 1970), p. 88.

[13] Studs Terkel radio interview with Diane Arbus, WFMT Chicago, 1968.

[14] Diane Arbus postcard to Marvin Israel, March 4, 1960.

[15] New York City telephone directory, 1932.

[16] Diane Arbus postcard to Marvin Israel, February 17, 1960.

[17] Doon Arbus interview with Stewart Stern, February 1972.

[18] Elisabeth Sussman interview with Stewart Stern, February 12, 2001.

[19] *Ibid.*

[20] Diane Arbus 1940 autobiography.

[21] Elisabeth Sussman interview with Allan Arbus, April 12, 2001.

[22] Doon Arbus interview with Allan Arbus, February 17, 1972.

[23] Letter from Victor D'Amico to Katherine Frazier, head of the Cummington School, June 14, 1938, archives, Fieldston School, Riverdale, New York.

[24] Elisabeth Sussman interview with Alex Eliot, May 1, 2001.

[25] Doon Arbus interview with Alex Eliot, February 14, 1972.

[26] Diane Arbus handwritten letter to Alex Eliot, November 1938. Collection of Alex Eliot and Jane Winslow Eliot.

[27] Elisabeth Sussman interview with Stewart Stern, February 2, 2001.

[28] *Ibid.*

[29] Diane Arbus papers for Elbert Lenrow class, 1940, Fieldston School, copies in the Archive of The Estate of Diane Arbus.

[30] Elisabeth Sussman interview with Allan Arbus, April 25, 2001.

[31] Studs Terkel radio interview with Diane Arbus, WFMT Chicago, 1968.

[32] Studs Terkel interview, quoted from Doon Arbus and Marvin Israel, eds. *Diane Arbus*, p. 5.

[33] Typewritten letter from Howard Nemerov to Gertrude and David Nemerov, Collection of Gertrude Nemerov.

[34] New York City telephone directory, summer 1940.

[35] Newspaper clipping, *The New York Times*, April 11, 1941.

[36] Elisabeth Sussman interview with Allan Arbus, April 12, 2001.

[37] Doon Arbus interview with Alex Eliot, February 14, 1972.

[38] *Ibid.*

[39] Elisabeth Sussman interview with Allan Arbus, October 17, 2000, and April 12 and 25, 2001.

[40] Elisabeth Sussman interview with Allan Arbus, January 17, 2000.

[41] Richard Ellmann and Robert O'Clair, eds. *The Norton Anthology of Modern Poetry* (New York and London: W.W. Norton and Co., 1988), pp. 1017–18.

[42] Pati Hill, "Some Notes from My Life," pamphlet for *Wall Papers*, Hill's exhibition at the Bayly Art Museum, University of Virginia, Charlottesville, April 15–June 18, 2000.

[43] Diane Arbus handwritten letter to Alex Eliot, May 1951.

[44] Elisabeth Sussman interview with Allan Arbus, October 17, 2000.

[45] Doon Arbus interview with Allan Arbus, February 17, 1972.

[46] Alfred Stieglitz Collection, the Beinecke Rare Book and Manuscript Library, Yale University Library, New Haven, Conn.

[47] Note to Pati Hill, 1945, Archive of The Estate of Diane Arbus, gift of Pati Hill.

[48] Elisabeth Sussman interview with Alex Eliot, May 1, 2001.

[49] Allan Arbus U.S. Army discharge papers, Allan Arbus Collection.

[50] Nancy Newhall was Acting Curator of Photography at The Museum of Modern Art while her husband, Beaumont Newhall, was in the armed services during World War II.

[51] Books in the Archive of The Estate of Diane Arbus.

[52] Doon Arbus interview with Allan Arbus, February 17, 1972.

[53] *Ibid.*

54 Elisabeth Sussman interview with Allan Arbus, April 25, 2001.

55 Doon Arbus interview with Allan Arbus, February 17, 1972.

56 Diane Arbus handwritten letter to Alex Eliot and Jane Winslow from Barcelona, July 26, 1951.

57 Doon Arbus interview with Allan Arbus, February 17, 1972.

58 Doon Arbus notes from a conversation with Nancy Bellamy, circa 1980.

59 Richard Ellmann and Robert O'Clair, eds. *The Norton Anthology of Modern Poetry*, pp. 1017–18.

60 *The New York Times* announcement of the engagement of Renée Nemerov, circa August 1947.

61 Elisabeth Sussman interview with Alex Eliot, May 1, 2001; and interview with Allan Arbus, April 25, 2001.

62 *Ibid.*

63 Alex Eliot letter to Elisabeth Sussman, dated "first day of spring," 2002.

64 Doon Arbus interview with Allan Arbus, February 17, 1972.

65 Diane Arbus handwritten letter to Alex Eliot and Jane Winslow from Spain, June 22, 1951.

66 Alex Eliot letter to Elisabeth Sussman, dated "first day of spring," 2002.

67 Diane Arbus handwritten letter to Alex Eliot and Jane Winslow from Spain, June 22, 1951.

68 Diane Arbus passport. Elisabeth Sussman interview with Alex Eliot, May 15, 2001.

69 Diane Arbus typewritten letter to Alex Eliot and Jane Winslow Eliot on their honeymoon in Europe, 1951.

70 Doon Arbus interview with Robert Brown, February 1972.

71 Elisabeth Sussman interview with Stewart Stern, February 2, 2001.

72 Diane Arbus circa 1960 Notebook (No. 4).

73 Diane Arbus typewritten letter to Alex Eliot and Jane Winslow Eliot, May 30, 1952.

74 Edward Steichen, Director of the Department of Photography at The Museum of Modern Art (1947–62), organized the exhibition *The Family of Man*.

75 Doon Arbus interview with Allan Arbus, February 17, 1972.

76 Doon Arbus interview with Lisette Model, February 5, 1972.

77 From transcripts of tapes made by Ikko Narahara, a student in Arbus's master class who made the recordings to replay later in case he had trouble with the English. The class was given from January to March 1971 in a public room at Westbeth, the artists' residence where Diane lived in New York City. *Diane Arbus*, 1972.

78 Doon Arbus interview with Lisette Model, February 5, 1972.

79 Doon Arbus interview with Allan Arbus, February 17, 1972.

80 The following Lisette Model photographs were shown: Lower East Side N.Y., 1939–45; Coney Island Bather, N.Y., 1939–41; Sammy's, N.Y., 1940–44; World War II Rally, Lower East Side, 1942.

81 Application for fellowship, John Simon Guggenheim Memorial Foundation, New York. Received October 15, 1962. Archive, John Simon Guggenheim Foundation. Although many of these projects were dated in the Guggenheim application as originating in 1959, an examination of Arbus's contact sheets makes clear that most of these subjects were present in the work as early as 1956.

82 The thirteen appointment books (1959–1971) and a total of thirty-nine working notebooks are currently in the Archive of The Estate of Diane Arbus. The notebooks have been numbered by the Estate in an attempt to indicate their sequence and the years to which they apply. It is not clear whether these thirty-nine notebooks in Arbus's possession at the time of her death constitute a complete inventory of all the notebooks she had. There may have been others that were either lost or destroyed. The thirty-nine notebooks do, however, represent all years between and including 1959 and 1971.

83 Diane Arbus 1959–1960 Notebook (No. 2).

84 *Ibid.*

85 In 1959 she includes in her notebooks (Nos. 1, 2, and 3) excerpts from writings and books including: *Howl*, by Allen Ginsberg; "A Secret Society," "The Web of Life," and "Beyond the Screen," by Howard Nemerov from his collection *A Commodity of Dreams and Other Stories* (London: Secker and Warburg, 1960); Plato's *Symposium; The Art of Loving*, by Erich Fromm.

[86] According to her 1959 appointment book, other movies she saw during that year include Jean Cocteau's *Beauty and the Beast*, Ingmar Bergman's *The Seventh Seal*, Sergei Eisenstein's *Alexander Nevsky*, *Tall Story* (a comedy about college basketball with Tony Perkins and Jane Fonda, based very loosely on Howard Nemerov's novel *The Homecoming Game*), Akira Kurosawa's *Rashomon*, John Cassavetes' *Shadows*, and Robert Frank's *Pull My Daisy*.

[87] Typewritten letter from Diane Arbus to Lisette Model, September 25, 1962, Lisette Model Archives, the National Gallery of Canada, Ottawa.

[88] Elisabeth Sussman interview with Robert Benton, May 9, 2001.

[89] Typewritten letter from Diane Arbus to Robert Benton, circa October 1959. "Please get me permissions both posh and sordid...the more the merrier..." The *Esquire* Collection, Spencer Museum of Art, The University of Kansas, Lawrence.

[90] *Ibid.*

[91] List of permissions sought, with dates and indications of assignments completed, from Harold Hayes's office, probably maintained by his secretary, Toni Bliss. The Harold Hayes Collection, Special Collections Department, Z. Smith Reynolds Library, Wake Forest University, Winston-Salem, N.C.

[92] Harold Hayes letter to Deputy Police Commissioner Walter Arm, November 30, 1959. The *Esquire* Collection, Spencer Museum of Art, The University of Kansas, Lawrence.

[93] Diane Arbus typewritten letter to Robert Benton, circa October 1959.

[94] *Ibid.*

[95] It appears that only the letters from Diane Arbus to Marvin Israel during this period have survived, although it is clear from the nature of the letters that the other side of the correspondence existed. Her letters to Israel, mostly dated from 1959 through 1960 (although some later ones exist as well), are now in the Archive of The Estate of Diane Arbus, gift of Marvin Israel. The correspondence may have continued at this rate in later years, but is no longer extant.

[96] Diane Arbus handwritten letter to Marvin Israel, circa late January 1960.

[97] An examination of the 1959 appointment book suggests that this letter refers to the International Debutante Ball at the Astor Hotel on December 30, 1959.

[98] Diane Arbus typewritten letter to Marvin Israel, March 13, 1960.

[99] *Ibid.*

[100] In a postcard to Marvin Israel dated January 24, 1960, she writes parenthetically: "Maybe I will photograph Reverend Olford when I finish this *Esquire* thing. That will be like converting him (into 2 dimensions) (black & white magic)."

[101] Diane Arbus typewritten letter to Marvin Israel, January 29, 1960.

[102] Diane was given a portfolio of August Sander photographs published in the Swiss magazine *Du* in 1959, separated from the magazine and placed in a folder of its own by Marvin Israel.

[103] Diane Arbus postcard to Marvin Israel, circa April 1960.

[104] Working captions for *Esquire*, circa April 1960, from Harold Hayes's office, probably maintained by his secretary, Toni Bliss. The Harold Hayes Collection, Special Collections Department, Z. Smith Reynolds Library, Wake Forest University, Winston-Salem, N.C.

[105] Diane Arbus typewritten letter to Marvin Israel, circa April 20, 1960.

[106] From then unpublished 1965 article by Diane Arbus on the closing of Hubert's Museum entitled "Hubert's Obituary, or This Is Where We Came In." Published posthumously in *Diane Arbus: Magazine Work*, pp. 80–81.

[107] In a handwritten letter to Doon Arbus, circa 1960, Diane writes: "Hey Doon wouldja like me to make you curtains of this stuff?...it's like the scarves magicians pull out of tubes and make disappear...I have a dictionary of carnival lingo. A merry go round is a simp twister. Orange drink is Saniflush or internal douche. Candy apples are dentists' friends. Piggie bank is a fat girls stocking."

[108] A comparison between the contents of this letter and the 1960 appointment book suggests that Diane is describing Wirth's Circus in Hempstead, L.I., which she appears to have visited on April 5, 1960. In the original, the second sentence quoted here appears in the margin.

[109] Joe Loebenthal's name appears in this context in 1959 Notebook (No. 3), in the 1960 appointment book, and in a typewritten letter from Diane Arbus to Marvin Israel, August 27, 1960.

110 Elisabeth Sussman interview with James Randi, June 21, 2001. James Randi is a professional magician (The Amazing Randi), author, lecturer, amateur archaeologist, amateur astronomer, and founding fellow of the Committee for the Scientific Investigation of Claims of the Paranormal.

111 Diane Arbus typewritten letter to Marvin Israel, August 27, 1960.

112 This novel was made into an eponymous movie (1947) about a geek, with Tyrone Power, Joan Blondell, and Helen Walker.

113 Diane Arbus typewritten letter to Marvin Israel, August 27, 1960.

114 The Stratoliners, a club for tall people, appears several times in her 1959 and 1960 appointment books and notebooks, but apparently never results in a photograph; she does, however, photograph on a number of occasions the giant she first encounters at Hubert's.

115 Doon Arbus interview with Allan Arbus, February 17, 1972.

116 Doon Arbus interview with Amy Arbus, August 2002. Amy recalls that Israel had a Nikon Rangefinder (which Amy now owns), and that this is almost certainly the camera that Diane borrowed from him. In the letter, Diane adds, "...I am much too slow with yours, lining up those two images infuriates me, like I am fitting them for a pair of shoes before I take their picture."

117 Diane describes something of her camera dilemma to her brother as well. In an undated note to her Nemerov writes, "Fascinated with your camera problem; I'd never (of course) considered what a difference it might make. I hope you grow happily into the possibilities of the new one: is it a question of its vision rather than yours? Its handwriting? Frightening."

118 Diane Arbus typewritten letter to Marvin Israel, November 13, 1960.

119 Original typewritten letter in the Howard Nemerov Collection, Washington University Libraries, Department of Special Collections, St. Louis, Mo.

120 "They just raised the price at Hubert's...to 40¢ which made them all glow with pride and I said how worth it they were and they were. The man who ties himself in knots is there whom I had been thinking I should find because he is really a perfect eccentric...and there is a wry sword swallower who is the son of sword swallowers...and next week there will be some knife throwers and soon after an eight foot tall giant." Letter to Marvin Israel, circa 1960–61.

121 Diane Arbus appointment book, July 6, 1961.

122 Diane Arbus 1961 Notebook (No. 5).

123 Diane Arbus letter to Robert Benton and Harold Hayes about the Eccentrics project, circa November 1960.

124 *Ibid.*

125 *Ibid.*

126 Harold Hayes letter to Diane Arbus, February 16, 1961. The Harold Hayes Collection, Special Collections Department, Z. Smith Reynolds Library, Wake Forest University, Winston-Salem, N.C.

127 The date of this typewritten letter, in which she also refers to Moondog, is unclear.

128 The legendary blind beggar, Moondog, is among the people she considers for the Eccentrics project.

129 In her 1961 appointment book, Diane makes a note to herself that none of the six should be left out, and no text changes should be made without consulting her.

130 Harold Hayes letter to Diane Arbus, August 25, 1961.

131 Diane Arbus letter to Harold Hayes, August 28, 1961. The *Esquire* Collection, Spencer Museum of Art, The University of Kansas, Lawrence.

132 Diane Arbus letter to Doon Arbus, circa August 1961.

133 Diane Arbus 1961 Notebook (No. 7).

134 The first mention of a twins convention appears in capital letters on a page of its own in 1959 Notebook (No. 3).

135 *Diane Arbus*, p. 9

136 Technical notes about the wide angle Rolleiflex camera, and about the Mamiyaflex camera appear on separate pages in her 1961 appointment book in March.

137 Doon Arbus interview with Lisette Model, February 5, 1972.

138 There are instances of Diane using both Rolleiflex and Nikon cameras in photographing people as well. One example, Girl on a stoop with baby N.Y.C. 1962 exists in both formats. The one she printed was the 2¼.

[139] Diane Arbus letter to Lisette Model, September 25, 1962. Lisette Model Archives, National Gallery of Canada, Ottawa.

[140] The actual text of the note says, "...I cant remember what you said about doing amy in clothes for Rae..." This is a reference to Rae Crespin, a fashion editor at *Harper's Bazaar*.

[141] These photographs, taken on June 26, were published in "Bill Blass Designs for Little Ones," *Harper's Bazaar*, September 1962, pp. 162–163.

[142] The full text of the The Silver Spoon project proposal, as sent to Nancy White, in 1962 Notebook (No. 8): "Silver Spoon (The Children of Good Fortune). I don't want to photograph the most distinguished and dazzling people of our time; I want to photograph their children. To discover the thousand ways they inhabit their rare and marvelous habitats, like princess and pirate (at once) in a predicament as poignant as it is pretty. Call it (perhaps) the Silver Spoon."

[143] The full text of the proposed Winners project in 1962 Notebook (No. 8) includes the following: "I guess there are four ways to win; by virtue of a test, or by an attribute, or to be chosen out of a hat, or immaculately conceived by a press agent without any contest at all. Even the Pope is a winner."

[144] Diane Arbus 1962 Notebook (No. 8).

[145] This project was originally intended for *Harper's Bazaar*. It is listed as "Seers" on Arbus's 1962 Guggenheim application. Application, courtesy of the John Simon Guggenheim Foundation. Ultimately, the pictures by Arbus appeared in *Glamour*, in January and October 1964, edited by Marguerite Lamkin for her column "What's New: The Witch Predicts." Elisabeth Sussman interview with Marguerite Lamkin Litman, April 2, 2002.

[146] Diane Arbus letter to Doon Arbus, summer 1960.

[147] In an interview with Doon Arbus on February 18, 1972, Bunny Sellers describes her first meeting with Diane Arbus, which took place around 1959.

[148] Bunny Sellers makes notes about fortune-tellers in Diane's 1962 Notebook (No. 10). The piece on fortune-tellers is published in Marguerite Lamkin's column "What's New: The Witch Predicts," in *Glamour*. Madame Sandra and Dr. George Darios are included on pp. 66–69 in the January 1964 issue, and Leslie Eliot and Doris Fulton are included in the October 1964

issue. The uncredited text accompanying the pictures is written by Lamkin, based on Diane's captions.

[149] Doon Arbus interview with Bunny Sellers, February 18, 1972.

[150] Diane Arbus letter to Lisette Model, September 25, 1962. Lisette Model Archives, National Gallery of Canada, Ottawa.

[151] Diane meets Lee Friedlander through Marvin Israel. In the early 1960s, Friedlander knew Israel when the latter was art director of *Seventeen* (1957–58). Diane knew Mary and Robert Frank from the mid-1950s. Mary Frank's name appears in her appointment books from 1959 through 1970. Elisabeth Sussman interviews with Lee Friedlander (March 6, 2002), Mary Frank (January 14, 2002), Allan Arbus (October 17, 2000).

[152] Diane Arbus letter to Lisette Model, September 25, 1962. Lisette Model Archives, National Gallery of Canada, Ottawa.

[153] In a letter dated October 30, 1962, Grace Mayer writes to Diane Arbus on behalf of Edward Steichen. She thanks Arbus for submitting a portfolio and the issue of *Infinity* containing her work. Mayer writes, "He finds your photographs 'good,' and feels that the *Infinity* piece did not do justice to your work, as you get the feeling of surrealism in the other subjects too. He has confidence in you, your undertaking and your ability to carry it out, and is, 'all for you on the strength of your portfolio.'" She concludes by saying he "will be glad to act as one of your sponsors..." Letter in Diane Arbus file, The Museum of Modern Art, New York.

[154] In the March 1962 issue of *Harper's Bazaar*, under the title "The Unposed Portrait," Israel publishes a group of Walker Evans photographs taken with a hidden camera while riding the New York City subways in 1938, 1940, and 1941. Walker Evans. Introduction by James Agee. *Many Are Called* (Boston: Houghton Mifflin Co., and Cambridge: The Riverside Press, 1966).

[155] Diane Arbus typewritten letter to Walker Evans. Walker Evans Archive, The Metropolitan Museum of Art, 1994. The date of receipt is marked on the letter, presumably by Evans, as 9/20/62. It reads as follows: "Dear WE, My grandmother was rather vulgar but superb, like a contemporary witch, and I often see something of her walking down Fifth Ave. although she is dead. In fact I am a bit enamored of vulgarity, excepting my own of course. When you asked about my literary tastes I forgot Celine...Meanwhile if you have news of Helen Levitt {the photographer} and she is anywhere near would you tell me?"

[156] Diane Arbus typewritten letter to Walker Evans, circa October 1962, with Guggenheim project proposal enclosed, "...for your criticism or approval." Walker Evans Archive, The Metropolitan Museum of Art, 1994.

[157] The earliest project that she lists is "children's games," from 1958; projects listed for 1959 are "movie theater interiors," "Vertical Journey (for *Esquire*)," and, "secret photos of steam bathers." She also lists more recent projects, such as "Female Impersonators," 1959–62; "photographs at the beach," 1959–61; and "sideshow," 1959–61. Application from the Archives of the John Simon Guggenheim Foundation and letter to Elisabeth Sussman from G. Thomas Tanselle, Vice-President, May 31, 2000.

[158] Included in her Guggenheim application, as required, is a list of people who will provide references (Guggenheim Fellows denoted by asterisk): "Richard Avedon, photographer; Leonard Bernstein, composer and conductor; Alexey Brodovitch, photographer; Victor D'Amico, Director of Education, The Museum of Modern Art; *Walker Evans, photographer; *James T. Farrell, writer; *Robert Frank, photographer; *Lee Friedlander, photographer; Marvin Israel, Art Director, *Harper's Bazaar*; *Helen Levitt, photographer; Lisette Model, photographer; Howard Nemerov (my brother) poet, novelist; James Thrall Soby, critic, Vice President and Trustee, The Museum of Modern Art." No letters were received from Brodovitch, Farrell, or Bernstein. Walker Evans did not write but spoke with Henry Allen Moe, chief executive of the Guggenheim Foundation at that time. Application from the Archives of the John Simon Guggenheim Foundation and letter to Elisabeth Sussman from G. Thomas Tanselle, Vice-President, May 31, 2000.

[159] The letter itself, in the Archives, Department of Photography, The Museum of Modern Art, has a handwritten note on it, probably written by John Szarkowski to his secretary, Pat Walker: "Pat: won't be back before October 15 deadline," and at the bottom of the page, in another hand, "telephoned September 28 to say not possible."

[160] Doon Arbus interview with John Szarkowski, February 11, 1972. Doon Arbus, "Diane Arbus, Photographer," *Ms.*, November 1972. Szarkowski's name appears in the 1961 appointment book on October 24, suggesting their meeting took place on that day.

[161] Szarkowski showed her Sander's book *Antlitz der Zeit* (*Face of Our Time*, 1929) and possibly *Deutschenspiegel* (*Mirror of Germans*, 1962).

[162] Pat Walker, John Szarkowski's secretary, responds on January 15, 1963, with the information Diane has requested. Diane Arbus file, The Museum of Modern Art.

[163] In the postcard she adds: "If what had to be done is still a problem I will try to help." The last line is probably a reference to her helping Model to write it.

[164] In light of the date of Model's recommendation, it appears that she did not take Diane up on the offer to help write the recommendation. Lisette Model Archives, National Gallery of Canada, Ottawa.

[165] See note 142 for complete text of Silver Spoon project from 1962 Notebook (No. 8).

[166] Letter to Paul Salstrom, Medical Center for Federal Prisoners, Springfield, Mo., January 9, 1963. Salstrom was one of the peace movement marchers Arbus had photographed for Thomas B. Morgan's "Doom and Passion Along Rte. 45" that appeared in *Esquire* in November 1962. Salstrom had written the leaflet about nonviolence that the marchers carried with them on their march from Hanover, N.H., to Washington, D.C. Salstrom was serving three years in prison for refusing to register for the draft. Elisabeth Sussman interview with Paul Salstrom, April 23, 2002. Collection of Paul Salstrom.

[167] Although the photograph of Penelope Tree was taken in 1963, the comment was made earlier, in 1962 Notebook (No. 8).

[168] Between 1962 and 1964 Arbus completes at least twenty-five assignments for magazines, including *Harper's Bazaar, Show, Esquire, Glamour*, and *The Saturday Evening Post*. For a more complete list and a discussion of Arbus's commercial activity, see *Diane Arbus: Magazine Work*.

[169] The Junior Interstate Ballroom Dance Championships take place in Yonkers, N.Y., on February 17, and a week later she photographs the winning couple. "Make sure children have trophies and formal clothes," she writes in her 1963 appointment book on February 25. Diane continues to work on the rituals and contests of everyday life as proposed in her Guggenheim fellowship application. Between January and October, she attends contests for "Mother of the Year," "Woman of the World," "Freckles," "spaghetti eating," and "Miss Lo-Cal."

[170] Doon Arbus conversation with Richard Avedon, June 2003.

[171] Diane Arbus letter to Henry Allen Moe, April 18, 1963, and his April 22, 1963, reply.

172 Diane Arbus postcard to Walker Evans, circa April 1963. Walker Evans Archive, The Metropolitan Museum of Art, 1994. They appear to have remained in touch prior to this postcard. In another postcard to Walker Evans, circa February 1963, Diane writes, "Dear Walker, On Sunday on the radio (WRVR-FM 106.7, 8:30 P.M) they are playing the tape of J. Baldwin's appearance at the Y. I don't think the curious mass masochism of the audience will be audible but he will be and he is important and I remember one very magnificent thing he said about the sonnets of Shakespeare..."

173 Diane Arbus postcard to Lisette Model, April 22, 1962. Lisette Model Archives, National Gallery of Canada, Ottawa.

174 In 1965, Howard Nemerov wrote in his memoir, *Journal of the Fictive Life*, "Here is a poem I wrote months before my father's death, on first seeing him in the hospital and learning that he was seriously ill:

GROWING A GHOST

From the time he knew / He groomed his hair / In a gray pompadour / And made grim his smile / fitly to represent / all that would be meant / When he arrived by growing / To that great dignity / Nondenominational / But solemn all the same / And

showing forth a force.

the stone jaw / the sharp nose / the closed lids

dreaming / nightmares for all / who looked their last / looking his best / the ancestral look / in evening clothes / to go underground / and have at last / in his folded hands / the peace of the world

the red clay

As my sister wrote me toward the end, 'he looks more like everyman than himself.'" Howard Nemerov, *Journal of the Fictive Life*, pp. 171–172.

175 Studs Terkel radio interview with Diane Arbus, WFMT Chicago, 1968.

176 Diane liked Vanderzee's memorial photographs of the dead where he manipulated the image to show the living person rising from the coffin. Szarkowski visited Vanderzee's studio after Diane told him about the photographer. John Szarkowski, e-mail to Elisabeth Sussman, April 17, 2002.

177 In the same 1963 Notebook (No. 11), under the heading "Mr. Vanderzee," Diane transcribes this quote: "If you stay in one place you become extinct."

178 Sunshine Park is called Sunrise Haven in "Notes on the Nudist Camp," unpublished, 1965; later published in *Diane Arbus: Magazine Work*, pp. 68–69.

179 *Diane Arbus*, pp. 4–5.

180 Other photos Diane makes at the nudist camp at this time are A young waitress at a nudist camp, N.J. 1963; Husband and wife with shoes on in their cabin at a nudist camp, N.J. 1963; and Nudist man and his dog in a trailer, N.J. 1963.

181 Although "Notes on the Nudist Camp" is written in 1965 in connection with an assignment for *Esquire*, it is largely based on notes from 1963 Notebook (No. 13). In 1965, she goes to a camp in Pennsylvania, but the *Esquire* assignment is never published. The complete article appears in *Diane Arbus: Magazine Work*, pp. 68–69.

182 *Ibid.*

183 Howard Nemerov was writer in residence at Hollins College in 1962–63, and Sudie Victor was a student of his in her senior year. In 1963 he received a one-year appointment as Poetry Consultant at the Library of Congress.

184 *Harper's Bazaar*, April 1964, pp. 162–167. Five portraits of trendsetters Reed Buchanan, Mia Villiers-Farrow, Patricia Merle Silver, Maria Christine Drew, Cynthia Boves Taylor.

185 *Harper's Bazaar*, April 1964, pp. 142–145. Text by Geri Trotta.

186 Diane Arbus appointment book, January 13, 1964.

187 Clarence J. Laughlin's name first shows up in Diane's 1962 appointment book in January, when she appears to have planned to call him and get his address in New Orleans. On April 15, 1962, she sends him the following postcard, apparently in response to his suggestion that they trade prints, and alluding to her difficulty changing from the Nikon to the Rolleiflex: "Dear Clarence, thanks for yr letter. Yes I wd like to exchange prints but may I wait a few months. I have been having serious growing pains changing cameras and relearning to photograph and progress has been so terrible slow that I hate to go back and print old things. So wd you wait until I know more where I am. Yes, I know which ones I want but I don't want to ask you for them yet. Thanks Clarence. I hope you are well. Diane." Original postcard in the Clarence Laughlin Archive, The Historic New Orleans Collection, New Orleans, La.

[188] Lee Friedlander discovered Bellocq's glass plate negatives in the late 1950s in New Orleans when they were in the possession of Larry Borenstein, who, with Al Rose (also from New Orleans), had bought the negatives after Bellocq's death. Friedlander told Arbus about Bellocq. Elisabeth Sussman interview with Lee Friedlander, December 2002. In her 1964 Notebook (No. 14), Diane attached Borenstein's card and copied Al Rose's address. She later acquired from Friedlander several of his prints of Bellocq's work.

[189] "Blaze Starr in Nighttown," *Esquire*, July 1964. Text by Thomas B. Morgan, photographs by Diane Arbus, pp. 58–62. On this trip, or on a separate one a few weeks later, also for *Esquire*, Diane photographs the atheist Madalyn Murray, a portrait published with an article by Bynum Shaw, "Nevertheless, God Probably Loves Mrs. Murray..." *Esquire*, October 1964, pp. 110–112, 168–171.

[190] Doon Arbus interview with Bunny Sellers, February 18, 1972.

[191] Diane Arbus typewritten letter to Marvin Israel, circa 1960.

[192] *Diane Arbus: Magazine Work*, pp. 48–53. In one of Diane's typewritten drafts of the text about the Bishop, she has included her own editor's note, which reads as follows, "The greatest stars of the human drama have always been the people who saw what no one else could see. Visionaries are by their very nature unbelievable... we (the editors) find ourselves unable to believe what the Bishop believes. But we ask your openmindedness, for if the Bishop can be believed this will indeed be a Holy Christmas."

[193] Dan Talbot claims to have been helpful in putting Diane in touch with Mae West. Talbot ran the New Yorker Theater, an art movie theater at W. 88th St. and Broadway.

[194] "Mae West: Emotion in Motion," *Show*, January 1965, pp. 42–45.

[195] Elisabeth Sussman interview with Robert Brown, April 2000. Robert Brown related that Diane went to see West for two days, and that at the end of the second day West gave her a hundred-dollar bill as a tip.

[196] "Mae West: Emotion in Motion," *Show*, January 1965, pp. 42–45.

[197] The opening spread includes a black-and-white portrait, and the next spread has two photographs, one of which is in color, of West in bed with her pet monkey.

[198] The title of the text as published in *Show*, "Mae West: Emotion in Motion," comes from the following West quote: "Sex is an emotion in motion." A variant photograph was also published in 1967 accompanying an article by Helen Lawrenson, "Mirror, Mirror on the Ceiling, How'm I Doin?" *Esquire*, July 1967, pp. 72–74, 113–114.

[199] Diane met Ruth St. Denis at a party with Stewart Stern. Elisabeth Sussman interview with Stewart Stern, February 2, 2001.

[200] Diane Arbus 1964 Notebook (No. 18).

[201] Diane comments in the same letter, "Partly I feel good like you do because it seems one thing is finished and what is next is vague enough to be at its most promising. If you see Bunny and Robert, ask them to show you the text of the Bishop..."

[202] Puerto Rican housewife, N.Y.C. 1963, and Sharon Goldberg, N.Y.C. 1965, are the only two photos of this series Diane actually prints.

[203] Diane Arbus postcard to Doon Arbus, August 5, 1960. She is reporting on Carlotta's car accident after she has been "quite decently sewed together."

[204] Diane Arbus 1964 Notebook (No. 15).

[205] Diane photographs the Red Shield Senior Citizens Club and its most renowned member, Mother Brown (born 1852) who turns 112 years old on November 17. In her 1964 Notebook (No. 15) she records a comment by one of the club members about Mother Brown: "It's terrible to live in the shadow of someone 112."

[206] Marguerite Lamkin, who is introduced to Avedon by her friend Marvin Israel, works on the book, arranging most of the sittings.

[207] In spite of John Szarkowski's enthusiasm for The Junior Interstate Ballroom Dance Champions, Yonkers, N.Y. 1963, this picture is not acquired by MoMA until 1969. Photography Department, The Museum of Modern Art.

[208] Diane Arbus artist file, The Museum of Modern Art.

[209] Diane Arbus 1959–1960 Notebook (No. 3). It is not clear what magazine she proposed this idea to but the format of it in the notebook suggests it was intended as such.

[210] Diane Arbus 1965 Notebook (No. 21) contains both quotes and a great deal more.

[211] The published article, "Fashion Independents: On Marriage," with text by Geri Trotta (*Harper's Bazaar*, May 1965, pp. 151–161, 184), includes portraits of the following nine couples: Paul Lester and Ingeborg Wiener; Armando and Georgiana Orsini; Frederick and Isabel Eberstadt; John Gruen and Jane Wilson; Herbert and Eliette Von Karajan; Gilbert and Kitty Miller; Mr. and Mrs. Howard Oxenberg; Otto Preminger and Hope Bryce. Other names appearing in this context on the March 10th page of her 1965 appointment book are the Clay Felkers, the Marcel Duchamps, the Wyatt Coopers, Theodorocropolis, Toppings, Guests, etc.

[212] "Familial Colloquies," *Esquire*, July 1965, pp. 54–57. Apparently somewhat later she also photographed Susan Sontag and her son, David, possibly for this project, but for whatever reason the photograph was never published. There is reason to think that in a few cases she attempted to make the separate assignments overlap. Her fascination with Jayne Mansfield appears to have preceded—and perhaps given rise to—"Familial Colloquies." Jayne Mansfield's married name (Cimber Ottaviano) appears in one of the lists for *Harper's Bazaar*'s "On Marriage" assignment.

[213] The only other assignment she published in 1965 appears in the "Fashion Independents" feature in *Harper's Bazaar*, July, pp. 90–93, the same month as *Esquire*'s "Familial Colloquies." It consists of four photographs of the Philadelphia socialite Mrs. T. Charlton Henry, with a text by Geri Trotta. On April 14, where Mrs. Henry's name appears, there is also a sentence that reads like a quote from her: "I like everything unrefined."

[214] She begins to visit Kerista in April. Kerista was founded in 1956 by John Presmont, a businessman turned prophet. (See John Gruen, *The New Bohemian*, New Jersey: A Cappella Books, 1990, pp. 52–60). She also attends a motorcycle rally in Watkins Glen, Laconia, N.H., in June.

[215] "It was really remarkable. And I found it very scary. I mean I could become a nudist, I could become a million things. But I could never become that, whatever all those people were. There were days I just couldn't work there and then there were days I could. And then, having done it a little, I could do it more..." *Diane Arbus*, p. 12.

[216] *Ibid*. This description of her work in Washington Square is one she gave in her master class in 1971.

[217] The texts, sometimes two or three copies of each —original and carbons—are in a yellow spring lock binder. The binder itself is similar to the blue one she later keeps in her darkroom that contains formulae and technical data.

[218] Unpublished typewritten text dated September 20, 1965. The names Jamie and Dexter appear on the July 5 page of her 1965 appointment book, suggesting this may be the day the events described occurred.

[219] *Ibid*.

[220] She may not have been the first of her era to employ the black borders, but we have been unable to determine who if anyone did it before her. For a complete discussion of this and various other Diane Arbus printing methods, see, Neil Selkirk, "In the Darkroom," *Diane Arbus Revelations*, pp. 267–275.

[221] On July 17, in her appointment book, she makes note of an Eastern Sunbathing Association convention. She had been visiting Sunnyrest off and on throughout July.

[222] The letter begins, "Dear John, everything is so superb and breathtaking I am creeping forward on my belly like they do in war movies. I have a foot in several worlds and I hope I can do what there is to do." She refers to the Elliot Erwitt Show as "absorbing and instructive" and ends with "my fingers are crossed." Diane Arbus artist file, The Museum of Modern Art.

[223] Letter from Harold Hayes, August 9, 1965. The *Esquire* Collection, Spencer Museum of Art, University of Kansas, Lawrence. Puerto Rican housewife, N.Y.C. 1963, is one of the photos related to the project.

[224] Israel continues to teach at Parsons School of Design. One of his students, Michael Flanagan, works for a time as Allan Arbus's assistant and recalls processing Diane's negatives and being with her on occasion in the darkroom when she was printing. Flanagan believes that she was using Agfa Portriga paper at this point— which it appears she had been doing for at least a year or two. Elisabeth Sussman interview with Michael Flanagan, May 2, 2002.

[225] The exhibition takes place in October. The nudist camp picture of the married couple at home was subsequently retitled twice by Diane, first as Man and wife at home, nudist camp, N.J. 1963, then, Retired man and his wife at home at a nudist camp one morning, N.J. 1963. The photograph of the female impersonators was retitled Two female impersonators backstage, N.Y.C. 1961. Diane cites this exhibition as well as one earlier in the year, in March (*Invitational Exhibition, 10 American Photographers*) in her Guggenheim application, dated October 31, 1965, as the only two shows in which

her work appeared. Archives of the John Simon Guggenheim Foundation, New York.

[226] The show took place at the School of Fine Arts, University of Wisconsin, Milwaukee, in March 1965. Ten photographers each chose a younger photographer. Lisette Model chose Diane, who was represented by five works. Archives of the John Simon Guggenheim Foundation, New York.

[227] *Ibid.*

[228] *Ibid.* In a letter to Gordon Ray at the Guggenheim Foundation dated November 7, 1965, she writes, "Months ago you wrote me in the customary way asking if I knew any people who ought to be candidates for fellowships and at the time it didn't seem to me that I did. I'd like to correct that oversight. Mary Frank is a sculptor of tremendous passion and constancy. I am not a chauvinist about womanhood, but her imagery is so authentically feminine that I look at it with a feeling like recognition. I think she is strong and delicate enough to last and not many women are. She has applied for a fellowship this year. Would you add my name to the list of those who vouch for her?" The year before, in a letter to Ray dated September 18, 1964, she had recommended Lisette Model and Marvin Israel for fellowships, "Lisette Model...is a photographer whose work is so profound, so amazing and subtle, that a whole generation of photographers is indebted to her...I hope she can be persuaded to apply or that some of the many people who believe in her could apply for her because her qualifications exceed everybody's. And Marvin Israel is a painter dedicated and daring enough to reward any trust." As indicated in Ray's response, Diane had recommended Israel the year before also but he had never applied.

[229] See Howard Nemerov, *Journal of the Fictive Life*, p. 146.

[230] Original letter in the Howard Nemerov Collection, Washington University Libraries, Department of Special Collections, St. Louis, Mo.

[231] Howard Nemerov, *Journal of the Fictive Life*, p. 80. He also acknowledges several pages later (p. 84) that his indictment of photography as opposed to writing is quite possibly a sophisticated version of what he and Diane used to do to one another as children, blaming each other and getting each other punished. Another example of Nemerov's preoccupation with subjects also of interest to Diane (the relationship of the image to the thing itself, issues of authenticity and fraudulence) is evident in the final stanza of Nemerov's poem "To Clio, Muse of History: On learning that the Etruscan Warrior in The Metropolitan Museum of Art is proved a modern forgery": (*The Next Room of the Dream*, Chicago: University of Chicago Press, 1962)

For I remember how / We children stared, learning from him / Unspeakable things about war / that weren't in the books; / And how the Museum store offered for sale / His photographic reproductions in full color / With the ancient genitals blacked out.

[232] In the letter to Howard Nemerov about *Journal of the Fictive Life*, she invites him to stay with her at Charles Street when he is in town. In her 1965 appointment book, a poetry reading of Howard's is noted on November 15.

[233] *Ibid.* A subsequent letter to Nemerov, probably written around the end of November, refers to Sudie Victor's imminent wedding to Michael Trazoff, which is to take place at Charles Street on December 8.

[234] *Diane Arbus: Magazine Work*, pp. 80–81.

[235] *Ibid.*

[236] *Ibid.*

[237] Letter from G. Thomas Tanselle to Elisabeth Sussman, September 14, 2000, "I have now looked into Diane Arbus's file to see whether the titles of the photographs she submitted with her two successful applications are present. We have no lists of titles; in each case, there is just a receipt signed by her, in which she acknowledges that the material submitted has been returned to her. The one in 1963 says, '2 Magazines, 76 Photographs.'" The list of accomplishments submitted with her application for the Guggenheim Fellowship may be found in the Archive, John Simon Guggenheim Memorial Foundation.

The April 1966 issue of *camera* (the official organ of the International Federation of Photographic Art) is primarily devoted to essays and a photographic portfolio of the Guggenheim Fellows in photography 1937–65. The issue coincides with an exhibition at the Philadelphia College of Art of the work produced by the Guggenheim Fellows of this period. It includes A widow in her bedroom, N.Y.C. 1963 and Teenage couple on Hudson Street, N.Y.C. 1963.

[238] Diane Arbus appointment book, February 8, 1966.

[239] Archive, John Simon Guggenheim Memorial Foundation.

[240] According to her appointment book entry, on January 6, 1966, she flies from La Guardia to Logan Airport on

assignment for *Esquire* to photograph Brenda Frazier (Mrs. Chatfield Taylor), the 1938 debutante of the year, in her home in Medfield, Massachusetts. The portrait appears in an article by Bernard Weinraub, "Girl of the Year, 1938," *Esquire*, July 1966, pp. 72–77.

[241] "James Brown Is Out of Sight," *New York*, Sunday magazine of the *Herald Tribune*, March 20, 1966, pp. 14–24, text by Doon Arbus.

[242] Elisabeth Sussman interview with Ruth Ansel, February 15, 2002.

[243] Elisabeth Sussman telephone interview, Lucas Samaras, New York City, February 18, 2002. Visiting Lucas Samaras, she saw his collection of antique French pornographic photography, which he subsequently brought to an Avedon workshop.

[244] "Not to Be Missed: The American Art Scene," *Harper's Bazaar*, July 1966, pp. 80–85, text by Geri Trotta. A later portrait of Ad Reinhardt appears in "Ad Reinhardt, or the Artist as Artist," *Harper's Bazaar*, November 1966, pp. 176–177, text by Annette Michelson.

[245] The article for *New York* was never completed. The dates and details of the Liddy raid vary in different accounts of the event. Leary was charged for possession of illegal drugs but the case was dropped on technicalities. Arbus gave a photograph she had taken at the Millbrook estate of members of The League for Spiritual Discovery, adding this inscription: "Dear Ralph {Metzner}. I hope these are of some use. Regards to tim and susan and rosemary and Eve and all. And you. Diane." The photograph, also inscribed "to Ro. Love Timothy, 7-22-95." This photograph is now in the collection of the San Francisco Museum of Modern Art.

[246] Margaret Sanger Papers Project, Newsletter #22, Fall 1999.

[247] Couple under a paper lantern, N.Y.C. 1966, Girl sitting in bed with her boyfriend, N.Y.C. 1966, Couple in bed, N.Y.C. 1966.

[248] Letter from Ruth Ansel to Elisabeth Sussman, February 15, 2002.

[249] Several years later, discussing the topic of sex and photography with her master class, she refers to "the greatest sex scene I've ever seen in my whole life." It is in a film called *Hunger*, based on the novel by Knut Hamsun. "The hero...looks through...a little crack in a door...and he sees his landlady who is a middle aged lady being fucked by her husband I guess...They've got their clothes on, except her skirt's up and his pants are open...there's like one movement you see...its like you never saw it before it's so accurate. It's really beautiful and there's nothing pretty about it...It's like you're there." *Authenticity* is the word she uses in her master class in 1971 in speaking of pornographic pictures and of the work of Tilo Kiehl.

[250] Lyon and Davidson, who had photographed the civil rights movement in the South, were to be included (with Lee Friedlander, Duane Michals, and Garry Winogrand) in a December 1966 show, *Toward a Social Landscape*, at the George Eastman House, Rochester, N.Y. Elisabeth Sussman interview with Bruce Davidson, April 22, 2002; Elisabeth Sussman interview with Danny Lyon, May 7, 2002.

[251] Colin Westerbeck and Joel Meyerowitz, *Bystander: A History of Street Photography* (Boston: Bulfinch Press, Little Brown & Co., 1994), pp. 373–88.

[252] From the wall label for the exhibition *New Documents*, curated by John Szarkowski, The Museum of Modern Art, February 28–May 7, 1967.

[253] From a text by John Szarkowski sent by him on February 15, 1973, to Shoji Yamagishi at *Camera Mainichi, The Mainichi Newspapers*, Tokyo. Archive, The Museum of Modern Art. The text was presumably written to be published in connection with the posthumous Diane Arbus retrospective at Seibu Museum in Tokyo, organized by Yamagishi and curated by Doon Arbus and Marvin Israel. This exhibition, which subsequently toured throughout Europe, Australia, and New Zealand, took place at the same time that The Museum of Modern Art retrospective began touring the United States and Canada.

[254] Archive, John Simon Guggenheim Memorial Foundation. Listed in her appointment book on June 13 are the following names of those who will require gamma globulin shots: "Amy, Doon, Allan, m[arvin]."

[255] Letter from Diane Arbus to James Mathias, July 5, 1966. Archive, John Simon Guggenheim Memorial Foundation.

[256] Note from James Mathias to Diane Arbus, July 6, 1966. Archive, John Simon Guggenheim Memorial Foundation.

[257] Letter from James Mathias to Diane Arbus, July 29, 1966. Archive, John Simon Guggenheim Memorial Foundation.

[258] Original letter is in the collection of Marilee and Stewart Stern.

259 Transcript of tape of master class at Westbeth.

260 Diane photographs the friend as well (Transvestite showing cleavage, N.Y.C. 1966).

261 As she further explained, "She lives always dressed as a woman and she whores as a woman. I would never think she was a man. I can't really see the man in her...I have gone into restaurants with her and every man in the place has turned around to look at her and made all sorts of hoots and whistles. And it was her, it wasn't me." *Diane Arbus*, pp. 13–14. The subject of this narrative is Vicki, and her friend's name is Jean. In one of Diane's notebooks (No. 26) she records a number of Vicki's observations about her life, including, "You make your own heaven and hell on earth."

262 Transcript of tape of master class at Westbeth.

263 Letter to Stewart Stern, circa 1967.

264 Postcard to John Szarkowski that begins, "Dear John, what a good time I had..."

265 In the *Newsweek* research report by Ann Ray Martin who interviewed Diane for the magazine's March 20, 1967, review of *New Documents*, the idea of making the large prints is credited to Szarkowski, "[Arbus] uses either a 35mm or a two and a quarter camera and prints the pictures at whatever size appeals to her based on the subject. For the exhibit she blew some of them up to life size at John Szarkowsky's [sic] suggestion." This is supported by the fact that a few of the Friedlander and Winogrand photographs in the exhibition are printed in a large format as well.

266 Postcard from Diane Arbus to John Szarkowski, circa 1966. Archive, The Museum of Modern Art.

267 A print she eventually gives him, presumably of his choosing, is Young girl at a nudist camp, Pa. 1965, 16x20. Collection of The Museum of Modern Art.

268 Doon Arbus interview with Amy Arbus, January 17, 2003. These fashion pictures appear to be the first work she has done in color since the photographs of Mae West for the 1965 issue of *Show*: "Mae West: Emotion in Motion," *Show*, January 1965, pp. 42–45, text by Diane Arbus. Her 1967 appointment book suggests she may have returned to New York by January 3. On that page and the next of the appointment book she has written: "print."

269 "Children in the Sun," *The New York Times Magazine Part II*, March 12, 1967, text by Patricia Peterson. Cover plus eleven color and black-and-white photographs.

270 Postcard from Diane Arbus to Paul Salstrom in Berkeley, Cal., March 7, 1967. Collection of Paul Salstrom.

271 The postcard from Diane Arbus to Howard Nemerov concludes, "Didn't know you'd be so willing to come so far so briefly (opening). Don't feel obliged but I am glad you think of it."

272 The checklist for *New Documents* includes: Burlesque comedienne, Atlantic City, N.J. 1963; Triplets, N.J. 1963; Girl with a cigar, Washington Square Park, N.Y.C. 1965; Young Negro boy, Washington Square Park, N.Y.C. 1965; Lady with swan sunglasses, nudist camp, Pa. 1965; Puerto Rican housewife, Jefferson St., N.Y.C. 1963; Young man on a sofa, E. 10th St. 1966; Transvestite at home, N.Y.C. 1966; Young man in curlers, W. 20th St., N.Y.C. 1966; Russian midget friends, 100th St., N.Y.C. 1963; Exasperated boy with toy hand grenade, N.Y.C. 1962; Transvestite with torn stocking, N.Y.C. 1966; Junior Interstate Ballroom Dance Champions, Yonkers, N.Y. 1963; Two female impersonators backstage, N.Y.C. 1961. Photography Department Archive, The Museum of Modern Art.

273 Doon Arbus interview with John Szarkowski, February 11, 1972.

274 *Ibid.*

275 *Ibid.*

276 *Newsweek* research report by Ann Ray Martin, March 6, 1967. Copy in Archives of The Estate of Diane Arbus. Excerpts used courtesy of Ann Ray Martin and *Newsweek*.

277 "An Interview with John Szarkowski," by Kelly Wise. *Views: The Journal of Photography in New England*, vol. 2, no. 4 (1982).

278 Doon Arbus interview with John Szarkowski, February 11, 1972.

279 List and letter from Diane Arbus to Pat Walker at The Museum of Modern Art, circa January 1967.

280 Diane Arbus 1967 appointment book, February 25 and February 26: "9 sasoon perm cut tips set $45; present for John, Bendel's party, etc."

281 Doon Arbus interview with John Szarkowski February 11, 1972. Szarkowski also recalls a present he received from the three photographers, although he suspects it was primarily Diane's doing. "I'm sure it was totally Diane's notion because it was the kind of thing a man wouldn't think of, certainly not Garry or Lee...They

bought me a bathrobe. Lovely, really very handsome, camel's hair bathrobe, elegantly embroidered across the back it said *New Documents* and across one sleeve it had [each of] their names...Like a fighter [would wear]. An elegant fighter."

[282] Elisabeth Sussman interview with Richard Avedon, August 22, 2002. Doon Arbus interview with Richard Avedon, February 14, 2003. Diane Arbus appointment book, February 28, 1967.

[283] Twins postcard to Stewart Stern from Diane Arbus, March 5, 1967. The photograph of Identical twins was exhibited that year at the Fogg Museum in a show called *The Portrait in Photography.*

[284] The rest of the postcard to the Meserveys reads: "Please Bob and Lyn get to The Museum of Modern Art between now and May 7 (30 of my photographs). It looks so good. Please call when you can come. Did you know my brother has moved to your town...Send me some word of you..."

[285] Postcard from Diane Arbus to Paul Salstrom in Berkeley, Cal., March 5, 1967. Collection of Paul Salstrom.

[286] "Showing It Like It Is," John Gruen's review published in *New York, The World Journal Tribune Sunday Magazine* with Teenage couple on Hudson Street, mistitled as 55th Street, says: "The New Document departs from the traditionally committed statement of the Thirties and Forties...in favor of observing, understanding and 'leaving alone' that which exists."

[287] Jacob Deschin, "People Seen as Curiosity," *The New York Times*, March 5, 1967. The Diane Arbus photograph, Miss Surf Beauty Contest, Venice Beach, Cal. 1962, accompanies the review.

[288] March 6 interview with Ann Ray Martin of *Newsweek.* A review by Martin, "Telling It as It Is," *Newsweek,* March 20, 1967, p. 110, reads in part, "She can capture the peacock pathos of a transvestite, the hygienic serenity of a nudist. She can evoke the scary sweetness of being a twin (or a triplet), the spotless sterility of a middle-class living room, the jaded grotesqueness of a burlesque queen, the togetherness of a trio of midgets."

She also receives a handwritten letter from Norman Mailer dated April 20, 1967, which reads: "Dear Diane, Saw your show. I think you're a remarkable photographer, splendid, extraordinary. My dear, you may select any word you wish in the Thesaurus. I'm so glad I saw it. All best to you, Norman Mailer."

[289] Postcard from Diane Arbus to Stewart Stern, circa March 1967, begins, "Dear S, Your letter was so heartwarming and rending and felt..."

[290] Letter from Diane Arbus to Peter Crookston, circa January 1969 (two years after Diane's first attempt to meet with Yaeger), proposing a story about Bunny Yaeger for *Nova,* a British magazine to which Crookston has recently been appointed editor in chief.

[291] Postcard from Diane Arbus to Marvin Israel from Florida, circa March 1967. Referring to the photograph on the front, "the beautiful Aqua Maids of the Cypress Garden ski show," she writes: "Dear m. This is a pornographic postcard for your class in case I do not return on time. It goes to show how clean it can be... Tomorrow I go to an authentic Italian Miami palazzo. And in the evening to the lady wrestlers..." Original postcard in the collection of Michael Flanagan.

[292] Postcard from Diane Arbus to Marvin Israel, circa March 1967. "The lady wrestlers were a little amazing, so emotional and vengeful and anguished. They plead and weep and sneer like hideous goddesses with orange and silver hair, but really they are housewives and mothers. They told me that there are midget women wrestlers who are 'adorable.' I was in Frank Sinatra's suite when he wasn't."

[293] Postcard from Diane Arbus to Ruth Ansel, circa March 1967. Original postcard in the collection of Ruth Ansel.

[294] Notes from Ruth Ansel to Elisabeth Sussman. February 15, 2002.

[295] *Ibid.*

[296] In April, two magazine assignments she began working on the previous year are published: a portrait of Thomas Hoving, director of The Metropolitan Museum of Art, for *Harper's Bazaar* ("Thomas Hoving Talks About the Metropolitan Museum," text by Geri Trotta, pp. 108, 112, 178–179) and a portrait for *Esquire* of a transsexual who became a woman in 1958 ("The Transsexual Operation," text by Tom Buckley, pp. 111–115, 205–208). In the latter instance, she did some research, read New York endocrinologist Dr. Harry Benjamin's book *The Transsexual Phenomenon* (New York: The Julian Press, 1966), and kept notes of her conversation with the subject of her portrait.

[297] Diane Arbus 1967 appointment book, April, May, and June.

[298] Postcard from Diane Arbus to Paul Salstrom at 591 Waller Street, San Francisco, circa June 1967.

[299] Letter from Diane Arbus to Howard Nemerov, circa fall 1967, following her trip to San Francisco. Topless dancer in her dressing room is the only picture she prints from this visit.

[300] Postcard from Diane Arbus to Paul Salstrom in Rock Island, Illinois, July 28, 1967. "Dear Paul, The drive was fun to Dallas and I got my money after a minimum of difficulty. which produced such an explosion out of me that the young man was rendered quite obliging and docile."

[301] Letter from Diane Arbus to Howard Nemerov, circa fall 1967, on the subject of the publication of his book *The Blue Swallows*, which has one of her photographs on the cover.

[302] Letter from Diane Arbus to Carlotta Marshall (Mrs. Louis Berger) in Holland, circa November 1967.

[303] Letter from Diane Arbus to Amy Arbus at camp, Tanager Lodge, summer 1967.

[304] "The New Life," *Harper's Bazaar*, February 1968, pp. 160–161, included a portrait of Anderson Cooper, infant son of Gloria Vanderbilt and Wyatt Cooper, and poems by Sandra Hochman. According to Diane's 1967 appointment book, this photograph appears to have been made on September 15 or 18.

[305] "God Is Back—He Says So Himself," text by L. M. Kit Carson, *Esquire*, February 1968, pp. 104–105, published with a portrait of Mel Lyman, author of *Autobiography of a World Saviour*.

[306] Diane made photographs at Camp Lakecrest during the summer of 1967 and her pictures were no doubt the inspiration for the subsequent publication by *The London Sunday Times Magazine* of an article by Hunter Davies entitled "Please Don't Feed Me," April 14, 1968, pp. 34–37, which included two of Diane's pictures.

[307] One of her assignments from *Cheetah*, a young people's magazine devoted primarily to music, is a portrait of the actor Michael J. Pollard, which is published along with the article "An Autobiography of Michael J. Pollard" by her daughter Doon, composed entirely of the actor's own words during a two-hour taped interview they did together. Pollard had a small but noticeable part in the 1967 movie *Bonnie and Clyde*, written by Robert Benton and his partner from *Esquire* days, David Newman, and directed by Arthur Penn.

[308] Elisabeth Sussman interview with Stewart Stern, February 2, 2001.

[309] In her appointment book on September 26 beneath the name John Berendt (an editor at *Esquire* since 1961), she has written the following names: Krishnamurti, Mel Lyman (author of *Autobiography of a World Saviour*), Meher Baba, and L. Ron Hubbard. She does eventually publish in *Esquire* a photograph of Mel Lyman, accompanying an article by L. M. Kit Carson ("God Is Back—He Says So Himself"). Her appointment book also reflects a number of Scientology sessions she attends in September and October in an effort to become "a clear."

[310] Letter from Diane Arbus to Howard Nemerov, circa October 1967 on the publication of his new book of poems, *The Blue Swallows*, on the cover of which a photograph of hers was used.

[311] The letter from Diane Arbus to Carlotta Marshall circa November 1967 continues with a description of Roxianne Lancelot, a woman Carlotta had met on the street several years earlier and had arranged for Diane to photograph. "Roxianne turned up about 30 lbs svelter as a result of going to one of those fancy NY drug doctors who make people feel so good they don't have to eat. She is living with a mysterious art dealer in a menage which seems to include his wife and assorted mistresses and housekeepers and a sense of perversion much wilder than it probably is. She asked me to photograph her there which is very much fun. She is still mean and ugly but has learned more about transforming herself into a sort of splendid creature, half beast half woman. She has shaved her eyebrows off and paints them on with consummate skill and about a thousand strokes like a giant exclamation mark in an awesome sunset. And apparently she wears sunglasses in bed. Thank you for finding her."

[312] Diane Arbus 1967 appointment book. There is a notation on October 24 that reads: "Peter Crookston... Room 403 Wentworth," and a second notation of his name for the evening of November 5. Also, see Peter Crookston, "Diane's all-devouring eye," *The Sunday Telegraph Review* (London), October 5, 1997.

[313] "Pauline Peters on People: Dr. Glassbury's Widow," *The London Sunday Times Magazine*, January 7, 1968, pp. 30–31. "Pauline Peters on People: How to Train a Derby Winner," *The London Sunday Times Magazine*, March 21, 1968, pp. 44–48. Both articles had texts written by Pauline Peters.

[314] It is not clear what photograph this refers to. It might be A widow in her bedroom or Woman in a turban or neither.

[315] Typewritten letter from Diane Arbus to Peter Crookston dated "Thurs Nov 30" with handwritten

annotations and numbered paragraphs. Paragraph 5 details her return visit to the diaper derby winner where she "photographed lots more...I will send those as soon as I can print them as well as the ones of Mrs. Henry (the rich lady)."

[316] Typewritten letter from Diane Arbus to Peter Crookston, dated by Diane "Dec 12 or so."

[317] Diane Arbus 1967 appointment book, December 14 and 15.

[318] Handwritten letter from Diane Arbus to Peter Crookston, December 19, 1967. The letter ends, "Happy New Year. Don't be sorry I'm not coming. When I see you I'll be glad. Uttermost thanks for your ingenuity, sweetness, zest, alacrity, generosity and smile..."

[319] Note from Diane Arbus to Peter Crookston, circa early January 1968, accompanying enclosed prints for Diaper Derby and two of Mrs. T. Charlton Henry, and supplying her new address.

[320] Note from Diane Arbus to Peter Crookston, circa late January 1968.

[321] In a note from Diane Arbus to Peter Crookston, circa March 1968, she writes, "Yes, too bad about the republicans." This note follows publication (January 7, 1968) of *The London Sunday Times Magazine* piece on Dr. Glassbury's widow ("I like Pauline's Mrs. G") and precedes the publication of the Diaper Derby story ("How to Train a Derby Winner," March 21, 1968).

[322] A 1968 notebook (No. 32) contains her customary record of the words of the subjects she encountered with Dr. Gatch on his rounds, as well as her account of some of his experiences.

[323] Studs Terkel radio interview with Diane Arbus, WFMT Chicago, 1968. The description she gives apparently reminds Terkel of the Walker Evans and James Agee collaboration, *Let Us Now Praise Famous Men* (New York: Houghton Mifflin, 1939). The title of the published piece in *Esquire*, "Let Us Now Praise Dr. Gatch," June 1968, pp. 108–111, 152–56, makes the same comparison. Three of Arbus's photographs were published with the article.

[324] The publication by *The London Sunday Times Magazine* of "Pauline Peters on People: Dr. Glassbury's Widow" (January 7, 1968, p. 37), and the 1963 photograph, A widow in her bedroom, prompts the widow herself to call twice, Diane reports in a May 18 letter to Crookston: "once in dismay and then again to say she found the story perfectly charming on

reflection and so did all her friends and to please send Pauline her particular regards and thanks." "Pauline Peters on People: How to Train a Derby Winner" (March 21, 1968, pp. 44–48) uses three photos. "Please Don't Feed Me," (April 14, 1968, pp. 34–37), with text by Hunter Davies, uses two photos. Apparently she is unhappy with these pictures and asks Crookston in advance not to give her a credit. In a typewritten letter to Peter Crookston circa May 1968 she says after seeing the piece, "I think the fat girl looks nice which just shows how unreliable I am."

[325] When *New York* became an independent weekly, Clay Felker remained the editor. Other founding staff members included Milton Glaser as art director and Gloria Steinem as contributing editor.

[326] Typewritten letter from Diane Arbus to Peter Crookston, circa May 1968. "La Dolce Viva," *New York*, April 29, 1968, pp. 36–41. Two portraits of Viva were published with the article.

[327] Dr. Frederick Wertham was a New York psychiatrist known for leading a campaign about the bad effects of comic and horror stories on children. His books *A Sign for Cain: An Exploration in Human Violence* (New York: Macmillan, 1966) and *Dark Legend: A Study in Murder* (Garden City, N.Y.: Doubleday, 1941) were in Arbus's library.

[328] Dr. Frederick Wertham's phone number appears on the May 22 page of her appointment book "after 3 Wertham," along with the titles of two of his books.

[329] In another letter a week or so later, she notes in a postscript, "The jewish giant is in calif having left his parents behind in ny for the present so forget that image I conjured up unless I can resurrect the old photograph." She does in fact return to this in 1970.

[330] The same pair of postcards to Peter Crookston include other suggestions as well. "There are also frequently those stories in the Daily News about the largest family and an association who pick the mother of the yr. They meet before Mother's Day [May 12] so that is over but I can call them to find out who the mother of the yr is. And what her family is like. Usually she is someone fantastically self-sacrificing but might be geographically difficult...I think I am supposed to work on some poverty photographs for an agency that is advertising poverty for the city. (!) The slogan is 'Give A Damn.'"

[331] On April 12 she calls the woman and eventually they make arrangements. She visits the family on June 16.

332 Typewritten letter from Diane Arbus to Peter Crookston, circa June 1968. On July 4, she writes Crookston, "I photographed the family in Westchester once and I must go back I think but they were fun and in August they will let me photograph at a party they are giving I will show you what I got when you come." The photograph she refers to having taken on June 16 is the photograph she eventually prints after all.

333 *Ibid.* Her mother and her mother's new husband, Phillip Rosenberg, were married on June 24, 1968. They were divorced within about a year.

334 Typewritten letter from Diane Arbus to Peter Crookston, circa June 1968.

335 This may be a reference to Mary Stevens Baird, who does eventually help her secure permission to photograph in some New Jersey institutions.

336 Although it is clear she had conversations with several publishers over the years, including those she considered adding to the MoMA invitation list for *New Documents*, there isn't any information as to what publisher she is referring to in this instance.

337 Typewritten letter from Diane Arbus to Peter Crookston, May 18, 1968.

338 Typewritten letter from Diane Arbus to Peter Crookston, circa June 1968.

339 Although apparently written in the same month, this letter is different than the one previously cited.

340 Typewritten letter from Diane Arbus to Peter Crookston, dated July 4. Most of the first page of the letter is devoted to ideas, including the average American family, family week at the Concord Hotel in upstate New York ("...an extraordinary vulgar place with indoor iceskating rink and things like revolving dance floor and more food than you have ever believed in."), and her progress, or lack of it, with the the generations of women, and the Mother of the Year ("...a dud..."), and her attempts to trace sets of twins who married twins.

341 Typewritten letter from Diane Arbus to Amy Arbus, circa July 1968.

342 Handwritten letter from Diane Arbus to Amy Arbus, circa July 1968.

343 Letter from Diane Arbus to Carlotta Marshall, dated by her "Aug 4 or 5," 1968.

344 *Ibid.*

345 Letter from Diane Arbus to Amy Arbus, August 8, 1968.

346 That same day Allan goes to the apartment to prepare things for her departure from the hospital and notices that Ishmael—the seven-year-old family cat and an offspring of Marvin's cat, Mouse—is behaving strangely and Allan takes Ishmael to the veterinarian. Apparently he was suffering from an incurable disease and died the next night.

347 Handwritten letter from Diane Arbus to Amy Arbus, August 8, 1968.

348 Four-page handwritten letter from Diane Arbus to Marvin Israel, circa mid-August 1968. Rene d'Harnoncourt died on August 13, 1968.

349 Letter from Diane Arbus to Stewart Stern, circa August 1968. Toward the end of the letter she remarks, "The hospital was wonderful. I learned Not to photograph and in the marvelous middles of the night walking the hospital corridors like a scene on TV I was both lost and found."

350 Typewritten letter from Diane Arbus to Carlotta Marshall, circa late August 1968.

351 Judging by her appointment book, the first class takes place on Friday, September 13, between 9 and noon.

352 Typewritten letter from Diane Arbus to Carlotta Marshall, circa October 1968, that begins, "I absolutely cannot bear to make you wait and I see it is a frustration for me not to answer everything you asked about in your letters."

353 The possibility of this job actually taking place persists for months and she meets with the producer, anticipating calls that are promised but are not made, followed by the unexpected arrival of the script. She remains ambivalent about the prospect throughout this period.

354 Crookston himself dates this letter—which is primarily devoted to information on the Brooklyn family—as "midsummer 1968," which may be correct although the letter also contains references to the *Catch-22* movie offer ("I don't know about the movie yet. I am to meet with the producer next week. He is rather fun but I have the oddest feeling I will blow the whole thing probably out of some deep snobbery which is quite uncalled for under the circumstances..."). She also mentions her efforts to locate the sets of double twins. ("There is an odd tidbit about these twins who marry

twins. One set live in identical houses with identical furniture but they are in missouri or somewhere... The book in which I found all this is called Twins and Super Twins by Amram Scheinfeld, J.P. Lippincott pub.") Most of this suggests that the letter was probably written in the fall.

[355] Probably on June 16.

[356] Letter to Carlotta Marshall, October 10, 1968, about photographing Mrs. Martin Luther King on October 2. The picture is published in "On a Photograph of Mrs. Martin Luther King at the Funeral," *Harper's Bazaar*, December 1968, pp. 106–107.

[357] Letter from Diane Arbus to Carlotta Marshall, circa November 1968. "I am supposed to do Agnew and McCarthy for *Esquire*." The Agnew sitting was never arranged. In a letter to Peter Crookston dated November 13, 1968, she writes, "*Esquire* hasn't been able to arrange it with Agnew in time for their deadline so as of yesterday they decided to use a caricature which I think (but didn't exactly say it like that because it seemed a bit sour grapes) looks awful since he IS a caricature and its sort of a vulgar looking one so you tend to assume it can't be true." The McCarthy photograph was not published. The image she printed appears in *Diane Arbus: Magazine Work,* p. 110.

[358] Letter from Diane Arbus to Howard Nemerov, November 10, 1968. In a postscript to the letter to her brother she says, "I don't think it will do to mention you to Agnew...I will just have to resort to something more elementary." Then she adds: "It is quite extraordinary how I cannot seem to take a photograph of a person that makes them look good. I don't think I ever have and the few times Ive made a special effort the photograph was rotten."

[359] "Tokyo Rose Is Home," *Esquire*, May 1969, photograph and text by Diane Arbus, pp. 168–169.

[360] "How Fat Alice Lost 12 Stone (Yes 12 Stone—The Weight of an Average Man!) and Found Happiness, God and the Chance of a Husband," *The London Sunday Times Magazine*, January 19, 1969, pp. 8–15. In a letter to Crookston in early 1969, following publication, Diane writes, "Alice wrote that she met a 6ft blond handsome boy who had to go back to Vietnam but when he comes back they will take up where they left off. I nearly cried with a kind of incredulous trepidation."

[361] Transcript of Diane Arbus 1971 master class, p. 18.

[362] Typewritten letter from Diane Arbus to Peter Crookston, circa December 1968, about *The London Sunday Times Magazine* issue on the family.

[363] Letter from Diane Arbus to Carlotta Marshall, circa November 1968.

[364] Letter from Diane Arbus to Peter Crookston, dated November 12, 1968.

[365] "Ready for Action," *The New York Times Magazine Children's Fashions* supplement, published March 16, 1969, cover and twenty-eight color and black-and-white photographs by Diane Arbus, with text by Patricia Peterson.

[366] Letter from Diane Arbus to Paul Salstrom. The letter includes a reference to teaching her last class of the semester at Cooper Union, which appears to have taken place on December 5, indicating the letter was probably written that day.

[367] Typewritten letter from Diane Arbus to David Halberstich, Division of Graphic Arts and Photography, Smithsonian Institution, Washington, D.C., circa January 1969. Diane Arbus file, National Museum of American History, Smithsonian Institution.

[368] Typewritten letter from Diane Arbus to Peter Crookston, circa February–March 1969. "Let me do something about very rich people (beyond my wildest dreams) when I come over. Maybe at least some of the Wives of Famous Men should be Enormously Splendid..." In another typewritten letter from Diane Arbus to Peter Crookston, circa February 1969, she writes, "congratulations. how fine" with regard to his new job at *Nova* and later says, "Of course I'll come over. And do the wives and the Who." Neither of these two projects transpire, but several other ideas replace them.

[369] Typewritten letter from Diane Arbus to Peter Crookston, circa late February 1969, also contains the following anecdote: "...did you hear the rather incredible reverberations caused in the Wall Street area several warm days last October when a very plain young girl from Bklyn whose bosoms measured 43 inches around gradually accumulated a crowd of 7000 men waiting to watch her walk from the subway station to work...She was swamped with offers to dance toplessly in nightclubs. What struck me about her was that I remembered several girls in school...who were sort of ugly and had enormous bosoms which they bore like an affliction...I remember how hard it was for them to walk, let alone run. Francine struck me as just such a girl and I have been quietly waiting for a little time to pass while she danced topless briefly, figuring that by March she would have gone back to being a keypunch operator and I would photograph her. But I just realized how it might very well have changed

her life permanently and she might still be wandering downward through the fringes of show business and might look extraordinary. Would she interest you?" This idea is not pursued.

[370] In October of 1968, she first made contact with Drs. Eberhard and Phyllis Kronhausen, experts in human sexuality and erotic art, and collectors of erotic art. They had published *Erotic Art: A Survey of Erotic Fact and Fancy in the Fine Arts* (New York: Grove Press, circa 1968). She makes note of the Kronhausens' other books, *The Sexually Responsive Woman* (New York: Grove Press, 1964) and *Pornography and the Law: The Psychology of Erotic Realism and Pornography* (New York: Bell Publishing Company, circa 1959).

[371] Typewritten letter from Diane Arbus to Peter Crookston, circa late February 1969.

[372] *Ibid.*

[373] On March 25, after photographing F. Lee Bailey in early March in New York, she visits him in his Boston office accompanied by the intended writer of the piece, Lady Alma Birk.

[374] The camera being advertised is manufactured by Zeiss Ikon and the color photograph taken by Diane Arbus is of a friend of hers, Bob Horowtiz, standing on a path in Central Park with the camera and a lot of pigeons.

[375] Diane Arbus letter to May Eliot, circa mid- or late June 1969.

[376] Judge Roy Mark Hofheinz. "The Greatest Showman on Earth, and He's the First to Admit It," *Sports Illustrated*, April 21, 1969, pp. 36–49.

[377] Appointment book, April 7, 1969.

[378] Typewritten letter from Diane Arbus to Peter Crookston, probably April 2, 1969. She asks him to send money for the airfare ($300) and advance expenses and an estimate of the number of pages she might do "because I use a particular film which I must bring." She adds, "If you do want to do that thing I wrote you about, about the stigma of Beauty, a marvelous example is Louise de la Falaise. I know her only slightly but she is marvelously perverse, headlong, doomed and wild. I think she's in Paris." The idea is not pursued.

[379] "People Who Think They Look Like Other People," *Nova*, October 1969, pp. 66–71. Eight portraits of look-alikes by Diane Arbus with text by Pauline Peters and Margaret Pringle.

[380] Peter Crookston, "Diane's all-devouring eye," *The Sunday Telegraph Review* (London), October 5, 1997.

[381] This text of an ad appears in her handwriting on the April 22 page of her 1969 appointment book.

[382] Letter from Diane Arbus to Amy Arbus in late April 1969 on Camden Court Hotel stationery. This project on the wax museum never appears in the magazine. Four of the photographs were published posthumously in *Diane Arbus: Magazine Work*, pp. 134–137.

[383] "Get to Know Your Local Rocker," *Nova*, September 1969, pp. 60–65. Six photographs by Diane Arbus with text by Peter Martin.

[384] Typewritten letter from Diane Arbus to Peter Crookston, circa October 1969. In a subsequent letter in November 1969 she asks Crookston to tell the art director of *Nova* to return any old prints of hers. "It might be prudent for me to acquire them. Just the Rockers and Lulu [a pop singer of whom nine photographs were published as "Lulu's Career Is Important," *Nova*, January 1970, pp. 30–33. Text by Helen Lawrenson]. I have J. Susann." The photographs were apparently not returned.

[385] Typewritten letter from Diane Arbus to Peter Crookston, circa late February 1969.

[386] Postcard from Diane Arbus to Ruth Ansel from London, circa late April 1969.

[387] Postcard from Diane Arbus to Richard Avedon from London, May 4, 1969.

[388] Typewritten letter from Diane Arbus to May Eliot, circa mid-May 1969.

[389] Typewritten letter from Diane Arbus to Peter Crookston, circa May 1969.

[390] May 25, travels to Florida, first to St. Petersburg to photograph old people in retirement homes living on Medicare, a project for the Social Security Administration. The photographs are published in the Social Security Administration's Public Information Circular on December 1, 1970, to be available upon request within the agency for promotional and public relations purposes.

[391] 1969 Notebook (No. 37) dates the visit to Ratoucheff and Krauze as May 26, 1969.

[392] Typewritten letter from Diane Arbus to Marguerite Lamkin Littman, circa June 1969. Diane had apparently

visited with Marguerite and her husband, Queen's Counsel Mark Littman, during her stay in London.

[393] "But Ladies, I am 76 Years Old, 'The World's Most Perfectly Developed Man', Now Lives Among the Aged in Florida. But Age, to Charles Atlas, Does Not Mean Being Reduced to a Seven Stone Weakling Again." *The London Sunday Times Magazine*, October 16, 1969, pp. 26–31.

[394] The speech is at the University of Florida, Gainesville, under the auspices of photographer Jerry Uelsmann, who taught there.

[395] Handwritten letter from Diane Arbus to Allan Arbus, probably June 6, 1969. Her speech to nuns takes place on July 14. It is arranged by the dean of Manhattanville College, Mother Brady, a Sacred Heart nun, who is a friend of Carlotta Marshall's and has instituted a graduate program for nuns to introduce them to issues of contemporary life. Gives lecture at Manhattanville. Her 1969 appointment book records: "July 14: Manhattanville 7:30 lecture $100."

[396] The photograph of the Joan Crawford fan was taken in the summer but was never published by *The London Sunday Times Magazine*. The photograph was published posthumously in *Diane Arbus: Magazine Work*, pp. 138–139.

[397] In June she begins to photograph women involved with the women's liberation movement for *The London Sunday Times Magazine*. These include Betty Friedan, Ti-Grace Atkinson, Roxanne Dunbar, Delores Alexander, Kate Millet, and the Red Stockings.

[398] Typewritten letter from Diane Arbus to Allan Arbus, circa mid-June 1969.

[399] Typewritten letter from Diane Arbus to Allan Arbus, circa late June 1969.

[400] *Ibid.*

[401] Typewritten letter from Diane Arbus to Allan Arbus, circa mid-June 1969. "I have $1656 unpd bills and 2000 in the bank...I have SOS ed to Peter [Crookston, at *Nova*] to estimate the # of pps I did in England and put through the bill for me, because the expenses are absolutely nil. I will call the Social Security today and bill them but the prints arent due till June 30. I have more work. For the London Times, the Feminists and a family portrait of total strangers this weekend. but none of it is much money. The museum owes me $750. I will bother them again, altho they say its in the works."

[402] *Ibid.*

[403] Typewritten letter from Diane Arbus to Allan Arbus, circa June 1969.

[404] Typewritten letter from Diane Arbus to Allan Arbus, circa July 1969. "Last night I dreamed I decided at last to go to a psychiatrist and I got to his great Oaken door and knocked and waited and at last the door opened and there he was...(guess who* see bottom of page for the answer.) [At bottom, upside down, she writes Richard Avedon.] This kind of thing is entertaining and appalling but I don't know what to do with it. In any event, the real situation is not bad."
In September, she begins seeing Dr. Helen Boigon.

[405] In a letter to Allan Arbus and Mariclare Costello, circa December 1970, she sends Allan a check from the account in the amount of $500 and encloses a stack of blank checks for his use, urging him to write his own whenever he needs any. "The account is still in your name, of course."

[406] The Metropolitan Museum of Art purchases Identical twins Cathleen and Colleen, Roselle, N.J. 1967, and Xmas tree in a living room, Levittown, L.I. 1963.

[407] Typewritten letter from Diane Arbus to Allan Arbus, circa late June 1969. Several years later the third photograph they intended to buy was included in the museum's collection as a gift from curator John McKendry's wife, Maxime de la Falaise, Boy in a straw hat waiting to march in a pro-war parade, N.Y.C. 1967.

[408] In February she sells five prints for a total of $125 to the Smithsonian Institution's History Photography Collection, part of the Division of Graphic Arts and Photography, the Museum of History and Technology. The prints are (in her shorthand): "Twins, Westchester Family, Boy and Girl (on 10th St.), Midgets, Transvestite [Transvestite with a torn stocking]."

[409] In February, her work is included in the exhibition *Thirteen Photographers* at the Pratt Institute in Brooklyn.

[410] In her 1969 appointment book, for June 2, she writes, "Mask, Bruce Cath [Naked man being a woman, which she crossed out], Xmas, Vicki [Transvestite with a torn stocking]."

[411] During the course of the exhibition, which continues for four years at venues throughout Europe, Latin America, and New Zealand, her print of Waitress at a nudist camp, N.J. 1963 is stolen twice and she is obliged to provide the museum with replacement prints.
In 1969 John Szarkowski and The Museum of Modern Art organized an exhibition, *10 Photographers*, for the United States Information Agency's U.S. pavilion at

the Japan World Exhibition in Osaka, 1969–70. Among the photagphers represented by approximately a dozen works each are Ansel Adams, Garry Winogrand, Lee Friedlander, Will Garnett, Bruce Davidson, and Diane Arbus.

[412] Typewritten letter from Diane Arbus to Allan Arbus, circa mid-August 1969.

[413] Letter from Jean-Claude Lemagny, Bibliothèque Nationale de France, May 31, 1969. "Dear Mrs. Arbus, As keeper in the 'Cabinet des Estampes' of the French National Library, in charge of the collection of photographs, I have the task of increasing this collection...Unfortunately...we cannot purchase photographic prints at their real price. Therefore, I must rely on your liberality and ask you whether you would let us have your prints rather cheap...I should like about twenty prints...I let you make your choice among your best and most famous photographs. I think, for instance, to the marvelous Identical Twins... P.S. Of course the reproduction of your photographs from our collections is strictly forbidden. Your copyright will be preserved."

[414] Doon Arbus interview with John Szarkowski, February 11, 1972.

[415] Typewritten letter from Diane Arbus to Allan Arbus, circa mid-August 1969.

[416] She also owns another Goffman book, *Asylums: Essays on the Social Situations of Mental Patients and Other Inmates* (New York: Doubleday, 1961).

[417] Typewritten letter from Diane Arbus to Peter Crookston, circa late March 1969. "Think of this: That Beauty is itself an aberration, a burden, a mystery, even to itself. What if I were to photograph Great Beauties (I don't know quite how they'd look but I think, like Babies, they can take the most remorseless scrutiny.)...Often they hate their noses or find their chins too long. Sometimes they feel painfully valuable like objects..."

[418] 1969 Notebook (No. 36) and again in No. 38. The subjects listed appear in different order, but almost all are included in the separate lists.

[419] Letter from Diane Arbus to Eugene Ostroff, Division of Graphic Arts and Photography, Smithsonian, June 13, 1969. Her 1969 Notebook (No. 38) records that she photographs at Vineland from July 29 to 31.

[420] In 1969 Notebook (No. 38) the first page of the five-page entry bears the dates July 29, 30, 31 which correspond to the entries in her appointment book. It also includes a

description similar to the following, which appears in an August 1969 letter to Amy: "One of the best times was when they played Simon Says in a field. Its a really a very serious game for them because when Simon Says Raise your hands high, some can some cant, some only just put their hands on their head. And when Simon says run in place the ones that can do it as if it was nearly impossible. Lots of them are pearshaped. Once during Simon says there was a pause and one girl sat down. Everyone knew it was important. She bent her head to her knees and with an odd shiver somehow the rest of her followed in what looked like the First Somersault."

[421] Typewritten letter from Diane Arbus to Allan Arbus, circa mid-August 1969. She continues on the same subject: "What I mean is of course that if I have to shoot at a 60th or a 30th so as not to underexpose the background too much...then if the figure moves and they are moving more...more lyrical and pastoral...then there is either a ghost or a total blur. if on the other hand I underexpose the bg too much it looks too violent and lit and nightlike...And what with trying more movement it is terribly tricky...I am going to look into fellowship possibilities...So I Have to make 20 prints of the NJ pix first next week."

[422] Five-page typewritten letter from Diane Arbus to Allan Arbus, November 28, 1969.

[423] Typewritten letter from Diane Arbus to Allan Arbus, circa early December 1969. She sends Allan a group of 8x10 prints from Halloween made on the Ektamatic Processor and apparently in answer to his comments about the quality of the prints, explains, "Those...were made on the machine, just roughs, and the machine paper is soft even {with} the hardest filter. They wont look like that." She continues to employ this method of producing rough prints for the rest of her career.

[424] Letter from Diane Arbus to Allan Arbus, circa November 28, 1969. "Talked more to Marvin. I think the portfolio will be a box of 8 or so prints (actual photographic prints) but he says and I think he's right, that I shouldn't make them, just supervise the making of them. it will be utterly simple. the pictures will be ones that have been shown like the twins, xmas, etc. no text except maybe a paragraph by me. an edition of a hundred or two, selling for, I dunno, 4 or 500 dollars or 3...it'll be a business proposition but pristine...and it wont conflict with the eventual book...I mean its like an edition of etchings or lithographs."

[425] Typewritten letter from Diane Arbus to Allan Arbus, November 28, 1969. Some of her concerns focus on the strategic issue of how to obtain funding for the

project. "I think I could get backing. The subject is so little known and people like Mrs Sargent Shriver have a passionate interest in it. The only tricky thing is which steps to make first...Im not sure whether to pursue an agent. Laura {Kanelous, Richard Avedon's representative} said Peter Schub (however you spell him I dread him)...she said to talk to Penn about him (he handles Penn) but talking to Penn is like talking to a pencil. Maybe I'd do better to pursue a fellowship for the retarded book. But I suppose I need both."

426 Letter from Diane Arbus to Allan Arbus, circa mid-November 1969. "In my relentless search for business I called Pat Peterson this morning on a most flimsy excuse. She was about to call me she said to ask about going to Barbados over Xmas."

427 Typewritten letter from Diane Arbus to John Szarkowski, November 6, 1969, The Museum of Modern Art. "What a nice lunch that was," she adds. They appear to have had a meeting on the subject on October 14.

428 Typewritten letter from Diane Arbus to Allan Arbus, November 28, 1969.

429 Typewritten letter from Diane Arbus to Allan Arbus, circa mid-December 1969.

430 Letter from Diane Arbus to Allan Arbus, November 28, 1969. "...and of all things halfway through the sitting his wife (he is the Macys santa, the parade one, a colossal idiot but pleasant and obliging) his wife volunteered 'how 'bout if I sit on his lap and ask him for the $200 gold pants suit I saw at Macys today.' So she did. perhaps I will take all my magazine pictures that way. Someone said J. Susann is angry at me."

431 Ground for the Westbeth building had been broken for the conversion in June 1968.

432 Typewritten letter from Diane Arbus to Allan Arbus, circa mid-October 1969.

433 Typewritten letter from Diane Arbus to Allan Arbus, early November 1969.

434 According to her appointment books she leaves for Barbados on Christmas Day 1969 and returns after January 5, 1970.

435 In the same letter she continues, "I swam in the rain yesterday. Our hotel is small and I have a marvelous air conditioned double room to myself...the rest of it is a bit seedy, that sort where you hear everyone's conversations and greet at breakfast, expressing attitudes about the weather."

436 Typewritten letter from Diane Arbus to Allan Arbus, January 16, 1970. She adds about Peterson, "I had spared her any knowledge of the near disaster of several sittings having been as much as 3 stops underexposed, which was very good and no one knew the difference so my professionalism hasn't been marred."

437 "Looking to Summer," *The New York Times Magazine Children's Fashions* supplement, was published on March 15, 1970, with text by Patricia Peterson, and cover as well as twenty-two photographs by Diane Arbus. The photograph she describes to Allan of a "black girl and a white boy about four years old holding hands" does not appear on the cover or in the magazine at all.

438 Typewritten letter from Diane Arbus to Allan Arbus, January 16, 1970. "I managed to get {an apartment} very like mine for Mary Frank who is separated from Robert and got sick and was in the hospital so I wrote a letter explaining her dire straits and she got precedence over the whole waiting list."

439 Typewritten letter from Diane Arbus to Allan Arbus, circa early February 1970. Among the items receiving the spray paint treatment are a set of wooden shutters which she makes silver and sets up as screens on either side of the alcove around her bed.

440 Typewritten letter from Diane Arbus to John Szarkowski, The Museum of Modern Art, New York. The letter, although undated, appears to have been written in January 1970.

441 Memo, John Szarkowski to Inez Garson, January 19, 1970, The Museum of Modern Art, New York. Szarkowski outlines the tasks required to "identify and locate the major sources of negatives and prints... retrieving original negatives, or of finding prints of quality adequate to produce good copy negatives."

442 *Ibid.*

443 Typewritten letter from Diane Arbus to Allan Arbus and Mariclare Costello, circa July 1970, "dunno what has happened about Chicago." And typewritten letter to Amy Arbus, circa early July 1970, "I haven't been able to get in touch with the *Esquire* editor about the Chicago job (the dying people) so I don't know what has happened about that, when or if I am going."

444 Typewritten letter from Diane Arbus to Allan Arbus, circa mid-November 1969.

445 Dr. Helen Boigon is a colleague recommended to her by Dr. David Shainberg, writer Lawrence Shainberg's older brother. Lawrence Shainberg is a friend of both hers and Marvin Israel's.

446 Handwritten letter from Diane Arbus to Allan Arbus, circa September 1969.

447 Typewritten letter from Diane Arbus to Marvin Israel, March 24, 1960. "You know what I hate? motivation and the whole notion that one does something BECAUSE of something and all of psychologic continuity and maybe historical continuity too."

448 In March, she works with Peter Bunnell, a curator, Department of Photography at The Museum of Modern Art, to compile a list of museums that might potentially buy photographs.

449 Her 1970 appointment book indicates a meeting with Lauro Morales on March 24, Eddie Carmel on April 10, and the Senior Citizens' Dance on May 22. On the practice sheet of vellum some of the titles are at variance with the way they finally appeared in the portfolio. About the twins: "notice their bobby pins and the difference in their stockings" and about the dwarf: "he is about thirty four or thirty eight, he has two girlfriends, one of whom he will marry."

450 Typewritten letter from Diane Arbus to Allan Arbus, circa early February 1970.

451 Handwritten letter from Diane Arbus to Allan Arbus and Mariclare Costello, circa June 1970. In a subsequent letter to Peter Crookston on June 28, 1970, she refers to Amy's departure in similar terms, "Amy has gone cycling in Europe with nine strangers who looked rather frightful at both our first glances. And she had babysat day and night to save $500 to make it possible."

452 From The Picture Press files, The Museum of Modern Art, New York.

453 One of these assignments is probably the feature on carnivals that takes her to Hagerstown, Maryland, on July 31 and is referred to in a letter from Hayes dated October 5, 1970, about payment for the story, which as it turns out is never published.

454 Typewritten letter from Diane Arbus to Peter Crookston, June 28, 1970. The letter refers to the fact that she is leaving the following day for Minneapolis to attend Richard Avedon's retrospective there, which Marvin Israel designed, "a tiny edition of 10 prints, boxed, which I am going to sell for $1000 to museums and collectors, I hope."

455 Letter from Diane Arbus to Peter Crookston, June 28, 1970. "Some of the things are glorious. Yesterday I found a picture of a lady looking lathered as if for a shave sitting cloaked in white between a doctor and a nurse. All for Beauty's Sake it is called...Harriet Heckman submits to plastic surgery by Dr. Nathan Smilee of Phila. as nurse assists. (5/21/35) Miss Heckman has asked for the perfect face and perfect figure and announces she is perfectly willing to face death to attain them. 'I want to do something about a body and face that have made me miserable' she says."

456 Marvin Israel also designs a portfolio of prints for Richard Avedon in the same year.

457 The project, which eventually became *The Sixties* (New York: Random House, 1999), began with Avedon's use of the 8x10 camera and entailed his portraits of artists and political and social activists. Doon conducted taped interviews with each of the subjects. Although a number of the Avedon portraits were published in the intervening years, the results of the project as originally conceived did not appear until the 1999 Random House publication.

458 Handwritten letter from Diane Arbus to Amy Arbus, July 2, 1970.

459 Typewritten letter from Diane Arbus to Allan Arbus and Mariclare Costello, circa early July 1970. This is the same letter excerpted in the text that follows, "I'm a bit sad to be back..."

460 Letter from Diane Arbus to Amy Arbus, circa late July 1970.

461 Letter from Harold Hayes to Diane Arbus, October 5, 1970. He writes, "I have put through a check for $371 for your Senior Citizens photograph, and an additional check for $500 against the assignment on Carnivals. However, I am loath to pay you the full amount for four pages until...I'm closer to booking the feature into an issue."

462 According to her appointment book she leaves for Florida on August 8 and returns sometime just before the 14th.

463 Marvin Israel had taken it upon himself to ask Richard Avedon if Diane and Doon could spend a few days there alone, and Avedon may have gone so far as to disinvite some people in order to make this possible.

464 Letter from Diane Arbus to Amy Arbus, circa late June 1970. "Meanwhile I'll enclose an article from

the VV by Paul Goodman (unless I forget) about not going to experimental schools. That should confuse you further." The article that she refers to is "Against 'Liberated' High Schools," *Village Voice*, June 25, 1970.

465 Typewritten letter from Diane Arbus to Carlotta Marshall, circa November 1970.

466 Typewritten letter from Diane Arbus to Allan Arbus, circa early November 1970.

467 Handwritten note from Diane Arbus to Allan Arbus, August 29, 1970.

468 Letter from Diane Arbus to Allan Arbus, circa mid-September 1970.

469 Handwritten note from Diane Arbus to Allan Arbus, August 29, 1970.

470 *The London Sunday Times Magazine*, January 3, 1971, "The Affluent Ghetto," six photographs of planned communities in America, with text by Ann Leslie, pp. 8–15.

471 Letter from Diane Arbus to Allan Arbus, circa early October 1970. She writes, "Detroit was a nightmare but it doesn't seem to matter." "Conversation: Ida Lewis and Rev. Albert B. Cleage, Jr.," Essence, December 1970, pp. 22–27. Includes one uncredited photograph of the altar of The Shrine of the Black Madonna and a portrait of its pastor by Diane Arbus.

472 "American Society of Magazine Photographers, Honors and Awards for 1970," *Infinity*, September 1970, pp. 16–17. "Of her present work Diane Arbus has said, 'I am still collecting things—the ones I recognize and the ones I can't quite believe. I think when you look anything squarely in the eye, it is different from how you thought it was.'" For the article she chose a photograph for which she provided a handwritten title, Miss Mary King and her dog Troubles, Carnival, Md. 1964.

473 Typewritten letter from Diane Arbus to Allan Arbus, circa early October 1970. She adds in describing the event, "Bruce was first and he was hilarious...like a kid at his birthday party...and he wants everybody to put on their paper hats and pay attention and stop talking while he makes a wish. At one point he was blah blahing on about how this all wouldn't have been possible without all these people and he suddenly said, 'I had my visual Proust and visual Dustyuskey: W. Eugene Smith and Diane Arbus to name just a few.' Gene Smith was good. like an old sea captain, funny and honorable."

474 *Ibid.*

475 *Ibid.*

476 Letter from Diane Arbus to Allan Arbus and Mariclare Costello, December 6, 1970.

477 Typewritten letter from Diane Arbus to Allan Arbus, circa early October 1970.

478 Typewritten letter from Diane Arbus to Allan Arbus and Mariclare Costello, circa late October 1970. In a subsequent letter to them sent in December she reports, "My mother is eyeing Palm Beach which means she is feeling better."

479 Handwritten letter from Diane Arbus to Carlotta Marshall, circa November 1970. Carlotta is now living in London.

480 Letter from Diane Arbus to Allan Arbus, circa early November 1970.

481 Typewritten letter from Diane Arbus to Allan Arbus and Mariclare Costello, December 6, 1970.

482 Letter from Diane Arbus to Allan Arbus and Mariclare Costello, circa late October 1970.

483 Typewritten letter from Diane Arbus to Allan Arbus and Mariclare Costello, December 6, 1970. "Both Dick and Hiro's assts use the cold light mostly. Of course they make harder negs..."

484 *Ibid.* Later in the same letter she adds, "One of Hiro's assts. {Neil Selkirk} is working with an 11x14 camera. He found two old ones in London. I saw a negative which looked gorgeous. Not tempting to me though. hardly." A subsequent letter in mid-December reveals that the film issue rages on, "Must call Ilford. They have something called Pan F but I don't think its made in 120. Would probably be good (ASA 50). There is one rated at 125 and another like Tri x but Id like a slower one. And then there is the problem of getting it. At this point I have in the cabinet 10-50 rolls of all sorts of different films. Must get that settled."

485 Typewritten letter from Diane Arbus to Gail Lineback, December 13, 1970. Lineback, unsolicited, sent a copy of this letter to Doon Arbus in 1972 suggesting it might prove to be of interest.

486 Letter from Diane Arbus to Allan Arbus and Mariclare Costello, December 6, 1970.

487 Letter from Diane Arbus to Peter Crookston, January 25, 1971.

488 *Ibid.* This refers to *The London Sunday Times Magazine*, January 3, 1971, "The Affluent Ghetto," six

photographs of planned communities in America, with text by Ann Leslie, pp. 8–15.

[489] Letter from Diane Arbus to Allan Arbus and Mariclare Costello, circa late January 1971.

[490] The account of this event that she gave to her master class in 1971 appears on pages 6 and 7 of *Diane Arbus*.

[491] Letter from Diane Arbus to Allan Arbus and Mariclare Costello, circa late January 1971.

[492] The name Bob Masochist appears several times in her 1970 appointment book in December.

[493] Letter from Davis Pratt to Diane Arbus, January 28, 1971. The letter goes on to say, "From the prints you kindly showed me here are the ones I would like to borrow for the exhibition. I will also attempt to purchase them for the Fogg." These are the images he lists: "Vicki (version 1. my notes say?), Man in curlers, Woman with accessories...Family on lawn, Giant, Dwarf, King & Queen."

[494] Letter from Diane Arbus to Davis Pratt, February 4, 1971.

[495] Letter from Davis Pratt to Doon Arbus, November 22, 1972.

[496] *Diane Arbus*, p. 3. "Sometimes I can see a photograph or a painting, I see it and I think, that's not the way it is. I don't mean a feeling of, I don't like it. I mean the feeling that this is fantastic, but there's something wrong. I guess it's my own sense of what a fact is. Something will come up in me very strongly of No, a terrific No. It's a totally private feeling I get of how different it really is. I'm not saying I get it only from pictures I don't like. I also get it from pictures I like a lot. You come outdoors and all you've got is you and all photographs begin to fall away and you think, My God, it's really different. I don't mean you can do it precisely like it is, but you can do it more like it is." This description was given by her to the class in the context of her response to the Walker Evans retrospective.

[497] Letter from Diane Arbus to Allan Arbus and Mariclare Costello, January 31, 1971.

[498] Transcript from Diane Arbus 1971 master class, p. 28.

[499] Transcript from Diane Arbus 1971 master class, pp. 16–17, 32–33. In the context of a discussion about various photographers she says of Cartier-Bresson, "In general I find the whole lyricism in Bresson...that sort of gentle sort of radiant pale silver that he photographs with—I just find it begins to separate out from the subject for me. I don't get that terrific kick that I get from say, Brassai, who has this kind of darkness that thrills me." About Brandt she says, "If you go through a hundred of his photographs you can really separate out that light [he has] and it's in the interior pictures, it's in the exterior pictures, it's in the lit ones, it's in the unlit ones, it's in the blackout pictures, it's extraordinary... It has something to do with the way he prints or something...[but] it comes from some mysterious deep place." About Ansel Adams, "One quarrel I've got with Adams is that—he's never lied in a photograph or even exaggerated—it's just that his prints are so sort of magnificent, he renders everything so incredibly...I mean I never saw a tree like an Adams tree...they're all silver and glowing and, you know, that sky...like something you might give for a wedding present, but not like trees. Not that I know trees very well." And about Robert Frank, "He is probably, well maybe outside of Cartier-Bresson, the most influential contemporary photographer there is. There's a funny thing in [his work] and it isn't even something I especially like but it always strikes me. It's a thing like a kind of hollowness in his work. I don't mean hollow like meaningless...I mean his pictures always involve a kind of nondrama...a drama in which the center is removed. There's kind of a question mark at the hollow center of the sort of storm of them, a curious existential kind of awe...It hit a whole generation of photographers terribly hard, like they'd never seen that before."

[500] The portfolio, titled *Walker Evans: Fourteen Photographs* (New Haven, Conn.: Ives Sillman, 1971) is printed by Thomas Brown, has an introduction by Robert Penn Warren, and is published in an edition of 100 on February 15, 1971. Fewer than a dozen are purchased during Evans's lifetime.

[501] Letter from Diane Arbus to Allan Arbus and Mariclare Costello, January 31, 1971. She adds, "Started to feel kind of grim: money, the sources drying up, Essence hasn't paid ($1000) and gives me a run around, I threatened them and finally asked Jay [Gold, lawyer, friend of hers and Marvin Israel's] to write em."

[502] Letter from Diane Arbus to Allan Arbus and Mariclare Costello, January 31, 1971.

[503] Note from Diane Arbus to Allan Arbus, February 2, 1971.

[504] *Ibid*. "Oh, Jay [Gold] got my ESSENCE money! it came this morning...AND my camera arrived from Japan. Going to Hiro's to get it."

505 Letter from Davis Pratt to Diane Arbus, January 28, 1971.

506 Letter from Diane Arbus to Davis Pratt, February 22, 1971.

507 Postscript to a letter from Diane Arbus to Allan Arbus and Mariclare Costello, January 11, 1971. This is probably a reference to the pugilist Max Schmeling who was the heavyweight world champion from 1930 to 1932 and who defeated Joe Lewis in 1936. There is no information about which magazine was involved.

508 Letter from Diane Arbus to Allan Arbus and Mariclare Costello, circa late February 1971.

509 *Ibid.*

510 Postcard from Marvin Israel to Diane Arbus, March 9, 1971.

511 Letter from Diane Arbus to Allan Arbus and Mariclare Costello, circa late February 1971. The party following the last Westbeth class takes place in her apartment.

512 *Ibid.*

513 Letter from Diane Arbus to John Szarkowski, February 27, 1971.

514 Szarkowski's letter of recommendation is dated March 24, 1971.

515 Henry Geldzahler's letter of recommendation is dated March 8, 1971.

516 It seems likely that her use of the phrase "quiet minorities" was a play upon the phrase "silent majority" which is often attributed to Richard Nixon. In fact, it appears John F. Kennedy actually originated the phrase in *Profiles in Courage* (New York: Harper, 1956). Nixon used the expression in a November 3, 1969, speech: "If a vocal minority, however fervent its cause, prevails over reason and the will of the majority, this Nation has no future as a free society...And so tonight—to you, the great silent majority of my fellow Americans—I ask for your support."

517 The quote continues, "Yet when you start talking about the different races, different racial qualities, you're paying allegiance to Hitler—so the conversation is verboten. Hitler was an extraordinary agent of the technological society, because for two or three decades he made it impossible to think politically about the nature of people."

518 Some of these contacts were initiated by the curators themselves, nonetheless it seems as though all the major institutional acquisitions that occurred during her lifetime were the result of personal contacts. These include John Szarkowski at The Museum of Modern Art, John McKendry and Henry Geldzahler at The Metropolitan Museum of Art, David Halberstich and Eugene Ostroff at the Smithsonian Institution, Jean-Claude Lemagny at Bibliothèque Nationale (one of the largest single institutional acquisitions), and Davis Pratt at the Fogg Museum.

519 According to her appointment book, she flies to Portland, Maine, on May 7 and returns on the 9th. Among the photographs she takes of the yurts and the members of the Study Travel Community School is one of Amy perched on the roof of her yurt.

520 Letter from Diane Arbus to Allan Arbus and Mariclare Costello, circa late April 1971.

521 *Artforum*, May 1971. A Jewish giant; Xmas tree in a living room; Young Brooklyn family; Mexican dwarf; Identical twins.

522 Apparently Diane first hears this joke at a dinner in 1960 with Allan and a friend of his. She gives Marvin Israel an account in a letter circa early November 1960. "Allan brought someone to dinner and we had a feast... his friend told a joke [which she recounts]...(How gorgeous. That is the real secret of these people I am pursuing, Uncle Sam, who I spent another afternoon with, and the lady who drinks Coca-Cola under water, and on and on. That joke would make me weep under water.)" She uses this joke in her November 1961 *Harper's Bazaar* piece "The Full Circle."

523 Letter from Diane Arbus to Allan Arbus, circa mid-May 1971.

524 *Ibid.* "This was her mistake. It made Marvin so mad he called and must have given her what for. In any event she called last night said she would stand by me and...would go to the top if necessary, totally changed in tone. He had somehow managed to transform it from a picayune, carping nuisance to an issue involving her own selfishness and indifference and she felt really ashamed because she knew he had done a lot for her."

525 The photograph of Germaine Greer for *New Woman* is never used either, although it is published posthumously in *Diane Arbus: Magazine Work,* p. 151. Following the first prints Diane submits to art director John Gerbino, she sends around a dozen more with a

quick note saying she likes them better. None include the photograph that appears in *Magazine Work*.

[526] Letter from Diane Arbus to Allan Arbus, circa mid-May 1971.

[527] Letter from Diane Arbus to Allan Arbus and Mariclare Costello, January 11, 1971.

[528] Letter from Diane Arbus to Allan Arbus, circa mid-May 1971.

[529] Diane Arbus completed the prints for eleven or twelve sets of the portfolio but did not sign them or prepare the individual title sheets until the sets had been sold. After her death, the remaining sets were designated by The Estate of Diane Arbus, on the advice of Marvin Israel and others, as artist's proofs. One was given by Doon and Amy Arbus to Allan Arbus as Diane had intended. One was purchased by the Fogg Art Museum in 1972. It remains unclear what happened to the two sets that would have been numbered 3/50 and 4/50. The probability is that they were set aside in anticipation of sales to specific purchasers that subsequently fell through and are included among the sets of artist's proofs.

[530] This letter is written after May 13, the date that she attempts to retrieve 500 rolls of film from Pan Am Cargo building, described as follows: "Finally got the 500 rolls of isopan after such scenes as only maybe you can imagine. Hours in the cargo bldg, pd the freight chges, then they couldn't find the package, many phone calls, the hiring of an agent to facilitate matters, no receipt, filing a claim for restitution, warnings that it may have been x-rayed (I still don't know about that) (some of Dick's Vietnam film was ruined) and suddenly I came home and there was the postman by chance and looking idly among his packages, there it was. Even PanAm doesn't understand how it got to the postman..."

[531] All previous correspondence between Davis Pratt and Diane Arbus on the subject of this exhibition refers to seven prints, and Boy with a straw hat (Bomb Hanoi) is not among them. This letter from Pratt, however, dated May 21, 1971, refers specifically to the return of

eight prints and to the Bomb Hanoi print as having been damaged.

[532] He goes on to say, "Thanks once more for loaning us your stunning prints and all agreed they were the guts of our smal exh. here." On August 11, 1971, Pratt sends a letter to The Estate of Diane Arbus expressing regret over her death and noting that, "During the spring we exhibited some of Diane's prints at Harvard. We had correspondence about the prospect of acquiring same when funds were available. This is now possible, so I wanted to learn whom I should contact." The Fogg subsequently acquires from the Estate a set of the artist's proofs of *A box of ten photographs* at the original purchase price of $1,000.

[533] Letter from Diane Arbus to Peter Crookston, circa mid-June 1971.

[534] The photographs she takes at Tricia Nixon's wedding are apparently never published, nor do the negatives or contacts appear to have survived.

[535] Letter from Diane Arbus to Peter Crookston, circa mid-June 1971.

[536] 1971 Diane Arbus Notebook (No. 39).

[537] Her June appointment book indicates that she goes to Hampshire College in Amherst, Massachusetts, from June 20 to 27.

[538] Doon Arbus interview with Lisette Model, February 5, 1972.

[539] *Ibid*.

[540] Letter from Vineland State School, dated June 14, 1971.

[541] These photographs appear on several contact sheets numbered in the 7400s.

[542] Elisabeth Sussman interview with Carlotta Marshall, March 27, 2001, and Doon Arbus interview with Carlotta Marshall, May 15, 2003.

[543] Diane Arbus handwritten letter to Carlotta Marshall, circa late October 1968.

A Chronology 1923–1971 was compiled with additional assistance from: Ruth Ansel, Allan Arbus, Amy Arbus, Richard Avedon, Bert Beaver, Robert Benton, Michael Blackwood, Irving Blum, Robert Brown, Peter Bunnell, Robin Clark, Wendy Clarke, Adrian Condon (Allen), Bernard Crystal, Bruce Davidson, Betty Dodson, Shelley Dowell, Alexander Eliot, May Eliot, Shirley Fingerhood, Larry Fink, Michael Flanagan, Miles Forst, Mary Frank, Lee Friedlander, Elizabeth Grady, Joy Hart, Nicky Haslam, Sarah Hermanson, Pati Hill, Toby Himmel, Jane Holzer, Lawrence Israel, Eleanor Jacobs, Ricky Jay, Jasper Johns, Carol Kismaric, Maraguerite Lamkin Littman, Richard Lamparski, Saul Leiter, Gideon Lewin, Jerome Liebling, Danny Lyon, Carlotta Marshall, Susan Meisel, Alexander Nemerov, Renée Nemerov, Michael Putnam, James Randi, Charles Reynolds, Paul Salstrom, Lucas Samaras, Allon Schoener, Mary Sellers, Larry Shainberg, Eve Sonneman, Judith Stein, Stewart Stern, Louis Stettner, Norma Stevens, John Szarkowski, Jacqueline Taeschler, Deborah Willis, Henry Wolf, LaMonte Young

BIOGRAPHIES

BY JEFF L. ROSENHEIM

BERENICE ABBOTT (1898–1991) is equally known for her advocacy of French photographer Eugène Atget, and for her comprehensive, Depression-era documentary project *Changing New York*, an extended photographic portrait of the city's nineteenth-century tenements, early-twentieth-century skyscrapers, and their common ground.

With historical captions by art critic Elizabeth McCausland, *Changing New York: Photography by Berenice Abbott* (1939) transformed how subsequent artists and publications have portrayed the urban experience in the United States.

Born in Springfield, Ohio, and raised in Cleveland, Abbott attended Ohio State University (Columbus) for a year, then moved to New York City to pursue writing, which she soon abandoned to open a sculpture studio. In 1921 she moved to Paris where, from 1923 to 1925, she worked as a darkroom assistant to the American artist, Man Ray, who had established a fashion and portrait studio. In 1925, she left Man Ray and opened her own business on the rue du Bac.

Abbott had her first one-person show in 1926 at the gallery Au Sacre du Printemps in Paris and exhibited her photographs in numerous group shows, including the influential 1928 international exhibition, *Film + Foto*, in Stuttgart, Germany. In 1927 she met and photographed

Eugène Atget, and after the artist's death in October 1928, purchased his archive of prints and negatives. She coordinated the first book on the artist, *Atget, Photographe de Paris* (1930) and organized his first New York show in 1930. Abbott regularly printed Atget's negatives, and in 1956 published *Eugène Atget Portfolio: Twenty Photographic Prints from His Original Glass Negatives*. She is also the author of *The World of Atget* (1964). Until 1968 when The Museum of Modern Art acquired the Atget archive from Abbott, she promoted the French documentarian's work through articles, exhibitions, and books.

Abbott returned to live in New York in 1929 and began to photograph the city as Atget had Paris. She participated in important shows in the early 1930s, and, in 1934, with Henry-Russell Hitchcock, the era's premier historian of modern architecture, produced an exhibition entitled *American Cities Before the Civil War: The Urban Vernacular of the Thirties, Forties and Fifties*. Her photographic project on New York, known as *Changing New York*, was sponsored by the New Deal's Federal Art Project. The exhibition opened in 1937 at The Museum of the City of New York, where the original negatives are still preserved.

In 1939 MoMA included Abbott as one of seven American photographers (including Man Ray and Walker Evans) in *Art in Our Time*, its tenth anniversary exhibition, and the first at its new building on 53rd Street. Arbus briefly studied technique with Abbott around 1946 at the New School for Social Research where she taught photography from 1935 to 1958.

Abbott had numerous retrospective exhibitions at, among other institutions, MoMA (1970) and The New York Public Library (1989), and beginning in 1976 published the first of several portfolios of her photographs. She was awarded many honorary degrees and citations, including the French government's Officer in the Legion of Arts and Letters (1988), and membership in the American Academy and Institute of Arts and Letters (1983).

RUTH ANSEL (B. 1936) graduated from Alfred University with a B.F.A. in ceramic design in 1957 and began her professional design career at *Harper's Bazaar* in 1961 working alongside Bea Feitler as an assistant to art director Marvin Israel. Two years later she and Feitler succeeded Israel as co-art directors of the magazine, a position Ansel kept until 1971. Ansel gave work to many of the era's most progressive artists, including Andy Warhol, James Rosenquist, Robert Rauschenberg, Bob Richardson, and Arbus. From 1974 to 1982 she was art director for *The New York Times Magazine* and eventually went on to art direct at numerous Condé Nast publications: *House & Garden* (1982–83); *Vanity Fair* (1983–88); *Vogue* (1988–89); and *HG* (1989–91).

In 1992 Ansel founded Ruth Ansel Design Studio and has designed numerous magazines, advertising campaigns, and books, including Richard Avedon and Doon Arbus's *The Sixties* (1999). *Hall of Femmes: Ruth Ansel*, a monograph of her work, was published in 2010 by Oyster Press.

ALLAN ARBUS (B. 1918) was born and raised in New York City. He attended DeWitt Clinton High School and entered City College of New York at the age of fifteen. A year and a half later he left and went to work at Russek's, a women's specialty shop that was owned by Max Weinstein and David Nemerov, Diane's father. Allan met Diane Nemerov at Russek's when she was thirteen and he was eighteen. They were married in 1941. During a vacation in Montauk, Long Island, he photographed her in the fashion picture idiom and when these pictures were shown to David Nemerov, a pioneer in the use of photography in advertising, he encouraged

them to pursue fashion photography. They were soon given what turned out to be successful assignments by the Russek's advertising department. When the United States entered World War II, Arbus became a Signal Corps photographer. While he was in Burma, the Arbuses' first child, Doon, was born in New York City. In 1946 Arbus was discharged and the couple established a studio on West 54th Street using the by-line "Diane & Allan Arbus." Condé Nast placed them under contract and their work appeared regularly in *Glamour* and *Vogue*. In 1954 their second child, Amy, was born.

The Arbuses continued to collaborate until 1956 when Diane left the business to pursue her own work. Allan continued the studio operation while simultaneously beginning a career as an actor. On the recommendation of a friend he began training with Mira Rostova, who had coached many prominent actors, including Montgomery Clift and Geraldine Page. He remained Rostova's student for eleven years, during which time he performed in Off-Off Broadway productions and appeared in his first movie, *Hey Let's Twist* (1961).

Although they continued to remain close friends, in 1958, Diane and Allan Arbus separated, and eventually divorced in 1969, when he moved to California to pursue his acting career. In 1976 he married Mariclare Costello, a fellow acting student. A year later their daughter Arin was born.

Allan Arbus is most widely known for his recurring television role as the psychiatrist Major Sidney Freedman on *M*A*S*H* (1972–83). He received great critical acclaim for his performance as Gregory Solomon in a 2001 stage production of Arthur Miller's *The Price* at the Laguna Playhouse in Los Angeles. In recent years, he has once more returned to making photographs. Arbus and Mariclare Costello live in California.

AMY ARBUS (B. 1954) is the second daughter of Diane and Allan Arbus. She is a professional photographer whose work has appeared in *The New Yorker*, *Egoïste*, *Vanity Fair*, *Rolling Stone*, and *The New York Times Magazine*, among other publications. After attending high school in New York City, she eventually spent a year at Goddard College in Vermont, then studied arranging and composition for two years at the Berklee College of Music in Boston. She soon left music for the visual arts, studying photography for a year at the School of the Museum of Fine Arts, Boston. In 1978 she returned to New York City to work as an assistant to the fashion photographer Jean Pagliuso. Two years later she began to freelance. Her monthly style feature for *The Village Voice*, "On the Street," ran from 1980 to 1991 and focused on street chic and the New York art and music scene in Soho and the East Village.

Amy Arbus has published four books of photography: *No Place Like Home* (1986), an examination of people and their unusual dwellings; *The Inconvenience of Being Born* (1999), a portrait series on infants; *On the Street 1980–1990* (2006), a collection of her *Village Voice* portraits; and *The Fourth Wall* (2008), featuring actors in costume and in character, out of the context of their plays. Her work is in the permanent collections of The Museum of Modern Art, The New York Public Library, the Columbus Museum of Art, and the Spencer Museum of Art in Lawrence, Kansas, and she has exhibited her photographs in numerous group and solo shows in the United States and abroad. Since 1995, she has taught portraiture at The International Center of Photography in New York, and has given workshops at Maine Media Workshops and The Fine Arts Work Center, among others. In 2008, *On the Street*, a documentary film based on her *Village Voice* subjects, premiered at The Walter Reade Theater at New York's Lincoln Center.

DOON ARBUS (B. 1945) is the first daughter of Diane and Allan Arbus. Since her mother's death she has managed The Estate of Diane Arbus. She produced the four posthumous books of her mother's work: *Diane Arbus: An Aperture Monograph* (1972), and *Diane Arbus: Magazine Work* (1984), which she co-edited with Marvin Israel; *Diane Arbus: Untitled* (1995), for which she wrote the Afterword; and *Diane Arbus Revelations* (2003), for which she coauthored *A Chronology*. The book won the International Center of Photography's Infinity Award as publication of the year.

After spending a year at Reed College, Doon Arbus returned to New York in 1964, and in addition to other freelance writing assignments, she collaborated with her mother on several magazine articles, contributing the text to "James Brown Is Out of Sight," *Herald Tribune Magazine* (New York), March 20, 1966; and "How Fat Alice Lost 12 Stone (Yes 12 Stone—The Weight of an Average Man!) and Found Happiness, God, and the Chance of a Husband," *The London Sunday Times Magazine*, January 19, 1969. In 1969, at the suggestion of Marvin

Israel, she began working with Richard Avedon on his new project, 8x10 photographic portraits of artists, and political and social activists. Thirty years later her recorded interviews of the portrait subjects became the text of *The Sixties* (1999), a coauthored publication of photographs and monologues focusing on the civil rights movement, Vietnam, the antiwar movement, space exploration, and the arts.

In 1973 she and Avedon produced a book based on her tape recordings and his photographs entitled *Alice in Wonderland: The Forming of a Company, and the Making of a Play* (1973), a chronicle of André Gregory's Obie award–winning (1969–70) production. In the mid-1970s she and Avedon collaborated on a series of commercial television and print advertising campaigns that relied on a similar approach. These included Catherine Deneuve for Chanel and Brooke Shields for Calvin Klein jeans.

In addition to her productive association with Avedon, she has also worked independently, contributing essays and criticism to *Rolling Stone* and *The Nation* on artists ranging from Peter Beard to Walker Evans. Her play, *Third Floor, Second Door on the Right*, was produced in New York by the International Fringe Festival in 2003. She is currently writing a work of fiction.

RICHARD AVEDON (1923–2004) was known for his portraits of Buster Keaton, Marian Anderson, Marilyn Monroe, Ezra Pound, Isak Dinesen, Dwight D. Eisenhower, Andy Warhol, and the Chicago Seven. He had numerous one-person museum exhibitions at, among others, the Minneapolis Institute of Arts (1970); the Whitney Museum of American Art (1994); and two shows at The Metropolitan Museum of Art: *Avedon: Photographs 1947–1977*, a retrospective of his fashion work in 1977, and *Richard Avedon: Portraits*, in 2002.

Avedon was born in New York City and attended DeWitt Clinton High School in the Bronx. He served as editor in chief of *Magpie*, his school's literary and arts magazine. Avedon's classmate and lifelong friend, James Baldwin, was the magazine's literary editor. In 1942 Avedon joined the U.S. Merchant Marine where he became photographer's mate second class. After World War II he returned to New York and attended Alexey Brodovitch's Design Laboratory at the New School for Social Research. He was chief photographer for *Harper's Bazaar* from the late 1940s to 1965, and for *Vogue* from 1966 to 1988.

In 1959, Avedon completed his first book, *Observations*, a volume of portraits designed by Brodovitch with text by Truman Capote. In 1964 he and James Baldwin completed *Nothing Personal*, a work about the civil rights movement designed by his frequent collaborator Marvin Israel. Avedon met Arbus in the 1950s and eventually purchased the first two sets of her portfolio designed by Israel, *A box of ten photographs* (1970).

Avedon discovered the work of Jacques Henri Lartigue and later edited *Diary of a Century: Jacques Henri Lartigue* (1970). The book and exhibition at The Museum of Modern Art helped launch the reputation of the then-unknown photographer of the Belle Epoque. In the late 1960s and early '70s, Avedon photographed American antiwar protesters, politicians, and military leaders. He was assisted by Doon Arbus, who made documentary tape recordings of all the subjects. After almost thirty years, Avedon and Arbus edited selections of these photographs and recordings as *The Sixties* (1999).

In 1979 the Amon Carter Museum in Fort Worth, Texas, commissioned Avedon to produce his largest series of portraits, a study of working-class American citizens. He worked for five years and photographed 752 people in seventeen Western states. The show *In the American West* opened in 1985 at the Amon Carter Museum, and the accompanying publication was designed by Marvin Israel. Avedon published two visual memoirs, *Evidence: 1944–1994* (1994), a book that accompanied his exhibition at the Whitney Museum of American Art, and *Richard Avedon: An Autobiography* (1993). From 1985 to 1992, Avedon's editorial work appeared exclusively in *Egoïste*, the French literary and arts magazine. In 1992, under the editorship of Tina Brown, *The New Yorker* named Avedon its first staff photographer in the history of the magazine.

Avedon died in Texas in 2004 while on assignment for *The New Yorker*. A year later, The Richard Avedon Foundation was established, and has since produced a number of exhibitions and books of his work, including *Woman in the Mirror: 1945–2004* (2005) and *Performance* (2008). A posthumous retrospective of his work, *Richard Avedon: Photographs 1946–2004*, was organized in 2007 for The Louisiana Museum of Modern Art in Denmark. It has since traveled to the Jeu de Paume in Paris, as well as to Italy, Germany, the Netherlands, and the United States.

RICHARD BELLAMY (1927–98) was born in Cincinnati, Ohio, the only child of two physicians. In the early 1950s, after a year of college, he moved to the East Coast and eventually settled in New York City having met Hans Hofmann and the artists in his school in Provincetown, Massachusetts. As director of the cooperative Hansa Gallery (1955–59), then later Green Gallery (1960–65), he emerged as one of the leading gallerists in America. Bellamy championed and represented many of the most important pop and minimalist artists of the era, including James Rosenquist, Donald Judd, Claes Oldenburg, and Dan Flavin.

When Arbus met Nancy Christopherson and Bellamy in the early 1950s their circle included abstract painters Willem de Kooning, Miles and Barbara Forst, and Alfred Leslie, as well as the photographer Robert Frank and his Beat friends Allen Ginsberg and Jack Kerouac. Between 1965 and 1974 Bellamy worked from an office in the Noah Goldowsky Gallery presenting exhibitions of Jo Baer, Richard Artschwager, Mark di Suvero, and Richard Serra, among many others. After managing a private gallery in the late 1970s, he opened the Oil & Steel Gallery in 1980. In his final decade of work Bellamy managed almost exclusively the installation and exhibition of di Suvero's large-scale sculptures. His correspondence, gallery records, and artists' files are in the archives of the collection of The Museum of Modern Art.

ERNEST J. BELLOCQ (1873–1949) was born into an aristocratic Creole family in New Orleans, Louisiana. After enrolling in classical courses at the College of the Immaculate Conception, he devoted his efforts to amateur photography. By 1898 Bellocq had become a prominent member of the New Orleans Camera Club, and by World War I he was working as a professional photographer specializing in shipbuilding. Bellocq's international renown, however, was established by a series of intimate, mildly erotic portraits of prostitutes working in Storyville, the city's infamous tenderloin district.

In 1966, photographer Lee Friedlander purchased eighty-nine Bellocq glass plate negatives from a New Orleans antiques dealer. Four years later when The Museum of Modern Art presented an exhibition of Friedlander's modern prints of these photographs, Bellocq was immediately recognized as a master of the modern, psychological portrait—an ancestor for a whole generation of contemporary artists, including Arbus, who acquired a few prints for her personal collection. Friedlander continues to print Bellocq's work and has published two editions of *E. J. Bellocq: Storyville Portraits, Photographs from the New Orleans Red-Light District, Circa 1912* (1970, 1996).

ROBERT BENTON (B. 1932) was born in Waxahachie, Texas, and is known for directing and/or writing such Academy Award–winning films as *Kramer vs. Kramer* (1979), *Places in the Heart* (1984), and *Nobody's Fool* (1994). After graduating from the University of Texas, he moved to New York City, worked on a master's degree in art and art history at Columbia University, then in 1954 took an editorial position in the art department at *Esquire* magazine. First as an assistant art director to Henry Wolf, then as his replacement in 1957, Benton contributed to the transformation of *Esquire* from a men's magazine to a graphically more sophisticated monthly featuring contemporary fiction, nonfiction, and photography. Benton met Arbus at *Esquire* in late 1959 and soon became one of the artist's most devoted advocates. Beginning with their seminal feature on New York's denizens of the night, "The Vertical Journey: Six Movements of a Moment Within the Heart of the City" (*Esquire*, July 1960), Benton provided Arbus with regular assignments through 1963 when he left the magazine.

Benton began writing screenplays while at *Esquire* in the early 1960s. His first effort (co-written with fellow editor David Newman) was *Bonnie and Clyde* (1967), a film directed by Arthur Penn that won him an Academy Award for best story and best original screenplay. Benton made his directorial debut with the revisionist Western *Bad Company* (1972). Among his recent films are *A Great Day in Harlem* (1995), *Twilight* (1998), *Double Jeopardy* (1999), *The Human Stain* (2003), based on a novel by Philip Roth, and *Feast of Love* (2007).

PAUL BIANCHINI (1928–2000) was a gallerist and art publisher born outside of Paris whose eponymous New York gallery (1958–67) presented avant-garde European and American pop and minimal art. For his infamous 1964 exhibition, *The American Supermarket*, Bianchini transformed his gallery into a super-market of fake food created by Jasper Johns, Claes Oldenburg, Andy Warhol, and others.

From 1967 to 1973 Bianchini worked as a private dealer and publisher of art books. Under his imprint, "A Paul Bianchini Book," he produced in the United States and Europe a series of books on artists, including Roy Lichtenstein, Alberto Giacometti, Willem de Kooning, Sol LeWitt, and Richard Lindner. He also published print portfolios and artists' books.

In 1960 Bianchini married the American author and visual artist Pati Hill, and together they raised their daughter, Paola, now a photographer. After he closed his New York business in 1973, the Bianchinis moved back to France where, in 1982, Bianchini assisted James B. Sherwood (then president of Sea Containers Ltd.) in restoring and launching the new Venice-Simplon-Orient-Express (VSOE). Returning to his primary passion, Bianchini opened in 1990 Galerie Toner in Paris, and then Galerie Jules Verne, in the town of Sens, both of which promoted artists working with toner, and then laser prints.

ALEXEY BRODOVITCH (1898–1971) was the art director of *Harper's Bazaar* for twenty-five years. He was also a professor of graphic design and one of the first to teach design as a professional discipline in America. Born in Russia, he moved to Paris in 1920 and began his career painting stage sets for Sergei Diaghilev and the Ballets Russes. Before moving to the United States in 1930, he worked as an art director for the famous French department store Aux Trois Quartiers, and designed street posters for Martini Vermouth, Le Printemps, and Au Bon Marché. In 1930 Brodovitch began what came to be called, three years later, the Design Laboratory. This workshop was conducted for more than two decades at various schools and private locations, including Yale University, the New School for Social Research, and the Corcoran Museum of Art. Brodovitch's philosophy of design influenced several generations of photographers and art directors, including Richard Avedon, Irving Penn, Garry Winogrand, and Marvin Israel.

As art director from 1934 until 1958 at *Harper's Bazaar*, Brodovitch incorporated the tenets of surrealism, abstract expressionism, and finally minimalism into the fabric of the magazine. He is credited for introducing Americans to European avant-garde artists. Between 1949 and 1951 Brodovitch and fellow editor Frank Zachary produced three issues of *Portfolio*, a journal of the graphic arts that is often cited as the most innovative visual experiment of the era. Brodovitch designed many books, most notably Richard Avedon and Truman Capote's *Observations* (1959).

ROBERT BROWN (B. 1926) was born in New Jersey, spent his childhood in the Bronx, New York, and is a stage, television, and screen actor best known for his television role as Jason Bolt, the oldest of three brothers in *Here Come the Brides* (ABC, 1968–70). He established his credentials as a stage actor in New York City in the 1940s and '50s where he studied alongside Walter Matthau and Rod Steiger at Erwin Piscador's dramatic workshop at the New School for Social Research. His first Broadway casting was in Lee Strasberg's *Skipper Next to God* (1948). Brown performed in Carson McCullers's *A Member of the Wedding* (1950) and in Maxwell Anderson's *Barefoot in Athens* (1951) and, in 1958, played Stephen Dedalus opposite Zero Mostel's Leopold Bloom in *Ulysses in Nighttown*. After moving to Los Angeles in 1959 Brown starred as Father Riccardo Fontana in the original Los Angeles production (and the national tour) of Rolf Hochhuth's *The Deputy* (1963).

Early in his New York stage career Brown lived in a small apartment adjoining Diane and Allan Arbus's on East 72nd Street, and later encouraged Allan to begin his training with the Russian acting coach Mira Rostova. Now retired from the theater, Brown does voice-overs for television and radio commercials, and is at work on a novel.

NANCY CHRISTOPHERSON (1924–2010) worked as a model, dancer, painter, and costume designer. Born in Cleveland, Ohio, she attended Cleveland College, Case Western Reserve University, then in the mid-1940s moved to New York City. She was briefly married to New York art dealer Richard Bellamy. Christopherson worked as a John Robert Powers model and posed for Diane and Allan Arbus. The Arbuses' daughter Doon, and Christopherson's daughter, Poni, were the same age and became close friends. Christopherson was interested in metaphysical disciplines, and long before it became popular in America, she introduced the Arbus family to the *I Ching, or Book of Changes*, the ancient Chinese (Taoist) wisdom and divination manual.

Soon after Christopherson moved to New York, she met Maya Deren, the Russian-born American avant-garde filmmaker and film theorist, who included her as a dancer in *Ritual in Transfixed Time* (1945–46), a celebrated short, silent film that features dance performances by Rita Christiani and Frank Westbrook, as well as Anaïs Nin. From the 1950s to the '70s, she designed costumes for several Off-Off-Broadway productions, including Al Carmines's show at the Judson Dance Theater.

MARICLARE COSTELLO was born in Peoria, Illinois, and is an actress, director, and teacher. She graduated from Clarke College in Dubuque, Iowa, attended the University of Vienna in Austria, and received a master's degree in theater from Catholic University of America. She worked as an actress Off-Broadway in a number of productions, most notably *The Hostage*. In 1962 she became a member of the original Lincoln Center Repertory Company, headed by Elia Kazan, Robert Lewis, and Robert Whitehead, where she trained and performed for four years. In its initial season she originated the role of Louise in Arthur Miller's *After the Fall* (1964). She appeared in a number of Broadway plays and began a long association with the renowned acting coach Mira Rostova. For two years she worked with Jerome Robbins in his experimental company, American Theatre Lab. She is a member of The Actors Studio, and studied improvisation with Viola Spolin.

Costello met Allan Arbus in 1965. Through him she met and subsequently developed independent relationships with Diane Arbus and the two Arbus daughters, Doon and Amy. In 1969 shortly after Allan Arbus moved to Los Angeles, California, Costello joined him there. They married in 1976. A year later their daughter, Arin, was born.

Costello's acting career broadened to include television and film. She acted in more than twenty movies, including *The Execution of Private Slovik* (1974). She has taught and directed children's theater and is currently a member of the theatre arts faculty at Loyola Marymount University in Los Angeles, for which she directed *The Skin of Our Teeth* by Thornton Wilder in October 2002. In February 2003 she directed another Wilder play, *Our Town*, for The Interact Theater Company in North Hollywood.

PETER CROOKSTON (B. 1936) has been a journalist for more than forty years. He first worked as a reporter and copy editor on newspapers in his hometown of Newcastle upon Tyne, then moved to London where he wrote for the

Daily Express. From 1961 to 1964 Crookston was picture editor for David Astor's *The Observer*, Great Britain's oldest Sunday newspaper. In his subsequent positions as assistant, then deputy editor at *The London Sunday Times Magazine* (1964–69), he came into contact with Arbus, whose photographs he soon featured.

Crookston published "Two American Families" (*The London Sunday Times Magazine*, November 10, 1968). As editor of *Nova* magazine (1969–71), a protofeminist women's monthly, he printed, among other series, Arbus's portraits of famous-people lookalikes: "People Who Think They Look Like Other People" (*Nova*, October 1969). With his former colleagues at *The London Sunday Times Magazine*, Crookston co-sponsored Arbus's productive April 1969 trip to England which resulted in three *Nova* articles and a series of portraits of wax figures in Madame Tussaud's Wax Museum that were published posthumously in *Diane Arbus: Magazine Work* (1984).

In 1973 Crookston rejoined *The Observer* and four years later became editor of *The Observer Magazine*, a post he held until 1982. He then went on to edit many other international publications. Since 1998 he has worked as a freelance writer for several newspapers, including *The Observer* and the *Daily Mail*. Crookston is the author of *Villian: The Biography of a Criminal* (1967). He is also the editor of a series of histories of England. *The Pitman's Requiem*, his book on the Durham coal miner and composer Robert Saint, was published in 2010.

VICTOR D'AMICO (1904–87) was founding director of education at The Museum of Modern Art from 1937 to 1969. D'Amico met Arbus early in his career while teaching at the Fieldston School in Riverdale, New York.

In 1960 d'Amico and his wife, Mabel (1909–98), a high school art teacher, founded the Victor d'Amico Institute of Art, also known as The Art Barge, a summer art school built on a refurbished World War I navy barge beached along Napeague Harbor at the eastern end of Long Island. In addition to his museum and institute programs, d'Amico was also the author of numerous books on art education, including *Creative Teaching in Art* (1942, 1953); and with Arlette Buchman, *Assemblage: A New Dimension in Creative Teaching in Action* (1972). His lectures, correspondence, audio and video tapes, and teaching slides are preserved at Columbia University in the Model School Library at Teachers College.

RENE D'HARNONCOURT (1901–68) was the director of The Museum of Modern Art, New York, from 1949 to 1967. Born in Vienna, he was schooled first in Graz, Austria, then at the university in Vienna. D'Harnoncourt studied philosophy and chemistry and was an amateur painter. In 1925 he moved to Mexico City and amassed an important collection of Mexican art. Dwight W. Morrow, then United States Ambassador to Mexico, convinced d'Harnoncourt to build a special collection of indigenous Mexican art to be shown in the United States. *The Exhibition of Mexican Arts* opened at The Metropolitan Museum of Art in 1930 and included 1,200 works of early and contemporary fine and decorative arts from the time of Spain's conquest of Mexico to the 1920s. It was the first major show on the origin and development of Mexican civilization through its arts.

Mexican Arts and its national tour circulated by the Carnegie Institute and the American Federation of Arts established d'Harnoncourt's reputation as a collector, curator, and impresario. A specialist in the art of indigenous peoples, d'Harnoncourt became a member of the Indian Arts and Crafts Board of the Department of Interior in 1936. In 1944 he joined the staff of MoMA and after five years succeeded Alfred Barr as the institution's second director.

Indian Art of the United States (1941), an exhibition catalog for a show at MoMA, was the author's first major academic publication. As director of MoMA, d'Harnoncourt provided introductions or was the coauthor of numerous museum publications including such standard texts as *Art of the South Seas* (1946) and *Ancient Art of the Andes* (1954). His last publication, *d'Hoodles* (1966), is a witty compilation of scribblings made by d'Harnoncourt during meetings at MoMA. D'Harnoncourt was killed by a drunk driver on Long Island, New York, a year after his retirement from the museum.

ALEXANDER ELIOT (B. 1919) is an art critic, novelist, and essayist who established his reputation with the book *Three Hundred Years of American Painting* (1957). After graduating from the Loomis School in Windsor, Connecticut, he went to Black Mountain College in North Carolina where he spent two years (1936–38) studying art with Josef Albers and stage studies with Xanti Schawinsky. Eliot moved to New York City in the early 1940s and worked at the Associated American

Artists Gallery, then for the March of Time Newsreel Service. From 1945 to 1960 he was a sportswriter, then art editor, at *Time* magazine where he wrote features about Pablo Picasso, Henri Matisse, and Diego Rivera, among other modern masters.

Among Eliot's more than twenty publications are *Proud Youth* (1953), a novel for which Diane and Allan Arbus provided an author's photograph; *Sight and Insight* (1959); *The Horizon Concise History of Greece* (1972); and *The Universal Myths: Heroes, Gods, Tricksters and Others* (1990).

In 1938, when he was nineteen, Eliot met Arbus, a fifteen-year-old fellow summer student at the Cummington School of the Arts near Northampton, Massachusetts. Eliot and Arbus remained friends for the next three decades. Arbus served as godmother to Eliot's daughter, May, from his first marriage to Anne Dick. For most of the 1960s and early '70s, Eliot, his second wife, Jane Winslow Eliot, and their two children lived abroad and collaborated on books about the myths of ancient civilizations, returning to the United States in 1976, and later moved to Venice, California.

WALKER EVANS (1903–75) is regarded as the progenitor of the documentary tradition in American photography. His 1938 publication and exhibition at The Museum of Modern Art depicted the daily lives of ordinary citizens.

Evans was born in St. Louis and raised in the Chicago suburb of Kenilworth. After a year at Williams College he moved to New York to pursue writing. By 1928 he had taken up the camera, and small selections of his photographs soon appeared in literary and arts magazines of the late 1920s and early '30s.

Like his Greenwich Village roommate Ben Shahn, Evans found employment in Franklin Delano Roosevelt's New Deal. From 1935 to 1937 he worked primarily in the American South as a photographer for the government's Resettlement (later called the Farm Security) Administration. Evans collaborated with the poet and writer James Agee to create a written and photographic portrait of three tenant farm families in Alabama, which eventually became *Let Us Now Praise Famous Men* (1941).

In 1938 Evans began a new project on subway passengers. Art director Marvin Israel published some of the images as "Walker Evans: The Unposed Portrait" in *Harper's Bazaar* in 1962, four years before they appeared in a book, with an essay by James Agee, entitled *Many Are Called* (1966).

From 1945 to 1965, Evans worked at *Fortune* magazine as special photographic editor and produced some forty portfolios. Evans served as a long-term member of the John Simon Guggenheim Memorial Foundation arts selection committee, and in this capacity encouraged numerous artists from Robert Frank (1955) to Arbus (1963) to apply for fellowships. He met Arbus in late 1961 and included her in his chapter survey of the eighteen most important artists in the history of photography in *Quality: Its Image in the Arts* (1969), edited by Louis Kronenberger. He taught photography at Yale University and produced his last photographs in 1973–74 with an SX-70 Polaroid. In 1994, twenty years after Evans's death, his complete personal archive of negatives, transparencies, papers, and collections was acquired by The Metropolitan Museum of Art.

BEA FEITLER (1938–82) was born in Rio de Janeiro but moved to New York to study design. A student of Marvin Israel's at Parsons School of Design, she was hired by Israel in 1961 as his assistant art director at *Harper's Bazaar*. After Israel was fired two years later, Feitler and another assistant, Ruth Ansel, jointly succeeded him. The collaboration of Feitler and Ansel defined 1960s magazine design.

Feitler co–art directed *Harper's Bazaar* for ten years until she left in May 1972 to design and launch *Ms.* magazine with Gloria Steinem. Six years later she became a consulting art director for Condé Nast Publications where she developed the graphic image for *Self* magazine. From 1975 to 1981 Feitler was art director of *Rolling Stone*, which she redesigned in 1977 and again in 1981. She taught design from 1974 until 1980 at the School of Visual Arts. When in 1970 Arbus produced her only portfolio, *A box of ten photographs*, Feitler purchased one of the few sets known to have been sold. It is now in the collection of the Smithsonian American Art Museum, Washington, D.C.

In addition to her magazine work, Feitler also designed album covers, books and their jackets, and even theatrical costumes, including the cover of *Black and Blue* for the Rolling Stones (1976) and Richard Avedon's *Diary of a Century: Jacques Henri Lartigue* (1970). She also designed *Cole* (1971), a massive volume of Cole Porter's lyrics, photographs, and discography. Her final magazine project was the redesign of *Vanity Fair*; the premier issue came out after her death of cancer. Feitler's personal archive of artwork, magazines, correspondence, and photographs is housed in the Adam & Sophie Gimbel Design Library at Parsons School of Design.

CLAY FELKER (1925–2008) was director of the Felker Magazine Center, University of California at Berkeley, Graduate School of Journalism. A 1951 graduate of Duke University, Felker began his journalism career covering sports for *Life* magazine, then in 1954 worked with Henry Luce and others on the development of *Sports Illustrated*. By 1957 he was features editor at *Esquire* and, along with Harold Hayes, Robert Benton, and David Newman, transformed Arnold Gingrich's men's monthly into a more sophisticated venue featuring contemporary writers and artists such as Vladimir Nabokov, Andy Warhol, and Arbus.

One of the architects of the literary movement known as New Journalism, his influential Sunday supplement to the *New York Herald Tribune*—the precursor to *New York* magazine—featured photographs by Arbus, and helped introduce the work of Gloria Steinem and Tom Wolfe into the pages of American magazines. He published Wolfe's two-part evisceration of William Shawn and *The New Yorker*, "Tiny Mummies! The True Story of the Ruler of 43rd Street's Land of the Walking Dead!" and "Lost in the Whichy Thickets: *The New Yorker*" (1965).

In 1968 he became the founding editor of *New York* magazine as an independent publication. For the magazine's fourth issue, Felker hired Arbus for a story entitled "La Dolce Viva," about the Warhol "superstar" Viva. The controversial story, which featured a nude portrait by Arbus, led to a major advertising loss for the fledgling magazine, but did not ultimately affect its success.

Felker also later served as editor of, among other magazines, *The Village Voice*. He authored *Casey Stengel's Secret* (1961) and served as editor of *The Best American Magazine Writing* 2000. In 1994, he joined the University of California at Berkeley's faculty as a lecturer, and the Graduate School of Journalism established the Felker Magazine Center one year later.

SHIRLEY FINGERHOOD (1928–2008) was born in New York City and was an attorney in private practice. She graduated from Fieldston School in 1940 in the same class as Arbus and their mutual friend Stewart Stern, the screenwriter. After graduating from Vassar in 1944, Fingerhood returned to the city where she renewed her friendship with Arbus. Fingerhood graduated from Yale Law School in 1951 and moved for a year to Washington, D.C.

In 1952 Fingerhood returned to New York and established a legal practice specializing in literary and First Amendment cases. In the course of her fifty-year career Fingerhood represented a wide range of clients in the fields of entertainment, the arts, and literature, including Arbus and three Pulitzer Prize winners. In 1978 she became a judge and sat on the Supreme Court of the State of New York from 1986 to 1994.

Arbus frequently consulted Fingerhood on legal matters from the mid-1950s until her death. Fingerhood served on the boards of several charitable organizations, and was a director of the Lawyers' Committee on Nuclear Policy (LCNP), a national nonprofit educational association founded in 1981 that uses national and international law to promote peace and disarmament.

MICHAEL FLANAGAN (B. 1943) was born in Buffalo, New York, and is a painter, graphic designer, and author. While studying painting at Parsons School of Design (1963–66), he met art director Marvin Israel through whom he was introduced to many artists, including Robert Frank and Arbus. Flanagan was greatly influenced by Arbus's first class at Parsons in the fall of 1965.

After his graduation and before he enrolled in Yale University's graduate painting program, he worked in the summer of 1966 for Allan Arbus as a darkroom assistant and contact-printed Diane Arbus's negatives. In 1969, after a year studying minimalist painting at Yale, Flanagan taught himself the art of book jacket design. With Marvin Israel he designed several notable photography books, including Clark Worswick and Ainslie Embree's *The Last Empire: Photography in British India, 1855–1911* (1976), and *Unseen Versailles* (1981) by Deborah Turbeville.

By 1981 Flanagan had his first one-person exhibition at Cordier and Ekstrom Gallery, New York. Numerous solo and group shows followed, as well as fellowships in painting from Yaddo (1988), the artists' community in Saratoga Springs, New York, and from the New York Foundation for the Arts (1986, 1987, 1992). Despite his success as a painter, however, Flanagan is probably best known for the critically lauded *Stations: An Imaginary Journey* (1994), a hybrid novel that integrates his artwork and original writing.

MARY FRANK (B. 1933) is known for her gestural, figurative sculptures, drawings, paintings, and monoprints. She is the recipient of two John Simon Guggenheim Memorial Foundation Fellowships (1973, 1983) and was elected to the American Academy and Institute of Arts and Letters in 1984. She has work in numerous public collections, including the Hirshhorn Museum and Sculpture Garden, The Metropolitan Museum of Art, The Museum of Modern Art, and the Whitney Museum of American Art. She is the subject of two major monographic essays: Hayden Herrara's *Mary Frank* (1990) and Linda Nochlin's *Mary Frank: Encounters* (2000), an exhibition catalog that accompanied a large painting retrospective at the Neuberger Museum of Art.

Born in London, Mary Frank came to the United States when she was seven years old and settled in Brooklyn with her mother, the American-born painter Eleanore Lockspeiser. While in high school she studied modern dance with Hanya Holm, then later with Martha Graham and José Limón in the first year of the summer dance program (later the American Dance Festival) at Connecticut College in New London. In 1950 she studied drawing and painting with Max Beckmann at the American Art School, and took life drawing classes with Hans Hofmann. That same year she married the Swiss photographer Robert Frank, with whom she had two children, Pablo and Andrea. Without any formal training, Mary Frank began to make sculpture in wood and plaster, then ultimately in clay, incorporating into her art her dance training and its reliance on gesture and movement. Mary Frank met Arbus in the mid-1950s through the art dealer Richard Bellamy who lived near the Franks on 10th Street.

Mary Frank first exhibited her sculpture in the 1950s at the Tanager Gallery in New York, and had her first one-person show at the Stephen Radich Gallery in 1961. From 1965 to 1970 she taught drawing at the New School for Social Research. In 1972 the Solomon R. Guggenheim Museum included her work in *10 Independents*, her first museum exhibition. Since 1968 she has had regular shows at the Zabriskie Gallery, and, since 1996, the DC Moore Gallery, both in New York City. Mary Frank separated from Robert Frank in 1969 and

after her divorce married Leo Treitler, a musicologist and pianist. She is an active antiwar protester and contributes her time and art to the cause.

ROBERT FRANK (B. 1924) is a photographer and filmmaker best known for his book of black-and-white photographs titled *The Americans* (1959), first published in Paris as *Les Américains* (1958). A compilation of two years of picture making across the United States courtesy of an extended fellowship (1955–56) from the John Simon Guggenheim Memorial Foundation, the volume includes an introduction by Jack Kerouac. The book presents a lyrical yet unvarnished look at even the most prosaic aspects of America from gas stations and barrooms to elevator operators and conventioneers. Subsequently published in several revised editions, *The Americans* endures as one of the post–World War II era's most influential monographs. Frank is also the author of numerous other books, including *New York Is* (1959), *The Lines of My Hand* (1972), and *Flower Is...* (1987). His archive is preserved in The Robert Frank Collection at the National Gallery of Art.

Frank was born in Zurich, Switzerland, and at the age of seventeen apprenticed himself to a local photographer, Hermann Segesser. In 1947 he showed the designer Alexey Brodovitch a small handmade book of his original photographs, *40 Fotos*, and was immediately hired by Brodovitch to work for *Harper's Bazaar*. Frank would soon provide fashion and editorial photographs for hundreds of articles in *Harper's Bazaar*, as well as in *Junior Bazaar*, *Life*, *Look*, *McCall's*, and *Fortune* magazines, and *The New York Times*.

In December 1949 *Camera* magazine published "Robert Frank," the artist's first important portfolio. The following year Frank appeared in *51 American Photographers*, curated by Edward Steichen at The Museum of Modern Art. Subsequently he would be included in such important MoMA exhibitions as *Post-War European Photography* (1953) and *The Family of Man* (1955). In 1961 the Art Institute of Chicago organized a retrospective exhibition, *Robert Frank, Photographer*. Other major museum shows would follow, including *Robert Frank: New York to Nova Scotia*, Museum of Fine Arts, Houston (1986); *Robert Frank: Moving Out*, National Gallery of Art, Washington, D.C. (1994); and *Robert Frank: Hold Still-Keep Going*, Museum Folkwang, Essen, Germany (2000).

Frank met Diane and Allan Arbus in the late 1950s when he was switching from still photography to motion pictures. His first film, *Pull My Daisy* (1959), a groundbreaking adaptation of Kerouac's play *The Beat Generation*, was followed by *The Sin of Jesus* (1960), and *Me and My Brother* (1965–68). Among his many films and videos is *Home Improvements* (1985) and full-length features like *Cocksucker Blues* (1972), a ninety-minute cinema verité film about the Rolling Stones's 1972 North American tour.

In August 2002 Frank received the Edward MacDowell Medal from the MacDowell Colony. His most recent film is *True Story* (2004) and his latest photography exhibition, *Looking In: Robert Frank's The Americans*, opened at the National Gallery of Art, Washington, D.C., in 2009, and traveled throughout the year to both the San Francisco Museum of Modern Art and The Metropolitan Museum of Art in New York.

TINA FREDERICKS (B. 1922) began her career as a magazine art director and is now head of the eponymously titled real estate firm in East Hampton, Long Island. As a *Glamour* magazine editor she gave Andy Warhol his first editorial assignment in August 1949. Born in Berlin, Germany, Fredericks is the daughter of the general manager of Ulstein Publishing, still one of Germany's largest publishers. After Hitler came to power, her family emigrated to the United States where her father took a job in 1934 at Hearst Publications. Fredericks attended Bennington College, but after winning a summer scholarship from *Mademoiselle* to work on the August "college" issue, she left school and moved to New York City. She began to sell fashion layout ideas to *Glamour* as a freelancer, and in 1943 Alexander Liberman hired her as assistant art editor under C. P. Penelis.

In 1947 Fredericks became art director of *Glamour* and gave many emerging artists their first jobs, including the illustrator Maurice Sendak, and Diane and Allan Arbus, whose first editorial photographs appeared in "The New Sweater Story Is a Long Story" (*Glamour*, May 1947). The previous month *Glamour* had featured the Arbuses among six other couples in "Mr. and Mrs. Inc." The Arbuses submitted their own portrait for the story. Known as a rebellious editor who appreciated new ideas, Fredericks left Condé Nast in 1953 to become picture editor at *Ladies' Home Journal*. After her first marriage ended, she moved to East Hampton, New York, where she established Tina Fredericks Realty.

LEE FRIEDLANDER (B. 1934) is the author of more than twenty books of photographs, including *The American Monument* (1976); *Like a One-Eyed Cat: Photographs by Lee Friedlander, 1956–1987* (1989); and *American Musicians* (1998). His first book, *Self Portrait* (1970), depicts the American social landscape in snapshots—many in which the artist appears only as a shadow on his generally unsuspecting subjects—of everyday life on city streets. A fellow of the American Academy of Arts and Sciences since 1999, Friedlander has received, among many other awards, three National Endowment for the Arts fellowships (1960, 1962, 1977), the Medal of the City of Paris (1981), the Edward MacDowell Medal for Lifetime Achievement in the Arts (1986), and a John D. and Catherine T. MacArthur Foundation Award (1990).

Born in Aberdeen, Washington, Friedlander took up photography in high school, and after graduation moved to California to enroll in the Los Angeles Art Center School. He met fellow jazz enthusiast Nesuhi Ertegun, a founder of Atlantic Records, who hired him to photograph music legends, from John Coltrane to Aretha Franklin. Friedlander would soon make record-cover portraits for Columbia, RCA, and Atlantic Records.

After moving to New York City in 1956, Friedlander began to work for *Seventeen*, *Esquire*, *McCall's*, and *Collier's* magazines. Through art director Marvin Israel he met and became friends with Walker Evans, Garry Winogrand, and Arbus.

Evans wrote about Friedlander's photographs of television sets broadcasting to otherwise empty motel rooms in a short essay entitled "The Little Screens" (*Harper's Bazaar*, February 1963); and ten years later provided an introduction to Friedlander's first portfolio, "Lee Friedlander: Fifteen Photographs" (1973). The following year Friedlander edited and arranged the publication of Evans's second portfolio, "Walker Evans: Selected Photographs" (1974).

In the late 1950s Friedlander discovered and later acquired and preserved the photographic negatives of Ernest J. Bellocq, the documentarian of New Orleans's red-light district known as Storyville. He printed, exhibited, and published the images in *E. J. Bellocq: Storyville Portraits, Photographs from the New Orleans Red-Light District, Circa 1912* (1970, 1996). Arbus acquired a few of Friedlander's prints of Bellocq's negatives and was among the first of his friends to appreciate their historical importance and psychological complexity.

Friedlander has had many exhibitions, beginning in 1963 with a solo show at the George Eastman House in Rochester, New York, and including *New Documents*, a group show with Garry Winogrand and Arbus that John Szarkowski organized in 1967 for The Museum of Modern Art. In 2000 and 2001, New York's Museum of Modern Art and the National Gallery in Washington, D.C., acquired a substantial number of prints from Friedlander himself. In 2005, New York's Museum of Modern Art hosted *Friedlander*, a major retrospective of the artist's work. A recent book of his photographs, *America by Car*, was published in 2010 by D.A.P./Fraenkel.

HAROLD HAYES (1926–89) was the editor of *Esquire* from 1962 to 1973. One of the architects of the literary movement known as New Journalism, he commissioned articles from Tom Wolfe, Norman Mailer, Gay Talese, Terry Southern, and Raymond Carver. While working as a features editor for an issue on New York City, primarily written by Talese, Hayes sent the still-untried Arbus into the streets with a press pass and letters of introduction from the magazine. The resulting article, "The Vertical Journey: Six Movements of a Moment Within the Heart of the City" (July 1960), complete with Arbus's own captions, served as the catalyst for her work of the 1960s.

Born in Elkin, West Virginia, the son of a Southern Baptist minister, and reared in Winston-Salem, North Carolina, Hayes graduated in 1948 from Wake Forest University. After two years in the marines, he landed a job as an editor at *Pageant*, a competitor to *Reader's Digest*. In 1956 he moved to *Esquire* where he worked with Clay Felker and Robert Benton under Arnold Gingrich, the founding editor of the magazine. As managing editor, Hayes promoted many of the era's most creative talents—from George Lois to Michael Herr. While with *Esquire*, Hayes edited a selection of essays by his writers entitled *Smiling Through the Apocalypse: Esquire's History of the Sixties* (1969).

In the early 1970s Hayes moved to California where he took over the editorship of *California* magazine. He ended his career writing books on Africa, including *The Last Place on Earth* (1977) and the posthumous *The Dark Romance of Dian Fossey* (1990). His November 1986 essay on Fossey for *Life* magazine served as the basis for the film *Gorillas in the Mist* (1988). Hayes's papers are in the Z. Smith Reynolds Library at Wake Forest University.

PATI HILL (b. 1921) is a writer and visual artist whose novels include *The Nine Mile Circle* (1957), *Prosper* (1960), and *One Thing I Know* (1962), which she dedicated to Arbus. The two met in New York City in the early 1940s when Hill was beginning her career as a fashion model. She and Arbus remained friends for thirty years.

In the late 1930s Hill left George Washington University for New York City and became a John Robert Powers fashion model, often seen in the pages of *Harper's Bazaar*. She also began her literary career, producing a monthly advice column for *Seventeen* magazine during its early years, and short stories for *Mademoiselle*. Hill first married Jack Long, an editor at *Collier's*, then in 1947 Robert Meservey, a photographer (later physicist). By 1950 she had appeared in advertisements by Diane and Allan Arbus for Russek's, divorced her first two husbands, and moved to Paris to model for Molyneux and other couturiers. She contributed short fiction to *The Paris Review* from 1953 to 1978 and completed her first published book, *The Pit and the Century Plant* (1955).

Hill moved back to the United States in the late 1950s and lived in New York and in Stonington, Connecticut, where she met the poet James Merrill, and Truman Capote, with whom she published "The Art of Fiction XVII" (*The Paris Review*, spring-summer 1957), an interview that anticipated the publication of *Breakfast at Tiffany's*. In 1960 she married the French gallerist and art publisher Paul Bianchini, and had a daughter, Paola (1962). In 1973, at the request of Doon Arbus, Hill translated, with Alain de la Falaise, the original text of *Diane Arbus* for the French publisher Editions du Chêne.

Hill began to work as an artist in 1975 and had three exhibitions at the Jill Kornblee Gallery in New York City. One of the pioneers of "copy art," she is recognized for her advocacy of xerography and for the quality that she demonstrated could be obtained through the use of toner as a print medium. She produced several artist's books with Kornblee, including *Slave Days: 29 Poems, 31 Photocopied Objects* (1975). The Versailles project, her chef d'oeuvre, is an ongoing work that is the subject of several published commentaries, including F. de Merdieu's *Pati Hill, or the Catalogue of Magical Objects* (Art Press, France, #76, December 1983). Hill's most recent exhibitions include 2005's *Pati Hill, vers Versailles* at the Musée Lambinet, France, and the 2000 exhibition of *Wall Papers* at the Bayly Art Museum, University of Virginia,

Charlottesville. Her artwork is in the collections of the Cooper-Hewitt, National Design Museum, Smithsonian Institution, and the Musée de Sens.

MARVIN ISRAEL (1924–84) was a painter, art director, graphic designer, and influential teacher. Born in Syracuse, New York, he briefly attended Ethical Culture School in New York City. He received a B.F.A. from Syracuse University in 1950 and in 1955 an M.F.A. in graphic design from Yale University. In 1950 Israel married the Cuban-born sculptor and ceramicist Margaret Ponce Israel (1929–87). Israel became art director at *Seventeen* in 1957. At *Harper's Bazaar* (1961–63) he replaced Henry Wolf, successor to Alexey Brodovitch with whom Israel had studied at Yale. Israel featured *Harper's Bazaar* star photographer, Richard Avedon, and also artists such as Arbus, Robert Frank, Lee Friedlander, Larry Rivers, and Andy Warhol, along with established masters such as Martin Munkacsi, Henri Cartier-Bresson, and Walker Evans. From 1957 to 1963 he worked as a freelance art director for Atlantic Records, designing record covers for the label's roster of jazz and blues artists.

Israel taught design and painting at Parsons School of Design (1959–64), School of Visual Arts (1965–67), and Cooper Union School of Art (1968–69); and in 1967 he conducted a master class in photography with Avedon, to which Arbus was an occasional guest artist. Israel produced many photography publications, including *Nothing Personal* (1964), by Richard Avedon, with text by James Baldwin; Lee Friedlander's *Self Portrait* (1970); and the first two of Arbus's posthumous publications, *Diane Arbus* (1972) and *Diane Arbus: Magazine Work* (1984). In the 1970s and '80s Israel's longterm collaboration with Avedon expanded to include the exhibition design for most of the photographer's large shows including *Richard Avedon*, a retrospective at the Minneapolis Institute of Arts; *Portraits, 1969–1975* (1975), at the Marlborough Gallery, New York, and the Seibu Museum of Art, Tokyo (1977); and *In the American West* (1985), which opened at the Amon Carter Museum, Fort Worth, Texas, a year after Israel's death.

Israel designed Arbus's only portfolio, *A box of ten photographs* (1970). The portfolio box—manufactured of clear plastic—served both as safe storage for the prints and as an exhibition frame for any one of the ten photographs. His simple but effective design is credited with inaugurating a new style of acrylic exhibition frames that soon dominated the New York gallery scene in the 1970s.

For the last twenty years of his life, Israel devoted much of his creative efforts to his own artwork; his paintings can be found in the collections of The Museum of Modern Art, the Whitney Museum of American Art, and the Art Institute of Chicago, among others. A documentary about his life and work, *Who is Marvin Israel?*, was produced by Neil Selkirk and Doon Arbus and premiered at The Metropolitan Museum of Art in 2005.

CLARENCE JOHN LAUGHLIN (1905–85) was born near Lake Charles, Louisiana, and in 1910 moved with his family to New Orleans where he lived for the rest of his life. In the mid-1920s he discovered the poetry and prose of the French Symbolists, as well as Edgar Allan Poe and Herman Melville, and began to write original poems and Gothic fiction, eventually earning a reputation as the "Baudelaire of the Bayou." Laughlin held a variety of jobs from 1924 to 1935, including a clerkship in a New Orleans bank, but by the late 1920s he was known regionally as an important bibliophile. By 1934 he had taught himself the rudiments of photography and soon began corresponding with a wide range of artists and writers from Margaret Bourke-White to Man Ray, André Breton, Eugene Berman, and Joseph Cornell. His photography also began to appear in *Photographie* (1939, 1954), *U.S. Camera* (1940), *Du* (1954), and *Life* (1942, 1960), among other journals and avant-garde publications.

Laughlin worked from 1936 to 1940 as a Civil Service photographer for the United States Army Corps of Engineers recording construction work on the Mississippi River levees between New Orleans and Vicksburg, Mississippi. He also began his thirty-year documentation of the region's nineteenth-century architecture. In 1936 he had his first one-person show of photographs at the Isaac Delgado Museum of New Orleans (now the New Orleans Museum of Art), then four years later exhibited his photographs of old New Orleans with Eugène Atget's photographs of Paris at the Julien Levy Gallery in New York City. Laughlin had in his lifetime more than two hundred solo shows at, among others, the Art Institute of Chicago and the Philadelphia Museum of Art. Laughlin is perhaps best known for *Ghosts Along the Mississippi: An Essay in the Poetic Interpretation of Louisiana's*

Plantation Architecture (1948), a book of his writings and photographs that blends documentary description with surrealism.

Arbus corresponded with Laughlin in April 1962 just after *Infinity* magazine published "The Full Circle," the reprint of her portraits of eccentrics, and around the time when a second edition of *Ghosts Along the Mississippi* was released. It is not known how they were introduced, but they likely met in person two years later when Arbus traveled to New Orleans to photograph Mardi Gras celebrations. Laughlin has been the subject of several monographs. His archive of master prints, negatives, papers, and correspondence is preserved by The Historic New Orleans Collection; the Louisiana State University in Baton Rouge houses his massive library of thirty thousand volumes. Upon his request, Laughlin was buried in Père Lachaise cemetery in Paris.

HELEN LEVITT (1913–2009) was born in Brooklyn, New York, and had her first solo show of photographs at The Museum of Modern Art in 1943. For more than half a century, she explored the nature of life on her native city's streets in black-and-white and color photographs, and also in documentary films. James Agee provided the introduction to her first book, *A Way of Seeing* (1965).

Levitt began her career as a motion picture camera operator and film cutter while assisting Helen Von Dongen, one of several editors working for Luis Buñuel at The Museum of Modern Art during World War II making short, pro-democracy documentaries for the U.S. government. In 1945 Levitt collaborated with Janice Loeb on *In the Street*, a documentary set in Harlem. With the filmmaker Sidney Meyers, Levitt and Loeb also worked together on *The Quiet One* (1948–49), a feature-length documentary about a delinquent boy that won first prize at the Venice Film Festival, among many other honors, including an Academy Award nomination for best story and screenplay.

In the 1950s and early '60s, while working in Hollywood, Levitt wrote a support letter for Arbus's first Guggenheim fellowship application. (The two artists did not meet until later in the decade and Levitt wrote her recommendation after reviewing a set of prints Arbus sent by mail to California at Walker Evans's suggestion.)

Levitt's photographs were featured in hundreds of museum exhibitions in the United States and Europe, including the 1991 retrospective at the San Francisco

Museum of Modern Art that traveled across the United States. Levitt published two expanded editions of *A Way of Seeing*, as well as many other volumes of photographs, including *In the Street* (1987); *Mexico City* (1997); *Crosstown* (2001); and *Here and There* (2003). In 2008, she published her final collection, the self-titled *Helen Levitt*, in conjunction with a retrospective show at Germany's Sprengel Museum Hannover.

ALEXANDER LIBERMAN (1912–99) was born in Kiev, Russia, and schooled in England and Paris, graduating in 1930 with a degree in philosophy and mathematics from the Sorbonne. He studied painting with the cubist painter André Lhote, architecture at the Ecole des Beaux-Arts, then worked as an assistant to the renowned designer, Cassandre. From 1933 to 1936 Liberman was assistant art director at *Vu*, the progressive Paris-based magazine dedicated to photography that was Henry Luce's model for *Life*. He left the monthly in 1936 to devote himself to painting and writing, and after the Nazi occupation of France emigrated to the United States. In 1941 Liberman became art director of *Vogue*. He held this position for twenty-one years, until he was promoted to editorial director of all Condé Nast publications, a title he kept until his retirement in 1994. Under his leadership, *Vogue* integrated high art and culture with the world of fashion by regularly including serious art criticism in its pages alongside commissioned work by Marcel Duchamp, Salvador Dali, Marc Chagall, and Joseph Cornell.

Throughout his fifty-three years in fashion, Liberman made paintings, photographs, and ultimately sculpture. His work can be found in most public collections worldwide. Liberman is the author of numerous publications, including *The Artist and His Studio* (1960); *Dietrich: An Intimate Photographic Memoir* (1992); and a personal memoir, *Then: Photographs 1925–1995* (1995).

MARGUERITE LAMKIN LITTMAN (B. 1929) is a director of the Elton John AIDS Foundation and a member of the national council for amfAR.

Littman was born in Monroe, Louisiana. She went to Miss Finch's Finishing School in New York City, then Newcomb College at Tulane University in New Orleans where she studied philosophy. In 1949 she moved to Los Angeles, following her brother, Speed Lamkin, the novelist and playwright. Littman continued her study of philosophy at UCLA and soon became friends with Dorothy Parker and Christopher Isherwood, as well as Tennessee Williams. In 1955 she taught Barbara Bel Geddes how to speak "Southern" for her role as Maggie in Elia Kazan's original stage production of Williams's *Cat on a Hot Tin Roof*; three years later she coached Elizabeth Taylor in the film version. Littman was for many years a dialect coach for the stage and screen and worked on more than ten Hollywood films, including Williams's *Baby Doll* (1956), and William Faulkner's *The Long, Hot Summer* (1958) and *The Sound and the Fury* (1959).

After a brief marriage to the screenwriter Harry Brown, Littman moved to New York City around 1960 and became the arts editor at *Glamour* magazine. In February 1963, at the suggestion of their mutual friend Marvin Israel, Richard Avedon hired her to work with him on his current photographic project—taken on various trips from New York to Louisiana—of civil rights demonstrations, racist politicians, elderly former slaves, and members of the Student Non-Violent Coordinating Committee. With James Baldwin's text, the project was published as *Nothing Personal* (1964).

Through Marvin Israel, Littman met Arbus and subsequently assigned and published "What's New: The Witch Predicts," *Glamour*, January and October 1964. The story features uncredited texts by Arbus about the most famous Los Angeles soothsayers whose clients included, among others, Elvis Presley, Jayne Mansfield, and Littman's friend, Elizabeth Taylor.

In 1962 Littman adopted the pen name Daisy and started a column in *Glamour* that advised lovelorn young girls on how to win and keep their men. She married her third husband, the barrister and Queen's Counsel Mark Littman, and moved to London.

CARLOTTA MARSHALL (B. 1939) was born in Atlanta, Georgia, and raised in Jacksonville, Florida. She graduated in 1957 from The Ethel Walker School in Simsbury, Connecticut, and after living with her grandmother in Paris moved at age nineteen to New York City. She met Arbus during her first week in Manhattan.

In 1959–60 Marshall attended poetry classes at Columbia University and at the New School for Social Research, and, with a friend, opened a small shop called The Bead Studio. She held various odd jobs related to photography, including working for filmmaker Robert Frank, the French photo agency, Rapho Guillumette,

commercial photographer David Attie, art director Alexey Brodovitch, and German-born photographer Hans Namuth. Marshall also modeled for an unpublished Diane Arbus feature for *Harper's Bazaar*.

She studied religion at New York's Union Theological Seminary, then in 1963–64 lived and traveled in Greece. Upon her return to New York City, Marshall met Sister Cora Brady, the distinguished professor of religion at Manhattanville College, a Catholic school run by the Society of the Sacred Heart in Purchase, New York. Sister Brady conceived and directed the Masters in Religious Education (M.R.E.) program.

In 1966 Marshall moved to Holland and married Louis Berger, a fellow theological student, and a year later gave birth to their son, Jamie. In the spring of 1968 Marshall visited New York and introduced Sister Brady to Arbus. While in Holland a few months later, Marshall developed encephalitis which triggered multiple sclerosis. She and Arbus corresponded steadily during the worst weeks of her severe illness.

In summer 1969, Sister Brady taught a Manhattanville College course for nuns, some from silent orders, who had recently left their convents. She invited Arbus to speak to her class and present slides of her work. Brady's objective was to introduce the sisters to life outside of the cloister. On July 14, 1969, six days before the historic moon walk and a month before the music festival at Woodstock, Arbus gave an evening lecture to the school entitled "The Still and All."

When Marshall's husband decided to pursue a monastic life in 1971, Marshall moved from Holland to London with Jamie who was then four years old. She became involved in childhood education, helping to facilitate the Early Education Project at the Froebel Institute. Marshall also supports the Campaign for Nuclear Disarmament (CND). She has lived in New York since 1997 and remains an active antiwar protester.

ROBERT MESERVEY (B. 1921) was born in Hanover, New Hampshire, and is a low-temperature physicist known for his research in superconductivity and magnetism at Massachusetts Institute of Technology (MIT). The son of a Dartmouth College professor, Meservey graduated from the college with a B.A. in physics in 1943 and was immediately drafted. A champion alpine skier, he became a rock climbing and skiing instructor in the Tenth Mountain Division, but by the end of 1944, instead of being sent overseas with the division, he was assigned to develop night-vision equipment at an army laboratory in Virginia, where he spent the rest of the war.

A lifelong devotee of photography, Meservey moved to New York City in the summer of 1946 to become second assistant to the fashion photographer Fernand Fonssagrives. Through Pati Hill, Meservey met and befriended Diane and Allan Arbus, who were just beginning their careers as fashion photographers. In early 1947 Meservey and Hill were married and left New York, traveling and working together on various photographic projects, including the contemporary photographs for Antoinette F. Downing and Vincent J. Scully, Jr.'s *The Architectural Heritage of Newport, Rhode Island, 1640–1915* (1952). Meservey and Hill separated in 1949, and for the next two years Meservey worked as a freelancer.

At the beginning of the Korean War, Meservey gave up photography for science and from 1951 to 1955 worked as a civilian physicist in night-vision research at the Army Research and Development Lab in Fort Belvoir, Virginia. In 1953 he married his present wife, Evelyn (Lyn) Miller Meservey, a painter then working in Washington, D.C., and two years later entered Yale University, where he earned a doctorate in 1961 in physics for an optical study of superfluid helium. After graduation Meservey conducted research on superconductivity at MIT's Lincoln Lab, then moved in 1963 to MIT's Magnet Lab (the Francis Bitter Magnet Laboratory). For more than thirty years he led a research team in low-temperature physics, superconductivity, and magnetism, and is known for the discovery of spin-polarized electron tunneling. Meservey retired in 1998, lives in Cambridge, Massachusetts, and continues to publish and write reviews as a visiting scientist at MIT.

JOSEPH MITCHELL (1908–96) was born on a tobacco and cotton farm in Robeson County, North Carolina, and attended the University of North Carolina for four years but left before graduating to take a reporting job in Durham. Mitchell moved to New York City in 1929 and spent his first decade there working as a newspaper reporter for the *Morning World*, the *New York Herald Tribune*, and the *New York World-Telegram*. In 1938 he moved to *The New Yorker* where he worked for fifty-eight years as a writer of "Talk of the Town" and of profiles of some of the city's most eccentric inhabitants and their milieu.

Mitchell's first book was a collection of his newspaper articles entitled *My Ears Are Bent* (1938). It was followed by, among others, *McSorley's Wonderful Saloon* (1943); *Old Mr. Flood* (1948); *The Bottom of the Harbor* (1959); and *Joe Gould's Secret* (1965). Arbus contacted Mitchell in early 1960, soon after reading *McSorley's Wonderful Saloon*. Although they never met in person, the two documentarians stayed in contact for almost seven years.

LISETTE MODEL (Née Elise Stern) (1901–83) was born in Vienna, Austria, and at age nineteen studied music harmony, counterpoint, and instrumentation with Arnold Schönberg, the influential Austro-Hungarian composer and theorist known for his atonal compositions. In 1926, after the death of her father, Model moved to Paris and eventually abandoned music for photography. In the summer of 1934 she produced her most famous series of photographs—intense, close-up studies of gamblers and pedestrians on the Promenade des Anglais in Nice, France. These and other photographs of Parisian vagrants soon appeared in the Communist periodicals *Regards* and *Lilliput*, and signaled the beginning of Model's career as a documentary street photographer.

After her marriage to the Russian-born painter Evsa Model, she emigrated in 1938 to the United States. She photographed on Wall Street, on the city's Lower East Side, and at Coney Island. Model worked for *Harper's Bazaar* from 1941 to 1953 and published her first photographs in the magazine in July 1941, a series of bathers presented in "How Coney Island Got That Way." Among her favorite subjects in the early 1940s were performers like Albert-Alberta, the half-man/half-woman at Hubert's 42nd Street Flea Circus, and the denizens of Sammy's on the Bowery, the infamous saloon and cabaret. The Museum of Modern Art presented her photographs in its survey exhibitions beginning in 1940, including *In and Out of Focus* (1948), *The Family of Man* (1955), and *Seventy Photographers Look at New York* (1957).

The Art Institute of Chicago organized Model's first solo museum exhibition in 1943, which was followed three years later by a show at the California Palace of the Legion of Honor, San Francisco. Model had career retrospectives at the New Orleans Museum of Art and the Folkwang Museum, Essen, Germany (1981–82). She is the subject of numerous monographs, including

Lisette Model (1979), designed by Marvin Israel, and Ann Thomas's retrospective book and exhibition *Lisette Model* (1990), based upon the artist's archive of negatives, papers, and related collections acquired by the National Gallery of Canada, Ottawa, in 1991.

Model taught photography at the New School for Social Research from 1951 through the 1970s in addition to giving private classes in her home. Arbus attended the first of several classes in 1956 and the two artists became friends. Model later served as a reference for Arbus's 1963 John Simon Guggenheim Memorial Fellowship. She also nominated Arbus in 1965 for the exhibition *10/10* at the Milwaukee School of the Fine Arts, University of Wisconsin. Although Model had applied unsuccessfully in 1949 for a Guggenheim Fellowship, Arbus encouraged her to reapply in 1964, and she was awarded a fellowship the following year for a project entitled "Glamour: The Image of Our Image."

In 1977 Graphics International published a portfolio of twelve photographs printed by Richard Benson. After thirty years of teaching, Model received an Honorary Doctorate in Fine Arts from the New School in 1981, and the following year the Medal of the City of Paris. In 2009, Jeu de Paume organized *Lisette Model*, an exhibition of approximately 120 of Model's most representative photographs.

THOMAS B. MORGAN (B. 1926) is a political writer and novelist known for his nonfiction essays for *Esquire* and *Look* magazines in the late 1950s and '60s. Born in Springfield, Ohio, he graduated with a B.A. in English from Carleton College in 1949, then moved to New York City to work as a freelance journalist. He became Arbus's landlord and neighbor on Charles Street in the mid-1960s.

Morgan's compilation of essays commissioned by *Esquire* on famous people, *Self Creations: 13 Imperson-alities*, was published in 1965. It includes a piece about Blaze Starr whom Arbus photographed for the original article. Morgan also wrote a novel, *Snyder's Walk* (1987), about a journalist covering the antiwar movement in the 1960s. For a long essay about a seven-hundred-mile peace march from Hanover, New Hampshire, to Washington, D.C., Morgan was paired with Arbus by Harold Hayes and Robert Benton at *Esquire*. For sixty-four miles and three days Morgan and Arbus recorded and observed thirteen pacifists on their march. When *Esquire* published

"Doom and Passion Along Rt. 45" in November 1962, the essay included Arbus's photograph of the pacifists on a two-page spread.

HOWARD NEMEROV (1920–91) was a poet, novelist, playwright, and essayist, and the third poet laureate of the United States (1988–90). The author of fourteen volumes of poetry, he was the recipient of the Pulitzer Prize in 1978, as well as the National Book Award, for *The Collected Poems of Howard Nemerov* (1977). The oldest of three children of Gertrude and David Nemerov, he graduated from the Society for Ethical Culture Fieldston School in 1937, then received a B.A. in English from Harvard University in 1941. Nemerov served as a pilot in World War II in the Royal Canadian Air Force and in the U.S. Eighth Army Air Force, then returned to New York to work on his first book of poems, *The Image and the Law* (New York: Henry Holt & Company, 1947). He published poems in the *Nation*, essays in *Sewanee Review*, then became associate editor of the literary magazine *Furioso*. In 1946 he began his teaching career at Hamilton College, then two years later left for Bennington College, where he taught for two decades. From 1969 until his death he was distinguished poet in residence at Washington University in St. Louis.

Nemerov's poems and essays reveal a dramatic range of style and subject matter, from wartime terrors to football, to the fall of ginkgo leaves. The trope of the camera and photography appear frequently in Nemerov's writings, especially in *Mirrors and Windows: Poems* (1958).

RENÉE NEMEROV (B. 1928) is a painter of impressionist-style landscapes, portraits, and sculpture. The youngest and only surviving child of Gertrude and David Nemerov, she graduated from high school intent on becoming a sculptor. Nemerov continued her studies with the Mexican painter Rufino Tamayo and the Swiss experimental portraitist John (Hans) Hansegger. In 1947 she married Roy Sparkia, later a writer of popular fiction and the author of more than thirty books, including *Boss Man* (1954), *The Vanishing Vixen* (1959), and *Doctors and Lovers* (1960). In 1954 she and Sparkia moved to Michigan and adopted a child, Lisa. Nemerov collaborated with Sparkia, producing resin furniture embedded with shells, pebbles, and stones that they collected on beaches near their home. Nemerov's most acclaimed work remains an installation at the Empire

State Building of public sculpture that exploits the varying refractive indexes of plastics. In 1963 the owners of the art deco landmark had commissioned Nemerov and Sparkia to produce a series of relief paintings depicting the Seven Wonders of the Ancient World. Following the death of her second husband, the painter Tom Brown, she moved to California.

PAUL SALSTROM (B. 1940) was born in Rockford, Illinois. He is currently associate professor of history at Saint Mary-of-the-Woods College in Indiana. A specialist in the history of the Appalachian region, he is the author of *Appalachia's Path to Dependency: Rethinking a Region's Economic History, 1730–1940* (1994). Before he received his doctorate in comparative history from Brandeis University in 1988, Salstrom, a lifelong Gandhian pacifist, homesteaded in West Virginia, raised goats, and from 1975 to 1978 was manager of Appalachian Movement Press.

Salstrom met and became friends with Arbus and the writer Thomas B. Morgan in May 1962 when they joined him and twelve other pacifists in New Jersey toward the end of the seven-hundred-mile "Walk for Peace" from Hanover, New Hampshire, to Washington, D.C. Salstrom had organized the event for the Committee for Non-Violent Action, one of three concurrent marches scheduled to converge on the nation's capitol from starting points in Hanover, Chicago, and Nashville. He is the hero of Morgan's November 1962 article for *Esquire* magazine, "Doom and Passion Along Rt. 45." Salstrom's friendship with Arbus continued throughout his three-year prison sentence for refusing to report for the selective service draft. In 1967 when she was at work on her second Guggenheim fellowship, Salstrom invited Arbus to San Francisco to stay at his house, then a haven for AWOLs and deserters from the Vietnam War. He then accompanied Arbus on a photographic excursion between San Francisco and Los Angeles, and from California to Oklahoma City.

AUGUST SANDER (1876–1964) was born in Herdorf, Germany, a small farming village east of Cologne. He began his photography training in 1896 while serving in the German army, and after World War I opened a photography studio, which he operated until 1944. In the 1920s he initiated a massive, unprecedented, lifelong portrait study of all classes of people known as "Menschen des 20 Jahrhunderts," or "People of the Twentieth Century."

Although Sander died before seeing his project fully realized, he envisioned its structure, organizing his portraits into seven broad categories representing the employment divisions and social structures of the day. Almost forty years after Sander's death, his grandson saw through the publication of *People of the Twentieth Century* (2002), a seven-volume opus that includes 619 photographs.

In 1929 Sander completed *Antlitz der Zeit* (1929), a preview of his grand project that became its first published expression. With a text by his friend Alfred Döblin, the German physician and author of the novel *Berlin Alexanderplatz* (1929), *Face of Our Time* remains one of the century's most distinguished publications. The straightforward documentary methods used by Sander to survey German society did not conform to the National Socialist ideal of a perfect society. After 1936 the Nazis confiscated all unsold copies and destroyed the book plates. But it was precisely the all inclusiveness of the work that attracted praise from multiple generations of artists and intellectuals from Walter Benjamin to Walker Evans to Arbus.

Sander did not have his first large show until 1951 at the Cologne Photokina where he exhibited his photographs of the city as it was before World War II. Three years later he met Edward Steichen, curator of photography at The Museum of Modern Art who was traveling in Germany researching for *The Family of Man* (1955). Steichen acquired eighty prints from Sander for the museum's permanent collection. It was this group of photographs that Steichen's curatorial successor, John Szarkowski, showed to Arbus in late 1962 when they first met at the museum. Arbus had already seen several of Sander's photographs in *The Family of Man* exhibition, which also included her and Allan's portrait of a father and son. She also owned the November 1959 issue of *Du* magazine, the illustrated monthly from Zurich which had published fifty-one portraits by Sander in a special feature on the artist.

The August Sander Archiv is preserved in Cologne at the Photographische Sammlung/SK Stiftung Kultur.

NEIL SELKIRK (B. 1947) is a photographer whose work has been published in magazines including *Esquire*, *Vanity Fair*, *Wired*, and *The New Yorker*. He maintains a studio in New York City and teaches photography at New York University. Selkirk is also the exclusive printer for The Estate of Diane Arbus, a responsibility he has had since the year of her death. "In the Darkroom," Selkirk's essay on printing Arbus's photographs was published in *Diane Arbus Revelations* in 2003.

Born in England, Selkirk graduated in 1968 from London College of Printing with a diploma in photography. From spring 1970 until summer 1971 he worked in the United States as an assistant to the fashion photographer Hiro. Selkirk met Arbus and Marvin Israel in Richard Avedon's studio and subsequently enrolled in her 1970–71 class taught at Westbeth in Greenwich Village. In the summer of 1971 he left the city to work for the German fashion photographer Chris von Wangenheim, shooting collections in Rome and Paris. After Arbus's death in July 1971 Selkirk returned to New York and helped Doon Arbus and Marvin Israel organize Diane Arbus's archive of negatives. He made prints of original Diane Arbus photographs for the 1972 Museum of Modern Art retrospective and the Aperture monograph.

The experience led him away from the commercial career he had been pursuing. He provided editorial portraits to *Andy Warhol's Interview* and *The New York Times Magazine*, where art director Ruth Ansel featured his full-page political portraits of Zbigniew Brzezinski, Jeb Magruder, and Henry Kissinger, among many others, during much of the early to mid-1970s.

In 1977 Selkirk opened his own studio where he began to produce advertising images and annual report illustrations for corporate clients. By the mid-1980s, Selkirk was concentrating on personal work. In March 1998 the designer Tibor Kalman commissioned Selkirk to photograph pedestrians in Times Square. The portraits were at first transformed into posters that papered the scaffolding on 42nd Street, then reconfigured as *1000 on 42nd Street* (2000), a *Photo District News* award-winning book designed by Yolanda Cuomo.

In 2006 Nazraeli press published a monograph, *See No Evil*, and the following year, *Lobbyists*, both designed by Cuomo. Selkirk has just completed a new project, "Certain Women," portraits made across America with an 11x14 view camera.

Selkirk's documentary film *Who is Marvin Israel?* premiered at The Metropolitan Museum of Art in 2005 in New York City.

MARY ELIZABETH SELLERS (B. 1936) was born in Philadelphia but spent her adolescent years in Stonington, Connecticut. After Sellers graduated in 1957 from Sarah Lawrence College in Bronxville, New York, she moved to New York City and began to write music. In 1958 she met Nancy Christopherson who introduced her to actor Robert Brown and his friends Diane and Allan Arbus.

Sellers, Christopherson, and Diane Arbus soon became close friends and Sellers often drove Arbus (who at the time did not have a driver's license) on various photographic expeditions. One of their earliest forays was a futile quest to New Jersey to find the Jackson Whites, an insular community of people of mixed descent (African, European, and Native American) living in the Ramapo Mountains near the New Jersey–New York state border. In 1960, Sellers married Robert Brown and later moved to Los Angeles where he had been pursuing his theatrical, television, and film career. Arbus visited them in Malibu in summer 1962 and again in 1964. Sellers accompanied Arbus when she photographed the soothsayers featured in "What's New: Witch Predicts"; the nighttime photograph A castle in Disneyland; and during her Santa Barbara sitting with Bishop Ethel Predonzan of The Cathedral of the Creator, Omnipresence, Inc. Sellers and Brown also drove Arbus to photograph Mae West in her luxe Hollywood home.

In the early 1970s, after her divorce from Brown, Sellers went back to school and received a master's degree in social work (M.S.W.) from the University of Southern California–Los Angeles in 1975. Sellers is a psychotherapist and Licensed Clinical Social Worker (LCSW) in private practice in Los Angeles.

LAWRENCE SHAINBERG (B. 1936) is a novelist, non-fiction writer, and humorist. Born in Memphis, he graduated in 1958 with a B.A. in sociology from Columbia University, where he studied under C. Wright Mills. Shainberg met Arbus in the 1960s through their mutual friend Marvin Israel, and Shainberg's neighbors, Mary and Robert Frank. Shainberg is the author of numerous short essays, including "The Hot Hand Sutra," a sports commentary for the premier issue of the quarterly *Tricycle: The Buddhist Review* (fall 1991), and, for the same publication in winter 1996, "Wheels of Dharma," a rumination about automobile ownership in a Zen community.

Shainberg is the author of *Brain Surgeon: An Intimate View of His World* (1979); *Memories of Amnesia: A Novel*

(1988); and *Ambivalent Zen: A Memoir* (1995), an autobiography that spans four decades of the author's life. Upon the publication of his first novel, *One on One*, a story about a 6'9" Jewish pro basketball player, Arbus pointedly gave Shainberg a print of one of her photographs of the Jewish giant at home with his parents.

Shainberg lives in New York City and Wellfleet, Massachusetts. His most recent novel, *Crust*, was published in 2008.

EDWARD STEICHEN (1879–1973) and his family emigrated from Luxembourg to the United States in 1880 and settled in Hancock, Michigan. By 1896 he had taken up photography and within a few years had created a series of landscapes that were first exhibited at the Second Philadelphia Photographic Salon in 1899.

In 1900 Steichen moved to Paris to paint, stopping in New York at the Camera Club where he showed his portfolio to Alfred Stieglitz, already the preeminent force in photography in the United States. In 1902, he moved to New York City, rented a studio at 291 Fifth Avenue, and with Stieglitz became one of the twelve co-founders of the Photo-Secession, the premier organization in America dedicated to the art of photography.

Upon his return to Paris in 1905 Steichen lent his New York studio to Stieglitz as an exhibition space for the Photo-Secession. Known simply by its address on Fifth Avenue, 291, the gallery simultaneously introduced photography and modern French art to America. Steichen arranged exhibitions for Stieglitz of the works of Auguste Rodin, Henri Matisse, Paul Cézanne, and Constantin Brancusi, among many others.

Steichen lived on and off in France from 1900 to 1923, making paintings and photographs, and winning numerous exhibition awards. In 1920 he gave up painting altogether to devote himself to photography and by 1923 he was living in New York City making fashion and advertising photographs as chief photographer for Condé Nast Publications. He quickly became the era's preferred portraitist. In 1938, the year that Steichen retired from commercial photography, the Baltimore Museum of Art presented the artist's first of many retrospective exhibitions.

During World War II Steichen served in the U.S. Navy as a lieutenant commander and was placed in charge of all Navy combat photography. In the same period Steichen curated several large exhibitions for MoMA,

including *Road to Victory* (1942), with texts by Carl Sandburg, and *Power in the Pacific* (1945). He began his new career as director of the Department of Photography at MoMA in 1947. In the next fifteen years, until his retirement from MoMA in 1962, Steichen organized more than one hundred large and small exhibitions, including *The Family of Man* (1955), the era's most popular photography exhibition circulated by the U.S. Information Agency and seen by more than nine million people in thirty-eight countries. The show featured more than 273 photographers and 503 photographs, including one by Diane and Allan Arbus.

In 1963, the year after his retirement, he was awarded the Presidential Medal of Freedom by President John F. Kennedy, and published his autobiography, *A Life in Photography* (1963). The Edward Steichen Photography Center opened at MoMA in 1964 and is the repository for his complete archive.

STEWART STERN (B. 1922) is a screenwriter and author best known for his screenplay for *Rebel Without a Cause* (1955), the cult classic featuring James Dean. He received Academy Award nominations for *Teresa* (1951), a World War II story directed by Fred Zinnemann, and *Rachel, Rachel* (1968), directed by Paul Newman and featuring Joanne Woodward, about the life of a schoolmistress in a small New England town. He won an Academy Award for Best Short Documentary for *Benjy* (1951). In 1977 Stern was awarded an Emmy for his television drama *Sybil* (1977), featuring Sally Field and Joanne Woodward.

Stern was born in New York City and attended Ethical Culture Fieldston School in the same graduating class as Arbus. He showed early acuity and interest in the visual arts. Through his uncle, Adolph Zuckor, the founder of Paramount Pictures, Stern was introduced to motion pictures. In 1941 he went to the University of Iowa to study painting, but graduated in three years with a degree in speech and dramatic arts. In 1943 he enlisted in the United States Army, was assigned to the 106th Infantry Division, and saw combat in December 1944 as a rifle squad leader during the Battle of the Bulge. Stern was hospitalized with frostbite and evacuated back to the United States in 1945. He received the Bronze Star for his role in the Ardennes Campaign.

After the war he worked briefly as an actor, appearing on Broadway in René Clair's production of the Joseph

A. Fields and Jerome Chodorov comedy *The French Touch* (1945–46). In 1947 he moved to Los Angeles and for two years worked for Joseph Fields as a dialogue director at Eagle-Lion Studios. He worked for several years in television, writing teleplays for NBC and the Philco-Goodyear Playhouse, including *Crip*, a story about a boy with cerebral palsy, and *Thunder of Silence* (1954), an investigation of an American farm family who adopts a family of refugees saved from the concentration camps in Europe which starred then relatively unknown actor Paul Newman. They formed a close friendship that led to many subsequent projects, including the films *The Rack* (1956) and *Rachel, Rachel* (1968). Stern is also the author of *No Tricks in My Pocket: Paul Newman Directs* (1989).

Stern has many other writing credits, including screenplays for *The James Dean Story* (1957), *The Ugly American* (1963), and *Summer Wishes, Winter Dreams* (1973). In 1962 while Arbus was in Los Angeles visiting Robert Brown and his wife, Mary Elizabeth Sellers, Stern helped her gain access to the back lot of Universal Studios and other Hollywood locations. He taught screenwriting at the University of Southern California School of Cinema-Television and at the University of Washington in Seattle, where he lives with his wife, Marilee, a former dance teacher at the School of the Pacific Northwest Ballet. In the summer he now serves as a regular creative adviser at the Screenwriters Lab at the Sundance Institute in Utah. Stern's papers are housed in the Special Collections Department in the library of the University of Iowa.

ALFRED STIEGLITZ (1864–1946) is widely considered the father of modern photography. Born in Hoboken, New Jersey, he moved to New York City in 1871. While studying at the Technische Hochschule in Berlin, Stieglitz acquired his first camera. Stieglitz worked in the photoengraving business from 1890 to 1895. In 1896 he became the founder and editor of *Camera Notes*, the journal of the New York Camera Club. In 1898 he published *Picturesque Bits of New York and Other Studies*, a photogravure portfolio of his own work, and the following year organized his first retrospective exhibition for the Camera Club.

In 1902 Stieglitz and eleven artists, including Edward Steichen, founded the Photo-Secession, the country's first modern photographic society. From 1903 through 1917 Stieglitz published *Camera Work*, the deluxe journal

known for its gravure reproductions, poetry, satire, and commentary on the history of photography and contemporary art. Stieglitz frequently showed his own work as well as photographs by the other members of the Photo-Secession at 291. He also promoted paintings and watercolors by a generation of emerging American artists, notably John Marin, Marsden Hartley, and Arthur Dove. He first showed the drawings of Georgia O'Keeffe in 1916, then began to collaborate with her on an extended photographic portrait. Between 1917 and 1937 he made over three hundred studies of O'Keeffe, whom he married in 1924.

For eight years following the demise of 291 in 1917, Stieglitz focused on his own career as a photographer and in 1921 began a new series of photographs of clouds that he called "Equivalents." In 1924 the Museum of Fine Arts, Boston, acquired a suite of his photographs for their permanent collection, as did The Metropolitan Museum of Art four years later. In the 1930s Stieglitz donated his collection of photographs by other artists to The Metropolitan Museum of Art and organized two retrospectives of his work at An American Place (1932, 1934). His last important series of photographs document the construction of skyscrapers in midtown Manhattan. In 1934 Stieglitz's friends commemorated his seventieth birthday with the publication of an influential volume of essays and photographs edited by, among others, Waldo Frank and Lewis Mumford: *America & Alfred Stieglitz: A Collective Portrait* (1934), which the Arbuses owned.

Steiglitz edited and/or published the monthly magazine *American Amateur Photographer* (1893–96); the quarterly *Camera Notes* (1897–1902); fifty issues of *Camera Work* (1903–1917); twelve issues of *291* (1915–16); and countless exhibition catalogs of gallery shows he organized from 1905 to 1946. In his lifetime he saw only one significant independent exhibition (and no such monographs) of his own photographs. The first major exhibition of his work, *An Exhibition of Photographs by Alfred Stieglitz* (1958), was held at the National Gallery of Art in Washington, D.C. This first show and its accompanying publication was followed by many others, most recently Sarah Greenough's *Modern Art and America: Alfred Stieglitz and His New York Galleries* (2001); and Greenough's two-volume compendium of the almost 1,600 photographs in the National Gallery's collection, *Alfred Stieglitz: The Key Set* (2002).

The Metropolitan Museum of Art is the custodian of his personal collection of other artists working in photography. Yale University preserves his papers in The Alfred Stieglitz/Georgia O'Keeffe Archive in the Yale Collection of American Literature at the Beinecke Rare Book and Manuscript Library.

JOHN SZARKOWSKI (1925–2007) was Director Emeritus of the Department of Photography at The Museum of Modern Art and one of the world's leading theorists and historians of photography. From 1962 until his retirement in 1991, he organized more than one hundred exhibitions and oversaw the dramatic expansion of the museum's photography collection, including the acquisition in 1968 of the Abbott-Levy Collection of Eugène Atget. Szarkowski curated landmark, monographic shows of such photographers as André Kertész (1964), Dorothea Lange (1966), Brassaï (1968), Walker Evans (1971), Diane Arbus (1972), William Eggleston (1976), Ansel Adams (1979), Eugène Atget (1981–82), Irving Penn (1984), and Garry Winogrand (1988). He also organized provocative survey exhibitions that integrated photographs by August Sander, Henri Cartier-Bresson, and Lee Friedlander with more functional, anonymous images that revealed the medium's vernacular traditions. From his first large museum show and publication, *The Photographer's Eye* (1964), to his last, *Photography Until Now* (1989–90), Szarkowski helped define and codify the language of photography.

Szarkowski was born in Ashland, Wisconsin, and graduated in 1948 with a B.S. in art history from the University of Wisconsin–Madison. From 1948 to 1951 he worked as a photographer at the Walker Art Center in Minneapolis, Minnesota, then for two years taught photography at the Albright Art School at the University of Buffalo, New York. While in Buffalo he became interested in the architecture and conceptual theories of Louis Sullivan, and in 1954 was awarded a John Simon Guggenheim Memorial Fellowship to produce the series of photographs in his first book, *The Idea of Louis Sullivan* (1956). Szarkowski was awarded a second Guggenheim Fellowship in 1961 to photograph the Quetico-Superior wilderness of Western Ontario, Canada. In 1962 Edward Steichen selected him to be his successor as director of the Department of Photography at MoMA.

Szarkowksi helped secure the reputations of many artists with his analysis of their work and its place in a historical tradition that was then in its infancy. He coauthored, with Maria Morris Hambourg, the four-volume treatise *The Work of Atget* (1981–85). Among Szarkowski's other books published by MoMA are *Walker Evans* (1971); *Looking at Photographs: 100 Pictures from the Collection of The Museum of Modern Art* (1973); *Mirrors and Windows: American Photography Since 1960* (1978); and *Winogrand: Figments from the Real World* (1988).

Szarkowski met Arbus in 1962 just after taking his post at MoMA. He became an early advocate for her work and in 1964 acquired seven photographs for the museum's permanent collection. In 1967 he organized *New Documents*, an exhibition that featured the work of Arbus, Lee Friedlander, and Garry Winogrand, and reflected his understanding of a shift in the poetics of the documentary tradition.

In 1970 Szarkowski hired Arbus to do preliminary picture research in the archives of the *New York Daily News* for a 1973 exhibition that eventually came to be called *From the Picture Press*. The exhibition was organized into seven sections defined by Szarkowski and Arbus as Ceremonies, Losers, Disasters, Alarums & Conundrums, Good News & the Good Life, Contests & Confrontations, and Heroes. For each of the photographs Szarkowski included the original newspaper captions.

In later years Szarkowski focused primarily on his own artwork. *Mr. Bristol's Barn* (1997) presents his photographs of the interior and exterior of a nineteenth-century wooden barn in East Chatham, New York. Szarkowski also, in official retirement, revisited the achievements of three of his favorite artists in several books: *Alfred Stieglitz at Lake George* (1995), *Atget* (2000), and *Ansel Adams at 100* (2001).

Szarkowski received numerous honorary degrees and taught at many schools, including Harvard University, Columbia University, Cornell University, and at his alma mater. In 2005, the San Francisco Museum of Modern Art presented *John Szarkowski Photographs*, a retrospective exhibition featuring forty-eight of Szarkowski's early works and twenty-seven of his later pieces.

SUZANNE VICTOR TRAZOFF (B. 1941) was born in Racine, Wisconsin, raised in Winnetka, Illinois, and graduated in 1963 with a B.A. in English from Hollins College in Roanoke, Virginia. Encouraged by her teacher Howard Nemerov, at the time the school's writer-in-residence, Trazoff moved to New York City and found an editorial trainee position at Random House. Through Nemerov she met Diane Arbus and shortly thereafter moved into her home to help take care of Amy Arbus, who was then nine years old.

After briefly moving in late spring 1964 to Iowa City to enroll in the master's program in creative writing at the University of Iowa, Trazoff returned to New York City in September to live and work in the Arbus household. She also assisted the essayist Thomas B. Morgan, who was their landlord and neighbor. At the time Morgan was traveling abroad and doing research for a book on anti-Americanism, later published as *Among the Anti-Americans* (1967). Trazoff married in 1965 and worked as an assistant editor at Bantam Books.

After Arbus's death in 1971, Trazoff assisted Doon Arbus and Marvin Israel with the cataloguing and organization of Arbus's photographs. She also transcribed tapes from Arbus's 1971 master class for the text of the 1972 Aperture monograph.

From 1977 to 1981 Trazoff served as a writer and editor for Manpower Demonstration Research Corporation (MDRC), a nonprofit, nonpartisan social policy research organization. She left MDRC to work as a writer (1982–86), then as deputy administrator in the Office of Public Affairs in the New York City Resources Administration (1986–90).

From 1990–1994, Trazoff served as Deputy Commissioner of the New York City Police Department in charge of Public Information, running the department's press office. In 1994 she moved to Maine and began a private practice as a consultant for nonprofit organizations on social services, health, and criminal justice policy issues. From 1999–2008, Trazoff managed the DaPonte String Quartet, a classical music ensemble based in Damariscotta, Maine.

JAMES VANDERZEE (1886–1983) is widely considered to be the most significant photographer of the Harlem Renaissance. His portraits from the late 1910s to the early 1930s of local celebrities, community leaders, and simple families helped forge a modern, urban identity among African-Americans in New York City and other communities. In 1924 he became the official photographer for Marcus Garvey and the Universal Negro Improvement Association.

Vanderzee was born in Lenox, Massachusetts, the son of the sexton of the town's Trinity Episcopalian Church.

His parents had formerly been the maid and butler of Ulysses S. Grant in New York City. Around 1900 he acquired a camera and began to teach himself the rudiments of portrait photography.

Vanderzee moved to New York City in 1906 and worked as a busboy and elevator man while studying violin at the Carlton Conservatory of Music in New York. He became first violinist with the John Wanamaker Orchestra, formed the Harlem Orchestra, and taught piano and violin in Harlem. Music did not provide steady income and to support his wife and family he took a position in 1915 as the darkroom technician in Gertz's department store in Newark, New Jersey. After a year he opened his first portrait studio, Guarantee Photos, on 135th Street in Harlem. Vanderzee would operate a portrait studio under various names until 1969, when he retired. During his half century in photography he would photograph a cross section of Harlem residents from work-a-day shopkeepers and their families to such celebrities as Bill "Bojangles" Robinson and Adam Clayton Powell, Sr.

Outside of Harlem, however, Vanderzee was not well known until The Metropolitan Museum of Art featured his photographs in *Harlem on My Mind*, the controversial 1969 multi-media exhibition organized by Allon Schoener that presented the history of Harlem from 1900 to 1968. The show brought almost instant fame to the eighty-three-year-old artist and his photographs were soon featured in numerous monographs, including Reginald McGhee's *The World of James Van Der Zee: A Visual Record of Black Americans* (1969) and *James Van Der Zee* (1973). With a foreword by Toni Morrison, *The Harlem Book of the Dead* (1978) focuses on Vanderzee's funeral portraits. In many postmortem photographs, Vanderzee added angels, biblical figures, and lifetime images of the deceased (often his own earlier portraits), which float like spirits over the open coffins. These last "double" portraits attracted Arbus, who visited Vanderzee's studio on Lenox Avenue in 1963, six years before he came to public attention. Arbus acquired a few prints for her personal collection and became an early advocate of Vanderzee's work.

WEEGEE (Usher, later Arthur, Fellig) (1899–1968) is one of the world's most well-known tabloid newspaper photographers. He is the author of *Naked City* (1945), a book that includes nighttime portraits of criminals, lovers, victims, policemen, and the residents of the

Bowery. The publication became a Hollywood film and quickly made Weegee an international celebrity.

Weegee himself made several short 16mm documentary films, including *Weegee's New York* (1948), *Cocktail Party* (circa 1950), and *The Idiot Box* (circa 1965). He also appeared as an extra in numerous Hollywood features, including the comedy *Every Girl Should Be Married* (1948) with Cary Grant. In 1963 the director Stanley Kubrick hired him as a special effects consultant for *Dr. Strangelove, Or: How I Learned to Stop Worrying and Love the Bomb.* Weegee also completed an autobiography, *Weegee by Weegee* (1961).

Weegee was born Usher Fellig in the city of Zlothev in the former Austrian province of Galicia, now part of Ukraine. In 1910 he immigrated with his family to the United States and lived in New York's Lower East Side. In the early 1920s, while living in boarding rooms on the Bowery, Weegee worked as a darkroom technician, first for *The New York Times*, then for Acme Newspictures, a major source of photographs for the *Daily News*, the *World Telegram*, and the *Herald Tribune*. One of his jobs was to squeegee wet prints and he became known as "Mr. Squeegee," possibly the origin of his adopted moniker. Another source may have been inspired by the Ouija board, an increasingly popular fortuneteller's game in which the Acme darkroom staff had quite an interest.

By the early 1930s Weegee was making his own photographs, and in 1935 he left Acme to work as a freelance police beat photographer. Two years later he published his first credited photographs in *Life* and *Popular Photography* magazines. In 1938 Weegee began to use his adopted name and to stamp his photographs "Weegee the Famous." From 1940 to 1945 he was staff photographer at the progressive evening newspaper *PM*.

In 1941 Weegee had two one-person exhibitions both entitled *Weegee: Murder Is My Business* at The Photo League, an organization dedicated to social and documentary photography. The Museum of Modern Art included his work in 1943 in the group show *Action Photography*, his first museum exhibition. Many more shows at MoMA would follow, including *Art in Progress* (1944), where his work was presented on the same wall with Lisette Model's, and *50 Photographs by 50 Photographers* (1948). Weegee then abandoned crime photography and devoted his talents to society, advertising, and to special effects motion picture photography, working in Hollywood, Munich, and Paris. He is the author of *Weegee's People* (1946), *Naked Hollywood*

(1953), and *Weegee's Creative Camera* (1959). He is also the subject of three documentary films, including *The Naked Eye* (1956) by Louis Stoumen.

Despite his success, Weegee was somewhat neglected at the end of his life when Arbus showed his work in 1965 to her students at Parsons School of Design. After his death, she discovered Weegee's archive, then in the possession of his common-law wife, Wilma Wilcox. Arbus brought the work to the attention of John Szarkowski while doing research for what became *From the Picture Press* (1973), an exhibition at MoMA on the tradition of news photography. She became an advocate of Weegee's work and introduced it to the gallerist Lee Witkin.

Weegee's work was posthumously the subject of many retrospectives at, among others, the Center for Creative Photography, University of Arizona, Tucson (1975) and the San Francisco Museum of Modern Art (1984). His photographs also appear in several major monographs, including John Coplans's *Weegee's New York: Photographs 1935–1960* (1982) and *Weegee's World* (1997), a comprehensive book by Miles Barth that accompanied a large exhibition at the International Center of Photography, New York.

GARRY WINOGRAND (1928–84) was born in New York City and raised in the Bronx. He graduated from high school in 1945 and subsequently served for two years in the Army Air Force as a weather forecaster in Georgia. He returned to the city, briefly studied painting at City University, then in 1948, on the G.I. Bill, entered Columbia University in the School of General Studies. His intention was to pursue painting, but after meeting the photographer George Zimbel he simultaneously began to photograph and make prints. In 1949 he left Columbia, and on a scholarship at the New School for Social Research, took classes with the art director Alexey Brodovitch, who helped him hone his mastery of the 35mm camera.

Winogrand received his first editorial assignment from *Harper's Bazaar* in 1951, the year he began his association with the Pix Photo Agency, soon followed by Henrietta Brackman Associates. He supplied the stock houses with a wide range of gritty images, including sweat-drenched boxers and dancers backstage at the ballet, street parades, and patrons and performers at the stylish El Morocco nightclub. His snapshot-style photographs began appearing in *Pageant*, *Sports Illustrated*, and *Redbook* and came to the attention of Edward Steichen, director of the Photography Department at The Museum of Modern Art, who included two of Winogrand's photographs in his exhibition *The Family of Man* (1955). Steichen subsequently featured Winogrand in *Seventy Photographers Look at New York* (1957–58).

John Szarkowski, Steichen's successor at MoMA, included Winogrand in numerous important group exhibitions in the 1960s, including *Five Unrelated Photographers* (1963) with Ken Heyman, George Krause, Jerome Liebling, and Minor White; *The Photographer's Eye* (1964); and *New Documents* (1967) with Lee Friedlander and Arbus. The last show became a legendary exhibition of photographs—a focused analysis of the conceptual innovations and formal traditions shared by the three artists. Nathan Lyons, curator at the George Eastman House in Rochester, New York, also featured Winogrand in several exhibitions, including *Photography 63* (1963) and *Toward a Social Landscape*, a 1966 show featuring four other artists, including Friedlander, that served in many ways as a preamble to *New Documents*.

His ironic study of caged animals and the captivated humans who stare at them became the subject for his first book, *The Animals* (1969), and a one-person show at MoMA. Winogrand compiled twenty years of his photographs of women in *Women Are Beautiful* (1975), later the subject of one of his four limited-edition portfolios.

Winogrand received three John Simon Guggenheim Memorial Foundation Fellowships (1964, 1969, 1978), a 1972 grant from the New York State Council on the Arts, and a National Endowment for the Arts Fellowship in 1975. His 1969 Guggenheim Foundation project "to study the effect of media on events" generated the book *Public Relations* (1977). Winogrand began his extensive teaching career in 1967 at New York's Parsons School of Design. He taught workshops worldwide and served on the faculty of many institutions, including the School of Visual Arts, New York (1968–71); Cooper Union for the Advancement of Science and Art, New York (1970, 1972); and the University of California, Los Angeles (1979, 1981).

Winogrand is the author of *Stock Photographs: The Fort Worth Fat Stock Show and Rodeo* (1980), his last book and a 1974 commission by the Fort Worth Art Museum. He is also the subject of numerous posthumous monographs, including *The Man in the Crowd: The Uneasy Streets of Garry Winogrand* (1999) and *Winogrand 1964* (2002). The Center for Creative Photography at the University of Arizona, Tuscon, is the custodian of the Garry Winogrand Archive.

HENRY WOLF (1925–2005) emigrated to the United States from Vienna, Austria in 1941. A designer, art director, teacher, and photographer, Wolf became art director of *Esquire* in 1952, then succeeded Alexey Brodovitch in 1958 as art director of *Harper's Bazaar*. In 1961 he left *Harper's Bazaar* to become the first art director of *Show*, the short-lived deluxe art magazine that featured Arbus, Robert Frank, and many of the most promising photographers of the generation. After the publisher Huntington Hartford sold *Show* to Hugh Hefner in 1965, Wolf left to become advertising director for Jack Tinker & Partners, McCann-Erickson, and ultimately Trahey/Wolf Advertising. He served as vice president of the Aspen Design Conference, president of the American Institute of Graphic Arts (AIGA), and was Mellon Visiting Professor of Art at Cooper Union School of Art. Among his many design awards is the Gold Medal from the AIGA in 1976. Wolf, author of *Visual Thinking: Methods for Making Images Memorable* (1988), was professor of art at Parsons School of Design, the New School, where he taught since 1954. He headed Henry Wolf Productions, and was known for his photographic advertising campaigns.

WITH ADDITIONAL ASSISTANCE FROM: MILES BELLAMY, JED BARK, ANDREA BAYER, LYLE BONGÉ, PHILIP BROOKMAN, ERIC BROWN, MALCOLM DANIEL, DOUG EKLUND, BARBARA FILE, MIA FINEMAN, LAURA T. HARRIS, TOBY HIMMEL, GALWAY KINNELL, CHRISTOPHER KOHAN, JOHN LAWRENCE, J.D. MCCLATCHY, FRED MCKISSICK, STEPHEN MAKLANSKY, LORI PAULI, STEPHEN PINSON, KELLYE ROSENHEIM, SHARON SNOW, JUDITH STEIN, NORMA STEVENS, DANIEL TALBOT, JEAN AND JOE TUCKER, JULIA VAN HAAFTEN

ORIGINALLY WRITTEN IN 2003, THESE BIOGRAPHIES HAVE BEEN UPDATED AS NECESSARY FOR THIS PUBLICATION.

INDEX

APERTURE

CHRIS BOOT: Executive Director

LESLEY A. MARTIN: Publisher, Books

MATTHEW HARVEY: Production Manager

SUSAN CICCOTTI, ANNA CARNICK: Project Managers

KRISTIAN OROZCO: Sales Director

PAUL COLARUSSO: Rights Manager

THE PUBLICATION OF THIS BOOK WAS MADE POSSIBLE IN PART
BY THE GENEROUS SUPPORT OF PIER 24 PHOTOGRAPHY AND CATHY M. KAPLAN.

A LESS TANGIBLE BUT EQUALLY INDISPENSIBLE FACTOR
HAS BEEN THE UNFAILING COMMITMENT OF JEFFREY FRAENKEL AND TIMOTHY TAYLOR.

ELISABETH SUSSMAN (coauthor, chronology and endnotes) is the Curator and Sondra Gilman Curator of Photography at the Whitney Museum of American Art. She served as co-curator for *Diane Arbus Revelations*.

DOON ARBUS (coauthor, chronology and endnotes) is the eldest daughter of Diane and Allan Arbus; since her mother's death she has managed The Estate of Diane Arbus.

JEFF L. ROSENHEIM (author, biographies) is curator of photographs at The Metropolitan Museum of Art.

MARY BAHR (editor, original texts) is the editor of *Diane Arbus Revelations*, which contained all the texts that appear in this book.

DESIGNED BY YOLANDA CUOMO

KRISTI NORGAARD ASSOCIATE DESIGNER

Aperture Foundation books are available
in North America through:
D.A.P./Distributed Art Publishers
155 Sixth Avenue, 2nd Floor
New York, N.Y. 10013
Phone: (212) 627-1999
Fax: (212) 627-9484

Aperture Foundation books are
distributed outside North America by:
Thames & Hudson
181A High Holborn
London WC1V 7QX
United Kingdom
Phone: + 44 20 7845 5000
Fax: + 44 20 7845 5055
Email: sales@thameshudson.co.uk

APERTURE
547 West 27th Street
New York, N.Y. 10001
www.aperture.org

The purpose of Aperture Foundation, a non-profit organization, is to advance
photography in all its forms and to foster the exchange of ideas among audiences worldwide.

DIANE ARBUS

A CHRONOLOGY

Library of Congress Control Number: 2010940598
ISBN: 978-1-59711-179-9

First Edition
Printed and bound in China by Midas
10 9 8 7 6 5 4 3 2 1

This book was typeset in Garamond 3 and ITC Cheltenham
and was printed on 130gsm Yulong Pure paper.

The texts in DIANE ARBUS: A CHRONOLOGY originally appeared in DIANE ARBUS REVELATIONS
(Random House, Copyright © 2003 The Estate of Diane Arbus LLC), published in conjunction with
the San Francisco Museum of Modern Art's exhibition of the same name.

Somewhere at the very end there is a joke

and even though I forget it there are moments when

I have fancied I knew just for a second what the punch line was.

—FROM A LETTER TO PETER CROOKSTON, MAY 1968